The House of Novello

The House of Novello
Practice and Policy of a
Victorian Music Publisher,
1829–1866

VICTORIA L. COOPER

ASHGATE

Published by
Ashgate Publishing Limited
Gower House
Croft Road
Aldershot
Hants GU11 3HR
England

Ashgate Publishing Company
Suite 420
101 Cherry Street
Burlington, VT 05401-4405
USA

Ashgate website: http://www.ashgate.com

British Library Cataloguing in Publication Data
Cooper, Victoria L.
   The house of Novello : the practice and policy of a
   Victorian music publisher, 1829–1866. – (Music in
   nineteenth-century Britain)
   1. Novello & Company – History 2. Music publishing – Great
   Britain – History – 19th century
   I. Title
   338.7'610705194'0942

Library of Congress Cataloging-in-Publication Data
Cooper, Victoria L., 1954–
   The house of Novello : the practice and policy of a Victorian music
publisher, 1829–1866 / Victoria L. Cooper.
      p. cm. – (Music in nineteenth-century Britain)
Includes bibliographical references and index.
   ISBN 0-7546-0088-2
   1. Novello & Co. 2. Music publishers–England. 3. Music
publishing–England–History. 4. Music–England–19th century–History
and criticism. I. Title. II. Series.

ML427.N69C66 2002
070.5'794'094109034–dc21

2002028116

ISBN 0 7546 0088 2

Typeset by Q3 Bookwork Ltd., Loughborough, Leicestershire.
Printed and bound in Great Britain by MPG Books Ltd., Bodmin, Cornwall.

Contents

Appendices

List of Figures and Tables

Figures

Tables

Acknowledgements

I am grateful to the following organizations and individuals for their assistance: the staff of Novello and Co. during the period of research, in particular Margaret Pace and the late Bernard Axcell; Mr D. Cox and Mr C. Sheppard, the Cowden Clarke Collection, the Brotherton Library, Leeds University; Margaret Cranmer, formerly of the Rowe Library, King's College, Cambridge; Richard Andrewes, Faculty of Music, Cambridge University; Chris Banks, Music Manuscript Division, the British Library; James Fuld; Jeff Kallberg; D. W. Krummel; the late Hans Lenneberg; and Nicholas Temperley. I would also like to thank Michael Hurd who was generous both with his time and information concerning the Novello archives. My thanks also to Margaret Christie and Kathryn Puffett for their help, and to Caroline Murray and Teresa Sheppard for friendship and assistance. I am indebted to Philip Gossett for the support and advice I received; he continues to be both mentor and friend to me.

I am grateful for the help and assistance I received from my editor at Ashgate, Rachel Lynch: in my own work as a Commissioning Editor I know too well the pitfalls and pleasures of the author/editor relationship; Rachel has made it nothing but a pleasure and an easy journey. I am also very grateful for the help and support I received from my copy-editor, Mary Worthington, and for the assistance at Ashgate from Donna Hamer and Kristen Thorner. I am also indebted to my series editor, Bennett Zon, for his encouragement and expertise. My parents, Wendy Knopf Cooper and Leon Cooper, and Shirley Cooper, have been supportive throughout this writing and long before this was even a glimmer of an idea. My interest in publishing was sparked by my great-uncle, Alfred A. Knopf; he instilled in me a love and fascination with the business of publishing, whether of music or words. My husband, John, and daughter, Julia, provided me with the time and space for my work and I am grateful for their quiet and strong support.

Music Examples. All music examples have been reset and do not represent the typefaces of the original editions quoted.

Introduction

Music publishing, by its very nature, involves a relationship with the social, economic, and artistic fabric of musical life. The development of these aspects of society often influences a publisher's decisions regarding quantity and content of the list. Thus, a study of a music publisher must range beyond the internal events of house policy, such as print run, relationships with composers, and editorial style, and examine these factors within a broader economic and social context.

The following study of the English music publisher Novello explores the growth of one firm in relation to the socio-economic forces that moulded and influenced its development. Founded as a personal endeavour by Vincent Novello (1781–1861) in 1811, the firm expanded under the management of his son Alfred (1810–96). From 1829 Alfred assumed the directorship of the house and in 1856 he passed responsibility for the firm to his protégé, Henry Littleton. Alfred completely sold his interest in the house in 1866.[1] In his mastery of the marketplace, Alfred Novello proved himself an astute businessman and spirited publisher. Thus, it is surprising that at the height of his career, with the house thriving and expanding, Novello would choose to retire. In October 1856, Alfred disclosed his desire to hand on the firm.[2] Michael Hurd has suggested that his early notification was perhaps influenced by the death of his mother two years earlier, and his management of the family business may have been more a matter of duty than personal devotion. It is clear, however, that Alfred planned to leave the firm under carefully selected new leadership – which he found in his protégé Henry Littleton. Littleton joined the company in 1841, serving first as a 'collector', picking up music from other firms not published or stocked by Novello's.[3] During the following two decades, Littleton earned Alfred's respect and admiration. Thus, at the beginning of the 1860s, the first of two contracts was drawn up to name Littleton partner and eventual owner. Briefly, the initial contract (transcribed as Appendix 1), dated 28 October 1861, bound Littleton to buy the firm over the course of the following ten years, at an

---

[1] There is a discrepancy in the sources concerning the year in which Alfred Novello began as director. Michael Hurd, *Vincent Novello – and Company* (London: Novello, 1981), p. 29, dates the beginning of Alfred's direction from 1830, although other published sources cite 1829 as the initial year.

[2] Ibid., p. 63.

[3] Ibid., pp. 47–8 for Alfred's early relationship and interest in Littleton's career.

annual rate of £5,000; the agreement could be nullified if the yearly sum was not available. Yet Littleton managed the house to such profit that he completed payment five years before the deadline. On 17 September 1866, Novello and Littleton signed their second contract (transcribed as Appendix 2) and Novello's passed into new hands.[4]

During Alfred's tenure, from 1829 to 1866, Novello's evolved from a small family enterprise to become one of the leading music publishers in England by the middle of the century, and it is this period of growth and integration into the fabric of Victorian musical life that will be of main interest to this study. The period of Alfred's management was marked by the most prolific economic, demographic, and industrial growth England had ever experienced: the close of the Georgian period and the advent of Victoria's reign brought with it a move from an agrarian-based to an industrially focused society. The new emphasis on manufacturing cannot be underestimated as one of the leading factors in the metamorphosis of English social and, to our interests, musical life. The period from the 1830s to the mid-1860s was one of unparalleled innovation, reform, and upheaval in all quarters of society. The changes in working hours, wages, occupations, and leisure time, the repeal of cumbersome paper and stamp taxes, the development of the music copyright law, and the technological advancements of the railways and the steam press all must be taken into account in the decisions Novello made regarding house policy and daily business operations.

Three studies of the firm of Novello's have been published, all by the house itself: Joseph Bennett, *A Short History of Cheap Music* (1887); Laurence Swinyard, ed., *A Century and a Half in Soho: A Short History of the Firm of Novello, Publisher, Printers of Music, 1811–1961* (1961); and Michael Hurd, *Vincent Novello – and Company* (1981). The 1887 study of 142 pages offers an introduction to the history of the firm and a large portion of its material is duplicated in Swinyard's 1961 publication. The most recent examination, by Michael Hurd, takes a chronological approach, from the beginning of the house (including Vincent Novello's background) to its state as part of the English organization the Granada Company. In 1988 Granada sold Novello's to the music publishing and film group Filmtrax. In January 1990, Novello's was sold by Filmtrax to CBS Records and the house journal, *The Musical Times*, was sold to Orpheus Publications, with additional changes in management to follow thereafter. The company is currently part of Chester Music, Music Sales Group. Through Hurd's access to Novello's private files he provides the most complete discussion of

---

[4]Both contracts, unpublished, are located in the Cowden Clarke Collection, the Brotherton Library, Leeds University Library; their contents are summarized in Hurd, *Vincent Novello*, pp. 64–5.

the three publications.[5] Yet by its task as an all-encompassing examination of 170 years and within the boundaries of a relatively short house monograph of 163 pages, here, too, the larger issues of social and economic climate and their influence on individual aspects of house policy receive limited discussion. In general, many publishing histories have tended to focus on the relationship of a publisher to a specific composer, examined in large part from the viewpoint of the composer, and to bypass the extramusical issue of the marketplace and economic environment. Such examinations generally emphasize one of three categories: the relationship of a composer to a firm; the correspondence between them; or the history of a publisher, often produced in-house as an anniversary volume.[6] Neglected, however, is the acknowledgement of music publishing at its most fundamental level: as a business.

---

[5]See the report by Michael Hurd, 'The Novello Archives', *The Musical Times* 126 (1986), pp. 687–8. For additional information see also Rosemary Hughes, 'The Novello Family', *The New Grove Dictionary of Music and Musicians*, 2nd edn, ed. Stanley Sadie and John Tyrrell (London: Macmillan, 2001), 18: pp. 214–17; and Harvey Grace and Peter Ward Jones, 'Novello and Co.', *The New Grove Dictionary of Music and Musicians*, 2nd edn, ed. Stanley Sadie and John Tyrrell (London: Macmillan, 2001), 18: pp. 218–19.

[6]Examples of these three categories are found in the following sources: studies concerning the relationship of a composer to a firm have included the issue of text variance in published editions and the composer's control; for a comprehensive example see Jeffrey Kallberg, 'Chopin in the Marketplace: Aspects of the International Music Publishing Industry in the First Half of the Nineteenth Century', *Notes* 39 (1983), pp. 535–69 and pp. 795–824. See also Luke Jensen, *Giuseppe Verdi and Giovanni Ricordi, with notes on Francesco Lucca: From 'Oberto' to 'La Traviata'* (New York: Garland, 1989). Publishing histories have also focused on specific composers; see Rudolf Elvers, ed., *Felix Mendelssohn Bartholdy: Briefe an deutsche Verleger* (Berlin: Breitkopf and Härtel, 1968); W. Altmann, ed., *Richard Wagners Briefwechsel mit seinen Verlegern: Briefwechsel mit Breitkopf und Härtel* (Berlin: Breitkopf and Härtel, 1911) and *Briefwechsel mit B. Schotts Söhne* (Mainz: B. Schotts Söhne, 1911). For studies produced by the firms themselves see O. van Hase, *Breitkopf und Härtel: Gedenkschrift und Arbeitsbericht*, 3 vols (Leipzig: Breitkopf and Härtel, 1917–19); *Der Bär: Jahrbuch von Breitkopf und Härtel 1929/30* (Leipzig: Breitkopf and Hartel, 1930); Rudolf Elvers, *Breitkopf und Härtel, 1719–1969: Ein historischer Überblick zum Jubiläum* (Wiesbaden: Breitkopf and Härtel, 1969); *Pasticcio auf das 250jährige Bestehen des Verlages Breitkopf und Härtel: Beiträge zur Geschichte des Hauses* (Leipzig: Breitkopf and Härtel, 1968). See also Claudio Sartori, *Casa Ricordi* (Milan: Ricordi, 1958) and n.a., *Music, Musicians, Publishing: 175 Years of Casa Ricordi, 1808–1983* (Milan: Ricordi, 1983); for further sources see the bibliography in H. Edmund Poole and D. W. Krummel, 'Printing and Publishing of Music', in Stanley Sadie, ed., *The New Grove Dictionary of Music and Musicians* (London: Macmillan, 1980), 15: pp. 232–74 and D. W. Krummel and Stanley Sadie, eds, *The New Grove Handbooks in Music: Music Printing and Publishing* (London: Macmillan, 1990). See also Stanley Boorman, Eleanor Selfridge-Field, and Donald W. Krummel, 'Printing and Publishing of Music', *The New Grove Dictionary of Music and Musicians*, 2nd edn, ed. Stanley Sadie and John Tyrrell (London: Macmillan, 2001), 20: p. 326.

A standard practice is to examine the publisher in chronological fashion. Yet a chronological study of a publisher provides only one part of the complete picture – for it suggests a linear history in which equal weight is afforded the activities and decisions which form daily business practices. Rather, a publisher responds to specific events, criticisms, government and economic policies and styles which cannot be charted in time-line fashion. A chronological approach must be supplemented by a methodology that incorporates social and economic factors and moves beyond a purely narrative discussion. I have therefore chosen to explore the development of the house of Novello's by focusing on particular issues which shaped the firm. Thus, the different phases of publishing – acquisition, editorial style, print run, and relationship with a composer – are examined in turn, divided into five chapters and a conclusion:

1. English economic, social, and musical life, 1829–66
2. House editorial style
3. Print run and demand: Novello's stockbook
4. Alfred Novello's business practices as illustrated in his acquisition policies, relationships with composers, copyright laws, and repeal of taxes
5. The role of Novello's house organ, *The Musical Times* as a reflection of house style and policy
Conclusion

To examine a publisher with both specific issues and the influence of the outside world in mind, all available documentation must be interpreted in a new light: stockbooks, for example, reflect not only productivity but also market demand; the analysis of a house journal may suggest the taste of the audience for whom the publisher printed; and a publisher's reaction to government policies (such as copyright laws) illustrates how a firm defined its role in society.[7]

Publisher's records have also been used to construct a composer's work catalogue. The *Druckbuch* of the music publisher Schott was employed for dating and editorial information in John Deathridge, Martin Geck, and Egon Voss, eds, *Verzeichnis der musikalischen Werke Richard Wagners und ihrer Quellen* (Mainz: B. Schotts Söhne, 1986). One article which examines the publishing records of a firm independently of their relationship to a composer or an in-house publication is James Fuld, 'The Ricordi "Libroni"' in Rudolf Elvers, ed., *Festschrift Albi Rosenthal* (Tutzing: Hans Schneider, 1984).

[7]This approach, examining the performing arts in light of their economic and social environment, has been explored in other disciplines as well. See, for example, Tracy C. Davis, *The Economics of the British Stage, 1800–1914* (Cambridge: Cambridge University Press, 2000).

That the early history of Novello's is bound up with the events of England in the nineteenth century was most eloquently recognized by George Grove in the Introduction to the first Novello study of 1887:

> Moreover, this record shows how dependent men and things are on one another and how secure those undertakings are which rise from small beginnings. Vincent Novello might have been as musical as he was, Alfred Novello as far-sighted, and Henry Littleton as enterprising and as accurate; but it would have been to no purpose but for the progress made in machinery and practical science, for the increase in communication, and for the removal of the taxes on literature, which have distinguished the reign of our beloved Sovereign; that removal being itself greatly aided by one of the three enlightened and energetic men just mentioned. The same causes which have created the immense periodical literature of our day have brought about the equally extraordinary cheap music which we now possess, and while they have given us the *Daily Telegraph* for a penny and the *Illustrated London News* for sixpence, have also given us a still more valuable acquisition – *The Messiah* and *Israel in Egypt* for a shilling. It is the division of labour, the spread of machinery, the extension of travelling and transport, the invention and use of labour-saving processes of all kinds unknown to former generations, and also the progress of education, helped by the foregoing mechanical improvements, and itself re-acting strongly on them – it is these characteristic achievements of the reign of Victoria which have effected so much in literature and music that is a mere commonplace to us, but which to our fathers and grandfathers was unknown, unexpected, impossible, and we may add, not desired, because the desire had not been evoked. When the house of Novello was founded no one could have dreamed of the change that was so soon to arrive.

CHAPTER ONE

The Economic and Social Environment in England, 1829–1866

It is not surprising that the house of Novello entered a phase of rapid development during the late 1820s, for the period from 1821 to 1836 is often recognized by historians as having offered an ideal climate for economic growth and expansion. S. G. Checkland summed up this moment of expansion as one in which new businesses developed and flourished and incomes grew:

> Real growth in wealth took place between 1821 and 1836. Indeed it has been suggested that the industrial revolution in Britain, far from tapering off in the twenties and thirties, was then at its height, in the sense of invoking and applying new capital. Men of business showed vigour and daring in the promotion of trade and industry. Real wages in many trades began to rise again ... Industrial output accelerated to produce the most substantial relative increase of the entire century. It seems likely that average real incomes, after a period of stagnation, 1800–12, showed a marked rise over the next ten years, and a significantly high rate of increase between 1822 and 1833.[1]

Although the country would encounter financial low points during the years Alfred Novello directed the firm, in general the period from 1815 to 1885 in Britain is considered an era of large-scale entrepreneurial and industrial expansion.[2] How the firm grew and prospered within this rapidly evolving environment and how Alfred Novello turned to his advantage the changes confronting him in technology, society, and business, reveal one publisher's successful participation in the contemporary climate.

This chapter will provide a brief survey of the socio-economic state of England during the period of Alfred Novello's management, focusing on three areas of change: (1) economic developments; (2) ecclesiastical and social reform; and (3) the musical environment. (The technological

---

[1] S. G. Checkland, *The Rise of Industrial Society in England, 1815–1885* (Harlow: Longman, 1971), p. 11. See also Roderick Flood and Deirdre McCloskey, *The Economic History of Britain Since 1700*, 2nd edn, vol. 1: *1700–1860* (Cambridge: Cambridge University Press, 1994).

[2] Pauline Gregg, *A Social and Economic History of Britain* (London: G. Harrap, 1965), p. 103.

advances made in the printing industry during this period will be examined in a separate discussion in Chapter 3.) Within each category we will also examine the Novello house list and determine whether external events influenced editorial decisions and style.

Economic Environment and Definition of the Middle Class

An examination of music publishing – especially concerning firms after the advent of an industrialized, and thus more economically and socially complex, society – must take account of the issues of occupation, wages, disposable income, and the availability of leisure time. Of primary importance was the shift in occupational focus from agriculture to manufacturing. In the course of the nineteenth century agriculture receded as the dominant occupation and was replaced by engineering, construction, and transportation. In the United Kingdom in 1851 the percentage of the population involved in agriculture was 20.9 per cent, compared to 32.7 per cent in manufacture. By 1861 the gap had widened with more of the population in manufacturing, 33 per cent, than in agrarian-related work, 18 per cent.[3] Within this new climate, with its emphasis on manufacturing and industrial expansion, the place of honour was reserved for the professionals who could build the factories, bridges, railways, and indeed entirely new towns which were in increasing demand. The value placed on such expertise is easily seen in the financial position of representative occupations and professions. In a table entitled 'Adult-Male Employee Classes and Their Approximate Mean Positions in the Nineteenth-Century Earnings Ranks for England and Wales', comparative percentages for annual incomes of both waged and salaried workers are listed in rising gradation.[4] The percentile position of engineers and surveyors, for example, increased markedly from 1827 to 1851 from 89th to 94th position; their advancement can be measured in the proximity to solicitors and barristers, who moved from 95th to 100th percentile during the same period.

With the shift away from agriculture and the move towards more urbanized and industrial occupations, working hours and wage stratification evolved as well. The influence of wages and working hours on the

---

[3]Geoffrey Best, *Mid-Victorian Britain, 1851–1875* (London: Fontana Press, 1971), p. 99, from the table 'Employment of the people of the UK 1851–81 as percentage of occupied population'.

[4]Peter H. Lindert and Jeffrey G. Williamson, 'English Workers' Living Standards during the Industrial Revolution: A New Look', *The Economic History Review* 36 (1983), pp. 1–25.

levels of disposable income and leisure time cannot be ignored where music – in printed form – is regarded as a commodity, available to those with the financial means and free time for purchase, study, and performance. However, the following discussion and analysis of wages must bear with it a caveat particular to studies of nineteenth-century English economic development. The definition of class and financial levels during the first half of the century is a difficult and imprecise exercise. This difficulty arises because there does not exist as much documentation concerning wages of the rural labourer as for the urban worker. The urban worker, for example, was often employed by a factory or in an occupation where wages and taxes were recorded. The rural worker, however, frequently received a wage from farm labour, with piecemeal work out of season – income not registered and therefore not easily determined. This lack of accurate data has been recognized by historians as one of the primary problems in quantifying Victorian social and financial levels. Moreover, different regions of England also produced varying economic environments. S. G. Checkland notes, for example, the difference in rural wages between the farm worker in Dorset or Devon who received only about half the income of his northern counterpart.

Because of the disparities of urban, rural, and regional factors, the figures which must be relied on are those gleaned from regulated work – from taxed, recorded employment – mostly located in urban centres. The following discussion of income therefore focuses on urban wages although this is not meant to suggest that the financial status, class definition, and buying power would be the same for the rural population.

A picture of the general wage-earning environment in England during the nineteenth century can be found in the article by Lindert and Williamson from which the following information is taken.[5] The cost-of-living index provided by Lindert and Williamson was calculated by computing the cost of commodities (that is, food, housing, and expenses) against wage rates.[6] Their scale indicates that in 1829 the figure was at 143.9 while by 1843 it had fallen to 109.6. With a slight increase the following year to 114.5, by 1849 it had again declined to 101.2. As the cost of living gradually fell between 1829 and 1849 it was coupled with an increase in wages. With respect to wage earning, Lindert and Williamson note that 'unless new errors are discovered or a host of new declining wage series added, it seems reasonable to conclude that the average

---

[5]Lindert and Williamson, 'English Workers' Living Standards', n. 3. Also informative is E. J. Hobsbawm, 'The Standard of Living during the Industrial Revolution: A Discussion', *The Economic History Review* 15 (1963), pp. 119–34.

[6]Lindert and Williamson, pp. 8–9, nn. 28–9 for a detailed explanation of sources used to determine the cost-of-living index.

worker was much better off in any decade from the 1830s on than in any decade before 1820'.[7] Indeed, even during the depression of 1841–3, 'no conceivable level of unemployment could have cancelled the near-doubling of full-time wages and left the workers of the 1840s with less than their grandfathers had had'.[8]

Thus, if we examine annual incomes from occupations representative of each class, we may observe this general rising trend. According to the table in Lindert and Williamson entitled 'Estimates of Nominal Annual Earnings for Eighteen Occupations, 1755–1851: Adult Males, England and Wales (in current £s [that is, the date of their research, 1983, value])' we find in almost every level of society wages increased. In 1835 'government low-wage' earners (defined as watchmen, guards, porters, and so on) earned £58.70 p.a. which increased by 1851 to £66.45. Following the same two sample years, members of the 'printing trade' (for example, compositors) were paid £70.23 in 1835 and £74.72 in 1851. In comparison, the upwardly mobile surveyors and engineers mentioned above held incomes of £398.89 and £479.00 respectively; and at the top of the scale solicitors and barristers annually received £1166.67 in 1835 and £1837.50 in 1851.

Within this environment of growing industry, increasing wages, and diminishing cost of living, we find that socio-economic portion of society broadly described as the middle class. If we focus now on this level of income we may use their statistics as the median point of reference for comparison with the classes both above and below their status. The notion of the middle class is frequently referred to in nineteenth-century studies in ill-defined and general terms. It is acknowledged that the definition can be employed to pinpoint groups of people from earlier centuries and other countries. For the purpose of this study, I refer to that portion of the population in nineteenth-century Britain within specific economic and occupational areas which will be defined below.

By following the records and assessments of tax returns, for example, Geoffrey Best, in his study *Mid-Victorian Britain, 1851–1875*, gave this description of the middle class: 'The earners of these incomes above £150 a year (alas! there is no means of knowing just how many of them there were; we know how many paid tax under each schedule, but not how many people paid tax under more than one schedule) were all in the

---

[7]Ibid., p. 12.

[8]Ibid., p. 13. It is of note that Lindert and Williamson's figures remain important and key references today and have become valuable resources for understanding the economic climate of the period. See Flood and McCloskey, *The Economic History of Britain Since 1700*, 2nd edn. See also P. H. Lindert and J. G. Williamson, 'Revising England's Social Table, 1688–1812', *Explorations in Economic History* 19 (1982), 385–408.

general sense "middle class" or higher: people with homes of their own and means to employ some domestic help.'[9] Yet even with such information available as provided by Best and by Lindert and Williamson, their definitions do not agree. While Lindert and Williamson mark the 'estimate of nominal annual earnings' for 1851 for solicitors and barristers as £1837.50, Best finds this sum as the annual payment for a 'chief clerk' (defined unclearly as 'principal officers') starting 'at around £1000'.[10] Lindert and Williamson, however, find 'government high-wage' (which may be close to Best's 'principal officers') at £234.87 p.a. It is likely that the Lindert/Williamson figures are more accurate but the wide discrepancy between the two illustrates the difficulty in forming correct definitions and determining prosperity and buying capability – difficulties which hamper the socio-economic study of a publisher.

We are, nonetheless, in a position to see which class levels held enough disposable income, as well as leisure time (discussed below), to participate in musical activities. That is, could the lower-middle-class clerk or the skilled labourer afford to be active in musical organizations which might involve personal expense? Clearly we know from the growth of the choral movement during the nineteenth century as well as from the growing activity in domestic music-making (both discussed below) that income was available. Table 1.1, illustrating the percentage of disposable income available for such activities and the extent to which such involvement was financially feasible, follows the categories presented by Weber in his study *Music and the Middle Class*.[11] Weber employs income statistics to determine the percentage that was spent on leisure activities. (Weber defines a 'modest clerical salary' as £250 p.a. and an income 'on the threshold of the upper-middle class' as £1,000.)

While Weber's table compares concert ticket prices and income, Table 1.1 substitutes income data from Lindert and Williamson and includes the cost of Novello editions (taken from a representative advertisement in *The Musical Times* of 1 March 1849). If we calculate what percentage of an annual and monthly income Novello's editions required, a picture of the Novello customer and the overall market begins to emerge. For this analysis, two of the firm's most popular editions are employed: Handel's *Messiah*, oblong format, piano-vocal

---

[9]Best, *Mid-Victorian Britain*, p. 102.

[10]Ibid., p. 107.

[11]William Weber, *Music and the Middle Class: The Social Structure of Concert Life in London, Paris and Vienna* (London: Croom Helm, 1975), pp. 25–6 and p. 160, table 10: 'Expense Brackets of Concert Prices'. See also William Weber, 'The Muddle of the Middle Classes', *19th-Century Music* 3 (1979), pp. 175–85.

Table 1.1   Annual and monthly incomes and percentage costs for
Novello editions and concert tickets

Occupation/income (annual)/monthly[a] (1851)	Percentage (annual)/monthly income: Novello edition	Concert ticket prices[b]
I. Novello edition: Handel, *Messiah*, oblong, price: 6s. (price from March 1849 *Musical Times*)		
Non-farm labourer: (£44.83)/£3.73	8/(0.66)	'lower price' bracket: 1s.–5s.
Printing trade (compositor): (£74.72)/£6.22	4.8/(0.40)	'middle price': 5s.–10s.6d.
Schoolmaster: (£81.11)/£6.75	4.4/(0.36)	5s.–10s.6d.
Engineer and surveyor: (£479.00)/£39.91	0.75/(0.06)	'upper price': 10s.6d.–21s.
II. Novello edition: Haydn, *Creation*, Octavo, in cloth, 5s.		
Non-farm labourer (£44.83)/£3.73	6.7/(0.55)	
Printing trade (compositor): (£74.72)/£6.22	4/(0.33)	
Schoolmaster: (£81.11)/£6.75	3.7/(0.30)	
Engineer and surveyor: (£479)/£39.91	0.62/(0.05)	

[a]Annual and monthly income figures from Lindert and Williamson, 'English Workers' Living Standards', p. 4.
[b]Concert ticket prices from Weber, *Music and the Middle Class*, table 5: 'Expense Brackets of Concert Prices', p. 160.

score ('adapted for piano-forte players', as it is described in the advertisement) and Haydn's *Creation*, octavo, piano-vocal score. Four income brackets are chosen, representing the occupational and financial levels of the population who might have purchased or performed Novello editions. The cost of concert tickets (as defined by Weber) is also included as a comparison to Novello's prices. Thus, the cost of a 'lower price' concert ticket of between 1s. and 5s. is close to that for the *Messiah* score at 6s. or the Haydn work at 5s.

Weber has calculated the percentage of annual income each social bracket devoted to 'entertainment':

> Several discussions of typical middle-class budgets indicate that less prosperous families would rarely spend more than 2% and in most cases closer to 1% of their income on entertainment. An English and an Austrian source each stated that persons with a modest clerical salary (£250 and 400 fl.) would spend about 3% upon medicine and incidentals (especially tobacco and beer) as well as trips to concerts or the theater. That the same writer said families on the threshold of the upper-middle class (£1000) would sink 2% into entertainment alone indicates that lesser ones would put but 1% into it.[12]

Weber's figures correspond to those in Table 1.1: if the 'less prosperous' normally spent an average of 1 per cent on music and theatre, then the cost of a Novello score, which would amount to 0.66 per cent of an annual income, would have been within this budget. The printer and schoolmaster's allowance of 1–2 per cent would permit the purchase of one Novello score per year in addition to limited attendance at concerts, while the engineer and surveyor could purchase as many as ten scores and still afford performance tickets within his 2 per cent budget. In addition to the individuals who purchased their own copies of Novello editions, it is most likely that a large number of copies were bought for their members by choral societies and organizations such as the Mechanics' Institute, many in the income bracket below the schoolmaster's £81 p.a. (as a report from a Mechanics' Institute concert, quoted below, indicates). Thus, we shall see that Novello's catered both to the individual eager to obtain his own score and perform at home (see the discussion below concerning domestic music) and to the growing number of choral society members for whom a large number of scores were purchased (Chapter 3 discusses these quantities as reflected in Novello's print runs and warehouse stockbook).

In addition to the increase in wages during the first half of the nineteenth century, mandatory working hours were gradually reduced; Checkland notes that the length of the work day in textiles, engineering, and house-building fell by approximately one-fifth between 1836 and 1886.[13] The history of working-hour reform cannot be detailed here but it is of note that the Ten Hours Act for Women and Young Persons of 1847 (with additional legislation in 1850 and 1853) is of note for the legalized reduction to a ten and a half hour day; the working hours for men would later come under reform as well. (Best cautions, however, not to assume that such reforms were widely embraced: shop assistants and

---

[12]Weber, *Music and the Middle Class*, p. 23.
[13]Checkland, *The Rise of Industrial Society*, p. 231.

shop workers, for example, would have to await future protection.[14]) An example of working hours within the music printing trade is also of interest. Following a general meeting of the London Typographical Music Association held in March 1861, a 'scale of prices' for work undertaken was printed, in the form of a sixteen-point flysheet, and circulated. Point fourteen states: 'Music-type Compositors employed by the week shall receive not less than £2 per week when wholly employed on music; 10½ hours to constitute a day's work.'[15]

The gradual increase in leisure – or, in any case, non-working – time now available to a growing number of the population brought with it concern for how these free hours would be spent. The notion of 'rational recreation' thus developed, encompassing the idea of relaxation with constructive activity, whether in education, technical training, or music (preferably in a church choir or choral organization but not in a music hall). While it must be acknowledged that, to some extent, the notion of 'rational recreation' remained more an ideal than a reality, nevertheless, the activities of the choral society, participation in a parish choir, and musical education in school for children and in organizations such as the Tonic Sol-Fa classes for adults comprised a large portion of mid-century musical activities and could be defined under the term. Novello's focused their editions and publications on these 'rational' musical genres rather than on the dance hall or brass band repertoire. The following discussion, therefore, will concentrate on the genres reflected in Novello editions: sacred choral music, music for singing societies, and music for domestic performance. The examination of leisure time in nineteenth-century England, and its social and economic implications, has developed into an extensive and independent branch of Victorian studies. What is of interest here is the impact of these reclaimed hours on the burgeoning participation in mid-century musical life, especially as it is reflected in the growing demand for printed music.

Ecclesiastical and Social Reform

The combination of wage increase and working-hour reform offered the Victorian more time for personal, educational, and recreational pursuits. But additional factors influenced the activities of mid-century English musical life and must also be considered. The impact of what came to be

---

[14]Best, *Mid-Victorian Britain*, p. 138; and Checkland, *The Rise of Industrial Society*, pp. 248–9.

[15]Flysheet, March 1861, 'Scale of prices of the London Typographical Music Association', located in the archive of the St Bride's Printing Library, London.

called the Oxford Movement may have suggested the kind of music Novello's chose to publish. A brief definition of this ecclesiastical reform will help us to determine how taste and practice of sacred music changed during the first half of the century. In 1833, on 14 July, John Keble (1792–1866) preached a sermon, entitled 'National apostasy', at the Church of St Mary the Virgin, Oxford. John Henry Newman considered the sermon as the beginning of a new approach to Church of England worship and thereafter marked this as the beginning of the Oxford Movement. The Movement was promoted through its own publication, *Tracts for the Times* (1833–41), and from this title followers became known as Tractarians.[16] At the heart of the Movement was the belief that the Church of England was the 'One Holy Catholic and Apostolic Church' for the country and held a relationship and link with the Church of Rome. Not surprisingly, this mention and connection with Rome gave rise to fears of popish influence and possible subversion of the English way of worship and life. Indeed, this philosophical tie with the Church of Rome eventually led some Tractarians to convert to Catholicism, most significantly John Henry Newman in 1845. On a practical level, Tractarian reform sought to revive the service of worship, enliven the congregation, and ultimately bring them spiritually closer to God; this was attempted through the use of particular surplices for the choir, the careful selection of chants and music, and the choice and placement of crosses and objects close to the altar. Although music in the Church was undergoing change well before the Oxford reforms, the importance of the Movement for the course of the Victorian sacred repertoire cannot be ignored.[17]

As a byproduct of the Oxford Movement, two conflicting attitudes developed concerning congregational participation, defined by Gatens as the 'ecclesiological' and 'cathedral' ideals.[18] The ecclesiological ideal supported participation by the congregation in the music for the service, especially for the responses and canticles and in chanting the Daily Prayer Book to Gregorian psalm tones.[19] The advocates of congregational singing

---

[16]Nicholas Temperley uses the terms 'Tractarianism' and 'the Oxford Movement' interchangeably to indicate this new philosophy. See Temperley, *The Music of the English Parish Church*, 2 vols (Cambridge: Cambridge University Press, 1979), 1: pp. 249 ff.; William J. Gatens, *Victorian Cathedral Music in Theory and Practice* (Cambridge: Cambridge University Press, 1986); and Bernarr Rainbow, *The Choral Revival in the Anglican Church* (London: Barrie and Jenkins, 1970), especially ch. 3: 'The Cradle of the Movement: S. Mark's College. Chelsea'. See also Bennett Zon, *The English Plainchant Revival* (Oxford: Oxford University Press, 1999).

[17]See Temperley, *Music of the English Parish Church*, 1: p. 249.

[18]Gatens, *Victorian Cathedral Music*, pp. 7–8.

[19]Ibid., p. 7; and Kenneth R. Long, *Music of the English Church* (London: Hodder and Stoughton, 1971), p. 327.

promoted their philosophy with a number of publications, including *The Psalter Noted* (1849) by the Revd Thomas Helmore (1811–90). Helmore prepared and published *The Psalter Noted* both to educate the St Marks students and to disseminate his instruction more broadly to other congregations in the art of chanting psalms. In 1850 *The Psalter Noted* was expanded to include canticles, 'a brief directory', additional instructions, and a new title, *A Manual of Plainsong*. It is worth pointing out the format of *The Psalter Noted* for it, in part, reflects the philosophy of the Oxford Movement. Helmore used his experience with students and singers at St Marks to transform the ancient chant style into one which would be suitable for contemporary performance, yet he also retained the earlier style of four-line staves, old clefs, and notation of longs, breves, etc. This reinforced the Movement's desire to uphold and yet make accessible the old style of music. Although Helmore's Psalter and chanting technique were successful at St Marks, his method proved too eccentric for the average parish congregation and his system was never widely accepted.

Other advocates of the 'ecclesiological ideal' founded their own organization, the Society for Promoting Church Music, in 1846. Its monthly journal, *The Parish Choir*, commenced publication in February of that year with the last issue printed in March 1851. The journal was an important instrument for this faction of the Oxford Movement as it provided music supplements with each issue to train and guide congregations in developing a repertoire. The journal also offered educational advice to the fledgling choir: the first issue included 'How to Begin' and 'Short Note on Chanting the Psalms'.[20] In part, the ecclesiological ideal may have gained a large portion of their following through the teaching reforms and subsequent influence of the graduates from St Mark's Teaching College in Chelsea. The founding of the College in 1841 introduced the first training institution for teachers in which an education in church music was recognized as an important part of the curricula. St Mark's was established by the Church of England under the initial direction of Reverend Derwent Coleridge as Principal; John Hullah, who would become famous as the founder of a nationwide sight-singing movement, joined the faculty as well. The repertoire for the daily service was far more ambitious than most contemporary church choirs could approach, but through the rigorous training as well as the advanced level of technique demanded by the works performed at the College, it was hoped that graduates would carry their knowledge and techniques to their students and congregations.[21]

---

[20]Rainbow, *Choral Revival in the Anglican Church*, pp. 95ff.
[21]Ibid., p. 50.

For advocates of congregational participation, the chosen repertoire featured technically accessible genres: the polyphonic music of the sixteenth and seventeenth centuries, English versions of Latin motets, and contemporary compositions written in this 'older' style.[22] Novello's editorial style for anthems and services is discussed in Chapter 2 but we may here briefly note that a number of his publications clearly were part of this 'ecclesiological ideal'. An examination of the firm's list during the 1840s and 1850s reveals that Alfred in fact published editions which suited this aspect of the Oxford Movement. Three publications in this vein are Maurice Greene, *40 Select Anthems*; (*c*.1840); Samuel Webbe, *Eight Anthems* (184-) and *Twelve Anthems*, described in the 1856 catalogue as 'particularly calculated for families or small choral societies'. We also find in this catalogue the following description accompanying *Turle's Chants*: 'The object of [the edition] is to combine sufficient choice with order, and, by publication of the arrangement, to enable the congregation to join the Psalms.' The 1863 catalogue also lists Helmore's *The Psalter Noted* and *St Mark's Chant Book*: 'being the chants used in the Collegiate Chapel of S. Mark, Chelsea ...'. Under a description of the first volume, 'A Hymnal Noted', is the comment: 'These melodies are eminently adapted for Congregational use, and have proved to answer better on the whole than more modern tunes.'

The second and ultimately more popular philosophy of the Oxford Movement was the 'cathedral ideal'. This approach to worship and ceremony held that parish churches should establish and maintain trained choirs to sing *for* the congregation (representing them both musically and spiritually). Following this viewpoint, parish churches sought to present a formal aura of ritual and tradition, usually associated with cathedrals, including the use of a surpliced choir and a repertoire of more ambitious and technically advanced music.[23] It is of note that from this local practice of the parish church to emulate the cathedral style of music and ceremony, a new standard of Anglican Church service developed which is today the expected norm:

> It is a remarkable development of the Victorian period that cathedral music came to be regarded as the normal music of the Anglican Church as a whole, not just the preserve of the choral foundation. The ecclesiological ideal, while essentially parochial, was destined not to gain wide acceptance. It was too closely tied to a much misunderstood and widely unpopular strain of churchmanship, and too firmly bound to a musical repertory of the remote past. While it was impractical, even undesirable, for all parish churches to adopt the

[22]Gatens, *Victorian Cathedral Music*, p. 7.
[23]Long, *Music of the English Church*, p. 328.

cathedral ideal wholesale, it was this ideal that had the potential for public enthusiasm, as adopted in the diocesan choral festivals, and as the cathedrals themselves raised their musical and devotional standards.[24]

Gatens dates the possibly earliest example of this 'philosophy' for the choral service from 1841 at the Leeds Parish Church where a desire had been voiced to establish daily choral services. The Novello catalogue includes an edition, 'The choral service as used in the Parish Church of Leeds ...', by James Hill and edited by Vincent Novello, published in 1841, intended, as the catalogue describes, for 'the Daily Prayer and Litany; consisting of the Chants, Versicles, and responses, arranged for the Priest and Choir'.

Analysis of the Novello list from the 1840s and 1850s suggests that, in part, Alfred was sensitive to the growing demand for music following the 'cathedral' style. In addition to the Leeds Parish Church edition, Novello published *Cathedral Voluntaries, from the works of Orlando Gibbons, Dr. Blow, Pelham Humphrey [sic] ... and other sterling church composers of the English school*, edited by Vincent Novello (c.1836); *Cathedral Music* (c.1849); *A collection of motets for the offertory and other pieces principally adapted for the morning service ...* (1840); and *169 Psalm and Hymn Tunes by eminent Composers with accomp. for organ or pianoforte ...* (c.1848). It is unfortunate that neither documentation nor correspondence appears to exist which would confirm a direct influence of the Oxford Movement on Novello's editorial decisions although it can only be expected that sacred editions would be published to attract both factions of the Movement, catering thus to the congregation and to the professional choir in the growing demand for printed music.

The Choral Movement

In addition to economic and ecclesiastical factors which may have influenced Novello's publishing programme, particular developments in Victorian musical life also helped to shape house policy. Among the most popular activities at mid-century were choral groups and societies; the growing participation in these organizations is frequently referred to as 'the choral movement'. A study of this phenomenon in nineteenth-century England carries with it a number of questions: what economic classes participated, what music was performed, what editorial formats were employed, and how large were the societies

---

[24]Gatens, *Victorian Cathedral Music*, p. 15.

involved?[25] The issue of editorial format will be addressed separately in Chapter 2 but we may here briefly examine the general environment of the choral singer and thus place Novello's editions within a musical and social framework of performance and demand. It has been noted above that the ecclesiological preference in the Oxford Movement and the training at St Mark's may have inspired the formation of choral groups and the advancement of music education beyond the environs of London. Two other factors influenced this expansion as well: the desire for education and the availability of leisure time. Contemporary accounts of choral festivals, for example, suggest the size of these gatherings as well as the social class which participated. *Aris's Birmingham Gazette* provides an informative observation in their issue of 28 September 1857 of the performance of *The Creation* by the Birmingham Festival Choral Society: 'It was an inspiring sight to mark the eager attention of the crowded auditory, the greater part of whom were of the working class, while hundreds followed the performance from the cheap editions of Novello and Cocks. This argues strongly for the increasing growth of an elevated musical taste among the masses.'[26] While the tone of the report treads into the realm of hyperbole, such documentation, coupled with cost-of-living and annual wage studies, sketch the social scene: the working-class – in great numbers – participated in music-making and purchased, or in any case obtained, Novello and similar editions. (A quantitative examination of the use of Novello editions by choral societies and their audience is discussed in Chapter 3 with an analysis of the Novello stockbook.) In the above examination of annual and weekly income, it was suggested that Novello editions were within the financial reach of the lower-middle class (that is, with an income above the labourer but beneath the surveyor). Contemporary reports, as quoted above, and the presence of concert series such as the 'Shilling Oratorios' in Liverpool and similar concerts in urban areas of Britain confirm a major participation by the working class. Contemporary accounts also indicate that organ accompaniments often replaced the orchestra. This would have made for less expensive productions in terms of numbers of performers required and may have also offered a more accessible presentation.[27] The musical preferences and format of choral society performances now become clear: concerts were frequently available at

---

[25]An extensive examination of the choral society and choral movement in England is found in Brian Pritchard, 'The Musical Festival and the Choral Society in England in the 18th and 19th Centuries: A Social History' (Ph.D. diss., University of Birmingham, 1968).

[26]Passage quoted Pritchard, 'The Musical Festival and the Choral Society', p. 598.

[27]See ibid., pp. 558–9.

an affordable price and were attended by the middle and lower classes; performances usually employed organ rather than orchestral accompaniment and both performer and, often, audience possessed piano-vocal editions. As we shall see in Chapter 2, Novello's neatly adapted to this demand by publishing inexpensive piano-vocal editions in octavo size which were easy to hold.

Participation in choral groups was also possible through the Mechanics' Institutes. These organizations, founded to provide additional education for artisans and skilled workers in technology and industry and to keep abreast of scientific advancements, were similar to societies already expanding on the Continent, and there was pressure to offer equivalent programmes at home. Education was not limited to scientific and practical subjects, however; music as well, especially in the form of singing groups and rudimentary training, was offered. A survey of contemporary music journals illustrates some of the musical activities connected with the Mechanics' Institutes. *Cocks's Musical Miscellany* for April 1852 reported the performance held in the Institute in Nottingham on 3 March of Mendlessohn's *Elijah*: 'Mendelssohn's oratorio *Elijah* was performed at the large hall connected with the Mechanics' Institution ... The choral body were [*sic*] most efficient – thanks to Mr. Fraser's efforts. Few towns of the same size as Nottingham could produce so effective a body of amateurs. The Hall was crowded.' The same issue also reported on a recent lecture: 'Brighton – Mr. Carte's lecture at the Atheneum was well received and the illustration admirable. Mr. Bond's Lecture on Vocal Music, with illustrations, delivered at the Mechanics' Institution, was unusually successful.' Yet the concept of the Mechanics' Institute, like the notion of 'rational recreation', held within it the patronizing sentiment of its creator – the middle-class manager – and eventually these organizations suffered from lack of enthusiasm by the participants.

An examination of the repertoire of the 'Shilling Oratorios' and the Mechanics' Institute concerts during their most active years suggests the compositions which were most popular, based on the repetition of specific works. Pritchard provides a list of the 'Shilling Oratorio' performances, and a sample from the years between 1854 and 1858 indicates that the most frequently performed works were Handel's *Messiah*, *Israel in Egypt*, and *Alexander's Feast*; Haydn's *Creation*; Mendelssohn's *Elijah* and *Hymn of Praise*; and Mozart's 'Twelfth Mass' (but see Chapter 2 for this spurious attribution to Mozart). A glance at any Novello catalogue from this period reveals these compositions to have been major editions in the house list, available in a number of editorial styles and formats. Not surprisingly, the Novello stockbook indicates that these works produced some of the largest print runs of the firm.

In addition to such specialized concerts and organizations, at mid-century the large choral festival reached its peak of popularity. Its massive scale, both in size of choir and audience, remains one of the predominant images of Victorian music-making. We find Novello a direct participant in the choral festivals both in the provision of scores and in the publication of compositions timed for special occasions. Thus, Novello published their edition of Mendelssohn's *St Paul* to coincide with its performance at the Liverpool Festival in 1836 and the firm was elected publisher for music at the 1851 Great Exhibition. Novello's commitment to suitable editions for congregations, choral groups, and amateurs is well illustrated in their numerous catalogues and advertisements: the August 1863 table of contents lists the editions for choral concerts as 'Music in separate vocal and orchestral parts, for the use of choral societies, singing classes, and church choirs'.

Domestic Music and Performance

The other side of Victorian music was found in the private domain of the home. As Nicholas Temperley has noted, during the period from 1800 to 1860 domestic music flourished:

> Music activity in the home in this period must have been very considerable judging from the amount of music published, which increased rapidly throughout the nineteenth century. Enormous quantities of piano music, songs and ballads, and chamber music for small ensembles poured from the rapidly expanding publishing houses; and from about 1840 onwards, the publication of vocal part-music was on almost the same scale. Very little of this music was performed in concerts.[28]

In her article 'Music-making in a Yorkshire Country House', Caroline Wood examines some of the collection of music found at Burton Constable Hall during the nineteenth century. From the archives and

---

[28]Nicholas Temperley, 'Domestic Music in England: 1800–1860', *Proceedings of the Royal Musical Association* 85 (1958/9), p. 32. Mary Burgan notes the portrayal of the piano in the home as a sign of accomplishment, education, and social status in Victorian literature. The piano appears as a symbol in novels such as *Pride and Prejudice*, *Vanity Fair*, and *Jane Eyre*. See Mary Burgan, 'Heroines at the Piano: Women and Music in Nineteenth-Century Fiction', in Nicholas Temperley, ed., *The Lost Chord: Essays on Victorian Music* (Bloomington, Ind.: Indiana University Press, 1989), pp. 42–67. See Caroline Wood, 'Music-Making in a Yorkshire Country House', *Nineteenth-Century British Music Studies* 1 (1999), 209–24.

material available Wood notes a fairly wide repertoire for performance including music for dancing and contemporary pieces by Thalberg, Chopin, Cramer, and Liszt, among others. From the research undertaken by Wood the music appears to have been played and performed. The conclusion one may be able to draw is that this was a collection created by a sophisticated and educated group. This quite differs from the domestic music-making repertoire of the middle and working classes – Novello's main markets – and suggests that any analysis of music-making in the home or in non-professional circumstances should be undertaken within socio-economic parameters, and generalizations incorporating all classes cannot be drawn.

The growing popularity of the piano was a major factor in the wealth of published music for domestic performance. The now commonplace presence in parlour or drawing room of the instrument led to an unprecedented expansion of the piano repertoire, including arrangements of recent operas, earlier oratorios, and classical works; accompaniments to vocal or instrumental music; and solos. Alfred Novello published editions which satisfied a portion of this market in domestic music-making: the firm specialized in piano-vocal reductions of sacred music, glees, and modern arrangements of madrigals from earlier periods. In addition to their presence in the choral society repertoire of piano-vocal editions of Handel and Mendelssohn (see Chapter 2 for a discussion of these arrangements), these editions were also adopted at home for small gatherings to practise, study, and perform.

Novello also published numerous collections of glees and songs suitable for performance around a domestic-sized piano (the small compact upright version, often referred to as the 'cottage' piano was the style found in most middle- and lower-class households).[29] At the 1851 Exhibition, cottage pianos were featured by a number of makers. As noted in the *Official Illustrated Catalogue of the Great Exhibition*, these pianos were especially suited to the more confined quarters of the lower-middle-class home: 'The small, upright piano-fortes, as now made by the best houses, are very good instruments, and are valuable for small rooms, from the little space they occupy and the facility with which they can be placed in any desired position. The upright form has the peculiar advantage that the strings are struck against their rests, which is generally

---

[29]The smaller pianos were about 4–5 feet high. The term 'cottage piano' was first applied *c*.1812, by the piano maker Robert Wornum (1780–1852). This smaller-scaled instrument was possible through the invention and development of a shorter piano-string length. See Arthur Loesser, *Men, Women, and Pianos: A Social History* (London: Gollancz, 1955). A comprehensive survey of the development of the instrument is Cyril Ehrlich, *The Piano: A History*, rev. edn (Oxford: Clarendon Press, 1990).

considered the most favourable direction for the blow, and much simpli-
fies the framing. Many attempts have been made to apply this method of
striking to the grand and square forms; but it has not yet come into
general use.'[30] Novello's approach to this kind of publication is illustrated in *Novello's Glee-Hive: A Collection of Popular Glees and
Madrigals* (c.1851: preface dated January 1851). The format was for
four and five voices with piano accompaniment. The homophonic style
of the songs offered both performer and listener the maximum amount
of harmony and sense of accomplishment with the minimum of technical
strain. The repertoire was predominantly English from earlier periods
and included, for example, compositions of Morley, Gibbons, Battishill,
Webbe, and Byrd. Each piece contained the price in the top right corner
('4s') as well as continuous pagination as the entire collection of songs
could be purchased singly or in a complete set (a pricing format also
employed in the piano-vocal scores). *The Glee Hive* was obviously a successful publication, and the 1863 Novello catalogue still advertised the
edition.

Domestic music-making also included the pursuit of musical education (another faction of 'rational recreation'). Music history, singing
technique, and music theory all could be studied at home if the proper
training books were purchased. Identifying this growing desire for histories and manuals, the firm began the series 'Novello's Library for the
Diffusion of Musical Knowledge'. The 1863 catalogue lists the Library,
separated into 'series' (these were published earlier but included here as
part of Novello's backlist titles available): the 'theoretical series'
included *Cherubini's treatise on Counterpoint* translated by Mary
Cowden Clarke (Vincent Novello's daughter married to the writer and
editor Charles Cowden Clarke). This series also includes *Dr. Marx's
General Music Instruction* and *Berlioz's Treatise on Modern Instrumentation*. The 'practical series' in part contained *Kalkbrenner's
Method of Learning the Piano-forte, with the aid of the Manual-Guide*;
Rink's Practical Organ School; and *Silcher's Succinct Instructions, for
the Guidance of Singing Schools and Choral Societies*. In addition to
the *Library for the Diffusion of Musical Knowledge*, Novello published
a number of vocal studies with at least six under the title *Sabilla
Novello's Vocal School*.

---

[30]Peter and Ann Mactaggart, eds, *Musical Instruments in the 1851 Exhibition: A Tran-
scription of the Entries of Musical Interest from the Official Illustrated Catalogue of the
Great Exhibition of the Art and Industry of All Nations, with additional Material from
Contemporary Sources* (Welwyn, Herts: Mac and Me, Ltd, 1986), p. 15.

In the domain of music at home the piano was the most popular instrument and, predictably, the demand for technically accessible compositions grew rapidly during the century.[31] Although Novello's focused, in large part, on the publication of vocal music, by 1856 the October catalogue contained an extensive collection of Mozart's works – primarily instrumental – edited by Cipriani Potter. The collection is arranged by genre: volume 1: airs with variations; volume 2: rondos; volume 3: duets; volumes 4 and 5: pianoforte sonatas; volumes 6 and 7: sonatas for the pianoforte and violin; volume 8: quartets and quintets; and volume 9: trios for pianoforte, violin and cello. In comparison with other composers published by Novello, the relatively large proportion of Mozart's instrumental repertoire in the catalogue is not surprising when we consider Vincent's early interest in the composer. As a founding member of the Philharmonic Society in 1813, Vincent saw that Mozart shared the programme equally with Haydn and other accepted composers of the day. In 1829 his enthusiasm led Vincent and his wife to make a trip to Vienna and Salzburg (described in *A Mozart Pilgrimage*) to present a donation to Mozart's widow and his sister.[32] In Novello's Mozart edition, compositions are listed in 'an analytical and thematic index, by Edward Holmes'. Edward Holmes (1797–1859), a music critic and editor of *The Musical Times*, was a music student of Vincent Novello. Through his association with the Novello circle – including contact with Mozart's students Thomas Attwood and Johann Nepomuk Hummel – Holmes developed his interest in Mozart later reflected in his biography, *The Life of Mozart* (1845, rev. 1878 and 1912).[33] Both Holmes's introduction to the entire collection and the brief descriptions accompanying each musical incipit in the index suggest the Novello audience for domestic piano music. The first paragraph of the Introduction to the 'Thematic Index' implies that among instructors and amateur pianists Mozart remained relatively unknown at this time or in any case unfamiliar performance territory:

> Nearly a century [counting back from the date of the Holmes Mozart catalogue] has elapsed since many of the works enumerated

---

[31]For a discussion of the growth of the piano as a domestic instrument see A. Loesser, *Men, Women and Pianos* and the bibliography for 'The Piano', *The New Grove Dictionary of Music and Musicians*, 2nd edn, ed. Stanley Sadie and John Tyrrell (London: Macmillan, 2001), 19: pp. 686–8.

[32]The complete account is available in Rosemary Hughes, ed., *A Mozart Pilgrimage*, transcribed and compiled by Nerina Medici (London: Novello, 1955; repr. London: Ernst Eulenberg, 1975).

[33]See John Warrack, 'Edward Holmes', in Stanley Sadie, ed., *The New Grove Dictionary of Music and Musicians* (London: Macmillan, 1980) 8: pp. 656–7. See also Leanne Langley, 'Edward Holmes', *The New Grove Dictionary of Music and Musicians*, 2nd edn, ed. Stanley Sadie and John Tyrrell (London: Macmillan, 2001), 11: pp. 642–3.

in the following catalogue were composed. In the meantime new generations of music and teachers have arisen, who, in compliance with the taste of the day, instruct their pupils in ephemeral and fashionable novelties, gradually losing sight of the valuable classics of the Pianoforte – the foundation of all true musical excellence. It is probable that not many of the younger class of instructors in music are familiar enough with Mozart's compositions, in their whole extent, to appreciate from the sight of a bar or two of the theme of a composition the true character of the work to which it belongs. To aid in their search, and to save the time and trouble of turning over a large bulk of music with a particular object in view, the following *catalogue raisonée* has been attempted.[34]

Novello's aim, clearly, was to familiarize his market with the repertoire as well as to aid in pianistic technical training. The majority of descriptions accompanying the incipits stress the technical feature of each piece. Thus, for the Variations on 'Unser dummer poebel meinst [*sic*]' (K. 455), Holmes notes 'It requires a player tolerably advanced with a strong left hand to execute extensions of octaves, and a good running finger.' Or, for the 'Sonata in D' (K. 205b=K. 284): 'Though the subject and some of the passages are slightly old-fashioned, the music is excellent and full of spirited phrases. The cross-handed passages in the second part bring back the age of Scarlatti, but the chromatic modulation at the return belongs to the more modern master. The variations with which this Sonata concludes are excellent, and demand strong and able fingers. There is much to do for both hands.' Both technique and aesthetic instruction were the benefits of Mozart's compositions as Holmes noted for the 'Sonata in F' (K. 547a/ Anh. 135): 'The contrasted effects of the brilliant and holding notes will infuse taste into the player.'

The inclusion of Mozart's chamber music within Holmes's edition also suggests demand for an ensemble repertoire within the technical boundaries of the non-professional. In his description of the Trio in B flat for piano, violin and cello (K. 254), Holmes clearly wished to attract the amateur: 'A Trio with a very easy bass part ... The rest of the music is very pleasant, and as it does not require uncommon powers of execution, is likely to be one much patronized in domestic performance.' And for the Trio for piano, violin and cello, he remarks: 'The music is elegant and melodious, and is adapted to the powers of a young performer who is being initiated in the family concert in the improving and pleasant art of playing with accompaniment.'

Within the increasingly complex economic and social environment of nineteenth-century industrial England, a response to changes and

---

[34]Novello catalogue, August 1863, p. 164.

reforms was mandatory to any successful business endeavour. It is not surprising, then, that through his observations of the social and economic climate of the day, Alfred Novello would lead the firm from its beginning as a family enterprise to become one of the leading English music publishers at mid-century. While Novello's glees, songs, and Mozart edition (to name only a sample) answered the demand for domestic performance in the growing amount of leisure time, the arrangements of oratorios offered a large and financially accessible repertoire to the choral movement. Although specific documentation does not exist to confirm that Novello's consciously published editions in line with the two factions of the Oxford Movement, catalogue descriptions and the editions themselves nonetheless suggest that the firm was sensitive to both aspects of the sacred music market.

In addition to the external factors which influenced the establishment of the firm, Vincent Novello was also guided by his own personal life as a Catholic. Vincent's Catholicism must also be acknowledged as an influential factor in his early endeavours as publisher. A full survey of the role and place of Catholicism in British society can be found in the discussion by Bennett Zon.[35] In general, restrictions on Catholics stretch back to Elizabeth I and hampered both public and private daily life. The establishment of foreign embassies in London for Catholic countries, such as the Portuguese Embassy, where Vincent Novello would begin his musical career in the Embassy chapel, offered a place for meeting, exchange of ideas, worship, and musical performance, not available elsewhere. In this regard the repertoire also differed from that found in Anglican churches, and yet its very 'difference' or sense of exoticism as it began to be seen attracted a non-Catholic audience. By the beginning of the nineteenth century the Portuguese Chapel was one of five remaining active, along with the Sardinian, Bavarian, Neapolitan, and Spanish Embassy chapels. An understanding of Novello's musical participation at the Portuguese Embassy helps to explain his choice of works to edit, seen especially in his first publication, in 1811, *A Collection of Sacred Music as Performed at the Royal Portuguese Embassy Chapel*.[36] Vincent's ability to mix his own personal musical concerns with the

---

[35]Bennett Zon, *The English Plainchant Revival*.

[36]For a detailed and valuable discussion of Vincent Novello's Catholicism and his early publications see Fiona M. Palmer, 'Vincent Novello and the Philharmonic Society of London' in Bennett Zon and Peter Horton, eds, *Nineteenth-Century British Music Studies* 3 (Aldershot: Ashgate, forthcoming) and Fiona M. Palmer, 'Vincent Novello in 1811: Entrepreneur or Antiquarian?', paper given at the Music in Britain Social History Seminar, February 2002. Palmer is also undertaking research on a critical biography of Vincent Novello which will examine further Novello's relationship with Catholicism.

requirements and demands of the market became the key to the success of the firm and can be seen in a number of decisions and activities throughout the early years of publishing. In this regard, Chapter 2 will examine the publishing policies and styles developed by Vincent and Alfred Novello to suit the technical capabilities and aesthetic sentiment of their audience and will illustrate the editorial practices developed in response to the demands of Victorian musical life.

CHAPTER TWO

House Editorial Techniques

Twentieth-century musicians have questioned the reliability of Novello's editions, denouncing them as inaccurate renderings. Discussing the Handel editions, Paul Henry Lang noted that 'the Novello scores are so lacking in elementary care that they cannot be considered in any scholarly, critical analysis'.[1] Although the Novello scores of the mid-nineteenth century do not today enjoy a reputation of accuracy, they nonetheless can be evaluated as documents of Victorian performance practice. The 'philosophy' behind the editing of music, the acceptance, use, and methodology of editions can tell us much about the period in which they were prepared and used. In their study of historical performance Colin Lawson and Robin Stowell indicate that earlier editions may not provide 'accurate' versions but can serve as windows disclosing much about perception of the work and the cultural climate in which it was created: 'For the discipline of editing, like performance and all critical undertakings, is undergoing continual change in response to the changing critical environment.'[2]

In this regard an examination of selected Novello editions will help us to understand how a large number of musicians in mid-century England became acquainted with the repertoire of Beethoven and Mozart as well as with the schools of seventeenth- and eighteenth-century English sacred composers such as Purcell, Boyce, and Greene. The following analysis of Novello's editions will investigate some editorial alterations that were made and what these changes disclose about the musical taste, technical capabilities, and demands of the growing amateur market. To understand the Novello editorial style, a few examples from the house catalogue will be analysed: the English sacred repertoire of Boyce, Greene, and Purcell and the sacred works of Beethoven, specifically his *Missa solemnis*. Each example represents a different facet of the Victorian repertoire and Novello's response to it. Novello's promoted performance editions of the eighteenth-century English school for a market which previously had to make do with old-style clefs and unrealized figured bass. In presenting a modern version, we shall determine what editorial licence was taken and why. The *Missa solemnis* was not

---

[1] Paul Henry Lang, *George Friedrich Handel* (New York: Norton, 1977), p. 672.

[2] Colin Lawson and Robin Stowell, *The Historical Performance of Music: An Introduction* (Cambridge: Cambridge University Press, 1999), p. 34.

an accepted part of the canon of amateur choral societies when Novello's published it *c.*1830, and in comparison to eighteenth-century works, it is important to understand how the firm presented their edition.

Sources of Novello Editions

Although Alfred had accepted responsibility for the firm by 1830, Vincent continued to participate in its management well into the 1840s both as editor and adviser for the numerous piano-vocal editions published by the house. One of Vincent's most important duties was to seek out music, whether from manuscript or from earlier published editions, which would tempt the Novello customer. Vincent's fund of musical sources was wide-reaching: he found new prospects in the music manuscript collections of the British Museum, the private libraries of his colleagues, and in his own personal library.[3] From the library of his friend, the composer C. I. Latrobe (1758–1836), Vincent also obtained a number of compositions which he cited in his published editions as either borrowed: 'from the manuscript score in the possession of the Rev'd C. I. Latrobe' or received: 'The gift of the Rev'd C. I. Latrobe'. Latrobe was an active participant in the early editions and a contributor to Novello's first publication, *Collection of Sacred Music* (1811). An example of the extent to which Vincent searched for new sources can be seen in his hunt for unknown compositions to include in his edition of *Purcell's Sacred Music*. Vincent outlines his search in the Introduction to the volume of the 1832 edition:

> Mr. Stevens of the Charter House, having informed the Editor that the private library belonging to the late King (George the Third), was *very rich* in MSS by Purcell, he thought it probable that it contained other compositions besides those enumerated by Dr. Burney, as being in Purcell's own hand-writing. The writer consequently went down to Windsor (on Wednesday, the 13th of May, 1829), and passed a very pleasant day with his kind friend Mr. C. Kramer, who was the Master of the King's Band at that time. They looked over together all the music books contained in the library of the King, (George the Fourth), but no manuscripts whatever by Purcell were to be found. The opinion of Mr. C Kramer is, that they were stolen by some one at the period of the death of George the Third, when the music was left in the greatest confusion, and without being placed in the custody of any responsible person ...

---

[3]As early as 1824 Vincent expressed his concern, in a letter to Henry Bankes, MP, a Trustee of the British Museum, over the state of its music collection. For a discussion of Vincent's relationship to the British Museum, see Alec Hyatt King, *A Mozart Legacy: Aspects of the British Library Collections* (London: The British Library, 1984), pp. 27–34.

Enquiries were afterwards made at the British Museum, under the idea that, as a large collection of books from the King's library were presented to that Institution, it was possible that the music in question might have been sent at the same time, but the search has not been successful. The editor likewise visited Oxford, to examine the MSS. bequethed [sic] to the library of Christ Church College, but although every search was made, no manuscripts whatever by Purcell could be found ...

Vincent's pursuit of Purcell manuscripts continued, as revealed in his letter of 22 November 1828, one month before the first volume of the edition was published, to a George Swilt:

You will perceive from the annexed Prospectus, that I am, at last, about to bring forward a collection of the masterly cathedral compositions of Purcell.

The list of MSS is already a pretty long one – and I am in expectation of enriching the collection still further through the exertion of my kind friends W. Shield, Dr. Crotch, W. J. B. Cramer, W. Thos. Adams, Dr. George Smart, W. Attwood, Mr. Jacob, W. Stevens of the Charterhouse, etc. who have all evinced the most gratifying [?] to assist my endeavors [sic] to render the Edition as *complete* as possible for Purcell's sake.

I wish to prefix a good portrait of Purcell if I can meet with one *authentic* likeness. The two best I have yet met with are those found in the possession of Dr. Burney, the one an oil painting and the other a small drawing by Sir Godfry Kneller.

The former was bought in [?] by Mrs Burney and the latter was published by Mr. Bartleman.

I find that the drawing was again sold at Mr. Bartleman's Musical sale, but *to whom* I cannot ascertain; for Mrs. Bartleman cannot inform me and Mr. White the Auctioneer who sold it is unfortunately lately dead.

It has struck me that you probably might be able to oblige me with the name of the person to whom it was sold at Mr. Bartleman's sales – as I know you occasionally made little memoranda of that nature in your copy of the catalogue.

If you can favour [me] with any information which will enable me to trace this drawing – or can tell me whether W. Hollaway (who made an engraving from it) is still in possession of the Plate – it will very much oblige me; and I have had such repeated proof of your kind readiness to promote the fulfillment of my wishes relative to publications of this class – to doubt for a moment your polite acquiecence [sic] in ceding to my request. As you have so fine a collection of the sterling old writers in your musical library perhaps you will have a rummage amongst them just to see whether you have any anthems by Purcell that are different from those enumerated in the Prospectus.

With Kind remembrance to Mrs. Swilt, V. Novello[4]

---

[4]Unpublished letter located in the Mary Flagler Cary Music Collection, series 2, The Pierpont Morgan Library, New York. MFC N9396 G994.

The introductory remarks Vincent published in his editions and the examples from correspondence are revealing for they suggest a vigorous pursuit of manuscripts and sources beyond the serendipitous acceptance and presentation of manuscripts received from friends or through loans. The search for manuscripts is also seen in Vincent's quest for Mozart's compositions. During his well-documented visit in 1829 to Mozart's widow and sister, Vincent also actively enquired after manuscripts.[5] Both Vincent and his wife Mary kept diaries of their journey to Salzburg and along the way through Belgium, Germany, Austria, and France. During his visit to the Mozart family, Vincent tried to obtain any unpublished manuscripts in the possession of the Mozart family; he wrote in his journal: 'Shown original manuscripts of two Kyries, in score, one in E flat and the other in C (different from any that I have published). He [Mozart] was about 22 when he wrote them.'[6] (See below for a discussion of the spurious nature of some of the compositions published under the composer's name.)

Editorial Philosophy

Throughout any analysis of Novello's arrangements, it is important to note that decisions concerning the organization, format, and marketing of the editions were largely dependent on the taste and demands of the firm's market. A number of Novello editions contain introductions or editorial prefaces which enumerate the different formats available and their advantages. These prefaces are especially important as they suggest the existence of an editorial philosophy which was inherent in the preparation and publication of the editions and, in turn, suggest the market Novello wished to attract. An especially detailed example is seen in the Preliminary Remarks to Novello's collection of Haydn masses (orchestral accompaniment edition, 1828) in which Vincent explains his editorial decisions (see Appendix 3 for a complete transcription). It is especially of note that Vincent kept as a primary objective the needs and limitations of amateur performing groups. Thus, although the edition reflects the complete instrumentation of the original score (see point 1 in the Preliminary Remarks), the edition has been arranged so that smaller forces, such as those of many amateur groups, can perform the works

---

[5]See Rosemary Hughes, ed., *A Mozart Pilgrimage: Being the Travel Diaries of Vincent and Mary Novello in the Year 1829*, transcribed and compiled by Nerina Medici (London: Ernst Eulenburg, 1975).

[6]Hughes, *A Mozart Pilgrimage*, pp. 76–7, n. 59. According to Hughes, Vincent probably refers to K. 323 (1779) and K. 221 (1771).

and still be satisfied (point 2): 'the prominent passages of the *Wind Instruments and Voices* are inserted in a smaller character, wherever the rests formerly occurred – so that the Leader may not only see what is going forward in the other parts, but will also be able to supply the place of the Flute, Oboe, Clarinet etc. – in case those Instruments should be deficient: – in the same manner, the second Violin will be enabled to supply the obligato parts of the Second Flute, etc. when necessary – the Viola of the Horns, etc. – and the Violoncello, of the Bassoon, when requisite.' In addition, as noted in point 4, the beginning of the first violin part contains a checklist of required instruments. Such features, clearly intended for the conductor and concertmaster, indicate Novello's desire to accommodate the market of choral society and non-professional performers. Vincent also understood that an amateur consort might be limited only to piano and voice and he therefore so arranged the edition 'To afford an opportunity for their performance by voices and piano alone – for which purpose the whole of the accompaniment for the latter instrument has been re-written and arranged so as to introduce several more of the features of the score (especially of the violin passages)'.

How Vincent recognized the technical abilities and instrumental limitations in many performance groups can also be seen in his introduction (dated December 1825) to *The Fitzwilliam Music* ('being a collection of sacred pieces selected from manuscripts of Italian composers in the Fitzwilliam Museum, now for the first time published by permission of the University of Cambridge by Vincent Novello'). Vincent notes the typographical design of the page and the editorial rationale behind it (see Figure 2.1 for the first page of the edition):

> The accompaniment for the organ or pianoforte and the vocal score are engraved in a larger character than that in which the instrumental score is engraved; the latter being of a size sufficient for the guidance of a copyist, when extracting the several parts for performance by a band, whilst the former is distinct and legible both by the player and the singers when performed in small parties, and without orchestral instruments. That accompaniment has been arranged and the directions concerning the use of different stops of the organ, added by the Editor. The one will be of service to those who are not accustomed to play from score; and he has had less scruple in giving the other, because the whole of the original manuscript having been retained, this addition may be disregarded when not approved ... the whole of the treble parts have been transposed to the G clef ...

The creation of well-designed editions, suitable for musicians and their performance requirements, was to become a hallmark of Novello publications. In an advertisement for the firm's *Cathedral Choir Book*

Figure 2.1 *The Fitzwilliam Music* (Novello, 1825)

(printed in *The Musical Times*, 1 September 1848) these features are highlighted:

> This work, of which the first number appeared some twelve months since, and which has continued to be published regularly on the first of each following month has now reached the completion of the first volume [with three formats available]:
>
>> 1. The organ score: folio, full music size: on the first of each month, is published, 16 pages in score, with separate accompaniment for the organ or pianoforte, in a very large type, both for the words and music, to compensate for the imperfect light in many churches.
>> 2. The vocal score. 8vo size. On the first of each month is published, 24 pages of vocal score (without accompaniment) to correspond with the music contained in the organ score. The size of the book will be convenient for the pew or hand.
>> 3. Separate vocal parts. 8vo size. First of each month published, vocal parts, each part 6 pages.

In further endeavours to assist untrained choirs and performers, Vincent also provided accompaniments solely for training and rehearsals. In his edition, *William Croft: 30 Select Anthems and the Burial Service* (1849), 'in vocal score with an organ or piano-forte accompaniment', he adds a note at the bottom of the 'Laudate Dominum': 'This accompaniment has been added in this edition for the accommodation of the performers in rehearsing this canon; but it had better be omitted when the voices do not require guidance or support. VN 1849.'

Here, then, lies the key to Vincent Novello's editorial technique: his editions should be accessible to the greatest number of people, whether professional performers, copyists, students, or scholars. The larger typeface for the organ part not only assisted the copyist but also the accompanist who possibly required additional guidance. For Vincent's edition of *Purcell's Sacred Music* (discussed below), we will see that he formed his editorial decisions and created an arrangement which would simultaneously suit the professional church musician and satisfy the musical demands of the choral society participant.

Despite Vincent's attempts to accommodate performance requirements, however, his editorial methods did not receive unanimous support from professional musicians and one particular criticism is of note. During the later years of his work with the firm, Vincent, not surprisingly, also commissioned others to prepare editions, following his editorial style of organ and pianoforte reductions. In 1840 he was in contact with the organist Thomas Adams (1785–1858), asking if he would prepare an arrangement of overtures from Mozart's operas. Adams wrote to Vincent on 1 April declining the offer, however. The organist believed Novello's arrangements to be unhelpful to students and amateurs. Adams found the compression of any full score into a limited number of staves difficult to read and unrepresentative of the actual sound:

> My previous intimation of your presence, made me extremely desirous of giving you pleasure; and I have, certainly, ample assurance that my wish was accomplished. I am sorry to differ with you in opinion concerning the *profitable* [sic] result of my publishing an arrangement of Mozart's overtures. It has always been my conviction that no written arrangement whatever will enable a student to give those effects which will be suggested to him (if he be a person of mind) by the power of reading score; and adaptations of full orchestral pieces which would approach the combinations of the band, would present to the general eye by far too great a crowd of notes to make such things saleable. These circumstances have given me an invincible antipathy to writing arrangements.[7]

In the discussion of Vincent's edition of Mozart's masses, below, further criticism is found that his reductions contained too many notes and formed a cramped page. Yet Vincent believed that large bodies of music were not available to the general musician and amateur and he continued to establish and develop his arrangements, taking in the eighteenth-century repertoire and more contemporary works in order to make them more accessible.

Editions of Eighteenth-Century Music

In the Introduction to his edition, *Purcell's Sacred Music* (1828–32), Vincent acknowledged the need for collections of English music, in editions within the technical capabilities of church choirs and amateur singers.[8] 'The editor is the more sanguine in anticipating the patronage of those gentlemen who have the direction of the various cathedral choirs in England ... he trusts also that [the edition] will be found a very acceptable acquisition to the choral societies which are now so prevalent all over the country, and that it will at the same time tend to preserve and improve the public taste for genuine, solid, and sterling compositions of the true English school.' In addition, Novello noted how he might make the repertoire more accessible: 'The text will be given from the best

---

[7]Quoted in W. Barclay Squire, 'Some Novello Correspondence', *The Musical Quarterly* (1954): pp. 206–42.

[8]The edition garnered sixty-two subscribers, including Thomas Attwood, Edward Taylor, and George Smart; the music collections of King's Chapel, Westminster Abbey, and St Paul's Cathedral; and his colleagues in publishing Samuel Chappell, J. B. Cramer, and Goulding and D'Almaine.

authenticated copies, and in addition to Purcell's own scores, the Editor intends to adapt a separate accompaniment throughout, for the organ or pianoforte, in which all the harmonies will be fully drawn out for the convenience and accommodation of those who are not accustomed to play from score.'

Vincent Novello was not alone in his interest in earlier music. By the second half of the eighteenth century, historical research was already reflected in the studies by Burney and Hawkins and in such organizations as the Catch Club and the Concerts of Ancient Music. An active curiosity in earlier literature was also mirrored in the quantity and quality of music found in private collections. Among the most comprehensive were those, predictably, of Burney and Hawkins and that of Lord Fitzwilliam.[9] An additionally large collection was also owned by the bass John Bartleman, a portion of which was later purchased by Vincent. The sale of Bartleman's library in 1822 was described in the auction as 'a very extensive and matchless assemblage of the most choice and scarce productions and works of all the great masters, ancient and modern'.[10] Similar to the generation before him, Vincent's fascination with earlier music could be seen in his personal library and, not surprisingly, a large portion contained eighteenth-century sacred works. Although an intact collection no longer exists, the contents can be surmised through the auction catalogues from two sales of his collection, in 1852 and 1862[11] and through his personal donations to both the British Museum and to the Musical Antiquarian Society.

Yet despite interest at the beginning of the nineteenth century in collecting and publishing music of an earlier era, performance editions suitable for the amateur and church organist were few. In general, continuo parts were unrealized, full scores printed 'old' clefs, and therefore an important repertoire remained out of reach to all but the initiated. From his first publication, *A Collection of Sacred Music as Performed at the Royal Portuguese Chapel in London* (1811), Vincent published music in a more accessible form, although he did not abandon all current editorial conventions at once. In this first edition, Vincent presented the more recent practice of an accompaniment part instead of an unrealized figured bass. However, he retained C clefs in the soprano and tenor parts. Vincent's decision to keep the C clef was enough of note to

---

[9]See A. Hyatt King, *Some British Collectors of Music c.1600–1960* (Cambridge: Cambridge University Press, 1963). See also Lenore Coral, 'Music Dealers and Antiquarians', in *The New Grove Dictionary of Music and Musicians*, 2nd edn, ed. Stanley Sadie and John Tyrrell (London: Macmillan, 2001), 17: pp. 477–80.

[10]Hyatt King, *Some British Collectors of Music*, p. 11.

[11]Ibid., p. 13.

warrant a remark in his 'Advertisement' (more accurately, Introduction), dated May 1811 placed at the beginning of the edition:

> It was suggested that it would be better to publish all the vocal parts (except the bass) in the treble clef, but as I consider this practice as an innovation, I was unwilling to afford an additional example of an erroneous custom that has already become but too prevalent. The treble clef when applied to the counter tenor and tenor parts, does not indicate the real or true notes that are required to be sung. The C clef does, and I trust therefore that no apology is necessary on my part for preferring truth to falsehood, or that which is proper, to that which is improper.

However, for the second edition (*c.*1815, no date or address is given; the title page is the same except for 'Second Edition' and new price), the C clef in the soprano part was replaced by the 'innovative' treble clef. Unfortunately, there is no Introduction to record Vincent's volte-face. The second edition is almost identical to the first except for the change of clef and the occasional instruction for organ pedal.

There exists further evidence revealing Vincent's editorial goal to prepare accessible editions suitable for both professional and amateur. During the late 1820s and early 1830s, Vincent transcribed a large portion of the music he had examined into a series of oblong books bound with blank manuscript leaves. For the purpose of this discussion they will be referred to hereafter as his 'workbooks'. In these notebooks, and frequently in the printed editions themselves, Vincent cited his original sources including the edition and year of publication or, with the methodical care of the archivist, the manuscript shelf number from the British Museum collection. (Vincent's distinctive handwriting, in red pencil, and his initials 'VN' can still be found on many of the manuscripts he consulted and transcribed into his workbooks; see below for a discussion of these notebooks.) A first glimpse of preparation is found in the workbooks which Vincent used from approximately 1828 to 1833 (see Table 2.1).[12] Within these books, Vincent included the complete dynamics, phrasing, and editorial comments for the final copy intended for the printer. At the beginning of each composition, in the top right corner, Vincent noted the source, while in the bottom left corner he wrote the name and number of the forthcoming publication (see Figure 2.2). The workbooks, in fact, must have been intended for engraver's copy as a number of pages also reveal printer's markings which indicate the ends of staves and the number of plates required. These markings

---

[12]The majority of the workbooks are located in the British Library Manuscript Music Collection. A collection of Novello workbooks is also in the archive of the Royal College of Music; this collection was unnumbered and uncatalogued at the time of examination.

Table 2.1   Catalogue numbers of the Novello
Workbooks located in the British Library,
Music Manuscript Division

Add. MS 9071–9074, 9076, 9077
Add. 17856
Add. 17857
Add. 17858
Add. 31120
Add. 33239

may have been made by Vincent himself as his daughter, Mary Cowden
Clarke noted in a commemorative article for *The Musical Times*, 1 April
1862: 'In "laying out" works for printing … he spared no trouble in
devising favourable turnings, with well-spaced bars, lines, and pages;
and frequently, when dividing his manuscripts for this purpose, he would
count up, with slight raps of his pencil on the paper, asking half aloud: –
"How many sevens in fifty?"'

Figure 2.2   Page from Vincent Novello's Workbook

Figure 2.2   continued

It is not clear what other stages existed before the workbooks, although it appears that initial editorial revisions occurred in other manuscripts now lost. In the same article, Mary Cowden Clarke suggested the presence of other worksheets: 'The majority of his manuscripts ... though most neatly and legibly written, were jotted down upon such mere odds and ends of music-paper, and generally stitched together (or rather, threaded together, like a file of papers), that they served but to be used by the printer, and then were thrown away or destroyed.' Fortunately, a representative proportion of Vincent's workbooks, as well as some of his music library, survived in storage at the Novello offices. In 1964, Walter Emery, of Novello's, offered the collection to the British Library; what the British Library did not take was then accepted by the Royal College of Music.[13]

The dates of some of the workbooks can be determined from Vincent's notes written within the margins or at the end of compositions. Some entries are dated, such as the transcription of the verse anthem 'I

[13]Jeremy Dibble, 'The RCM Novello Library', *The Musical Times* (1983), pp. 99–101.

will always give thanks': 'I transcribed this on Wednesday, June 16, 1830, V. Novello.' It is clear, however, that the workbooks were in use as early as 1828, to prepare portions of *Purcell's Sacred Music,* and until 1833 as noted in reference to the composer Charles Evans: 'This Gentleman, who is still living (1833) ...'.

From the repertoire of sacred English music published during the eighteenth century, in large part Vincent chose from the collections by William Boyce (*Cathedral Music* and *15 Anthems*) and by Maurice Greene (*40 Select Anthems*). Because Vincent carefully noted specific editions, we know that in place of the original publication of Greene's *40 Select Anthems* (1743), he employed the Birchall version, *A New and Correct Edition of 40 Select Anthems in Score, Composed for 1–8 Voices, 2 volumes* (London, 1795) – the citation 'Birchall edition' is duly noted for the appropriate compositions in Novello's *Cathedral Voluntaries.* (Hereafter, Greene's *40 Select Anthems* will be referred to as the Birchall edition.) Thus, the editorial genesis for a number of Novello's publications can be viewed in three stages: source – workbook – Novello edition (see Table 2.2). It is not precisely documented why Vincent did

Table 2.2   Three stages for publication of English sacred music of the eighteenth century by Vincent Novello: a selection

---

1. **Published original source:** Birchall edition (1795),[a] vol. 1, p. 25, 'O Let my Soul Live'
2. **Novello Workbook:** British Library Add. MS 31120, fol. 62
3. **Novello edition:** *Cathedral Voluntaries* (*c.*1831), No. 37

1. **Published original source:** Birchall edition, vol. 1, p. 59 'All the Kings of the Earth'
2. **Novello Workbook:** Add. MS 31120, fol. 64v
3. **Novello edition:** *Cathedral Voluntaries,* No. 38

1. **Published original source:** Boyce, *Cathedral Music* (1760–78), vol. 2, p. 59: 'O clap your Hands'
2. **Novello Workbook:** Add. MS 31120, fol. 18
3. **Novello edition:** *Cathedral Voluntaries,* No. 5

1. **Published original source:** Boyce, *Cathedral Music,* vol. 2, p. 276, 'Be merciful unto me O God'
2. **Novello Workbook:** Add. MS 9073, fol. 53
3. **Novello edition:** *Purcell's Sacred Music,* No. 31

---

[a]*A New and Corrected Edition of 40 Select Anthems in Score, composed for 1–8 Voices,* 2 vols (London, 1795).

not simply mark up the original sources as engraver's copy when he prepared vocal editions from vocal music. However, as noted above, Vincent was especially concerned with 'laying out' the compositions for printing to offer the most convenient page turns and organization of bars per stave. It may have been that by recopying the music into his workbooks Vincent could simultaneously edit and create the page layout exactly to his wishes. The process of recopying, in fact, offered complete control of the editorial process and lessened the chance of mistakes and features from the source edition being included.

The following examples, taken from the two primary Novello publications of English sacred seventeenth- and eighteenth-century music, *Cathedral Voluntaries* and *Purcell's Sacred Music*, reveal the kinds of editorial alterations Vincent incorporated. The Novello editions under examination represent two different editorial transformations: *Cathedral Voluntaries* is a collection of *instrumental* arrangements from choral pieces. In turn, *Purcell's Sacred Music* is an edition of *vocal* music derived from vocal works. The two Novello editions are discussed together, however, as they represent Vincent's interpretation of the repertoire prepared for his specific market. In large part, Vincent's editorial changes, seen in the following examples, may disappoint – there are no major additions or omissions – yet even the small alterations he imposed suggest the areas of performance practice where Vincent anticipated technical difficulties and thus these changes, however slight, provide clues to the requirements of the amateur musician of the early decades of the century.

For his editions of seventeenth- and eighteenth-century music, Vincent focused his alterations in four areas: phrasing; octave doubling and the pedal; ornamentation; and rhythm. Within the category of phrasing, he frequently made changes according to the performance medium: Vincent's editorial decisions depended on whether his arrangement was to be vocal or instrumental. In the change to an instrumental medium from a vocal source, for example, Vincent frequently omitted the phrase markings which might have aided a singer but were perhaps not needed for a performance by organ or piano. This is found especially in the voluntaries Vincent prepared from sung anthems. An example is seen in the Chorus, 'Blessed be God', (Examples 2.1 and 2.2) where the phrase mark over 'blessed' in the Birchall edition is omitted in the Novello version. In turn, when Vincent did not change medium, but prepared a new vocal edition from an older vocal source, he often *added* slurs. In Example 2.3b, Vincent added slurs in his edition of *Purcell's Sacred Music* for 'Be merciful unto me, O God', although the original source, Boyce's *Cathedral Music* (Example 2.3a), does not contain any over the semiquaver passage for 'fighting' and 'troubling'.

Example 2.1   Greene, 'Blessed be God', in Birchall, *40 Select Anthems*

Example 2.2   Novello's transcription of 'Blessed be God' in his *Cathedral Voluntaries*

Example 2.3a   Purcell, 'Be merciful unto me, O God', in Boyce, *Cathedral Music*

Examples 2.4a and 2.4b illustrate a second instance in the same anthem with a slur added by Novello over 'rejoice'. The presence of slurs in Novello's edition may be the mechanical indication of text declamation; but in addition, their inclusion may have been motivated by

Example 2.3b   Purcell, 'Be merciful unto me, O God', in Novello, *Purcell's Sacred Music*

Example 2.4a   Purcell, 'Be merciful unto me, O God', in Boyce, *Cathedral Music*

Novello's perception of his performers' capabilities and experience. Although one can see in the Boyce version that the semiquavers over 'fighting' form a group on one syllable and should be sung as an unbroken phrase, the addition of the slur, almost as an *aide-memoire*, makes this instantly clear.

The second category of alterations, concerning pedal technique and octave doublings, is of special importance as it highlights the nature and development of the organ in England at the beginning of the nineteenth century – a time when both construction of the instrument and performance technique were evolving. At the turn of the century, the English organ differed in major characteristics from its Continental counterpart: the English organ was still tuned in meantone and based on an F or G

Example 2.4b Purcell, 'Be merciful unto me, O God', in Novello, *Purcell's Sacred Music*

compass rather than on C as the German model, which had already adopted equal temperament (pitch names here and elsewhere follow the Helmholtz system). And, unlike the German instrument, few English organs had pedals and thus, only a minority of English organists were familiar with them.[14] An example of the standard of pedal technique is seen in the first set of Twelve Voluntaries (1804) by William Russell with the pedal as a slow bass line or pedal point, a technical level which was to remain the average until around the 1840s.[15] Nicholas Temperley has noted that 'As late as the 1830's there were still only half a dozen organists who could give an unassisted performance of Bach's organ works; they were sometimes played as organ duets, or with the pedal part arranged for double-bass by Dragonetti.'[16] Temperley's observation that 'pedal parts in most English organ music before 1850 are either rudimentary or altogether lacking'[17] is reflected in Vincent's limited utilization of the pedal throughout his early arrangements. A typical example is seen in 'O praise our God ye people', from *Cathedral Voluntaries*. For the closing cadence Novello marked G″ for the pedal while the manual played the upper parts (Example 2.5: Birchall edition, *40 Select Anthems* and

---

[14]Nicholas Temperley, ed., *Music in Britain: The Romantic Age, 1800–1914* (London: The Athlone Press, 1981), pp. 435ff.

[15]Nicholas Thistlethwaite, *The Making of the Victorian Organ* (Cambridge: Cambridge University Press, 1990), p. 104.

[16]Ibid., pp. 435–6.

[17]Nicholas Temperley, *The Music of the English Parish Church*, vol. 1 (Cambridge: Cambridge University Press, 1979).

Example 2.5   Greene, 'O praise our God ye people', in *Birchall, 40 Select Anthems*

Example 2.6: Novello's Workbook sketch re-editing, typeset here as music example). Similar elementary passages are common throughout his editions; indeed, Vincent frequently employed the pedal simply to add an extra octave below the bass line and thus 'expand' the compass.

Example 2.6   Novello's reworking of 'O praise our God ye people' in his Workbook

In the third category, ornamentation, Vincent was especially conscious of the effect of additional notes on the overall texture of his keyboard reduction. In the chorus, 'O let my soul live', the Birchall edition indicates a trill over the motive: ♩♪♪ (Example 2.7a) although Vincent omitted the flourish (Example 2.7b). In the keyboard reduction for *Cathedral Voluntaries*, the necessity of quick motion from the dotted quaver to the semiquaver, with a trill in the right hand, might create a blurred texture as well as technical difficulties Vincent no doubt wished to avoid. Yet the Novello edition retained trills in slower passages and where a clear texture was possible. An example is seen in the same

Example 2.7a   Greene, 'O let my soul live', in Birchall, *40 Select Anthems*

Example 2.7b   Novello's transcription of 'O let my soul live' in his *Cathedral Voluntaries*

Example 2.8a   Greene, 'O let my soul live', in Birchall, *40 Select Anthems*

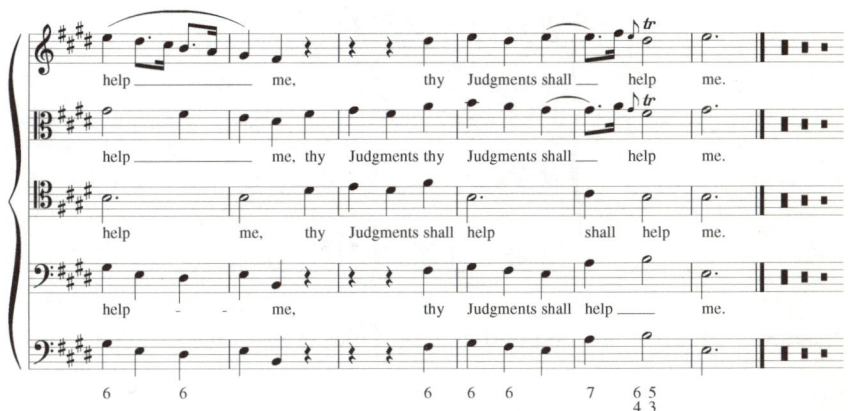

anthem (Examples 2.8a and 2.8b), where the ornament remained, since the longer note value and cadential function made possible a clean execution. Novello's redefinition of the appoggiatura as two equal crotchets can also be considered an appropriate interpretation. Spohr notes in his

Example 2.8b   Novello's transcription of 'O let my soul live' in his *Cathedral Voluntaries*

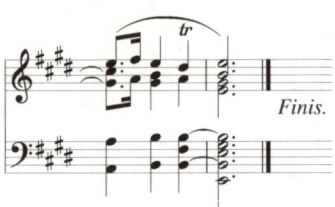

treatise, *Violinschule* (1832): 'If the appoggiatura stands before a note which can be divided into equal parts, it obtains the half of its value ...'. At other instances, where this application of the appoggiatura could have been used, however, Vincent demurred. In 'O let my soul live', (Example 2.9b) the appoggiatura on A, in the Birchall edition (Example 2.9a), would have caused a cross-relation to the A sharp in the organ transcription and was therefore not included.

To create a more homophonic texture or to integrate a motif within a phrase, Novello occasionally also altered note values, the fourth area of editorial modification. An example is seen in the 'Hallelujah' of 'O God,

Example 2.9a   Greene, 'O let my soul live,' in Birchall, *40 Select Anthems*

Example 2.9b   Novello's transcription of 'O let my soul live' in his *Cathedral Voluntaries*

thou art my God'. The two notes of the Birchall edition: ♪ ♪ (Example
2.10a) are transformed by Vincent into the figure: ♪. ♪ (Example 2.10b),
a rhythmic pattern found throughout the piece. By altering the two quavers to conform to the presence of this motif elsewhere, Vincent sought a
more uniform texture. In other instances, to create a more homophonic
fabric, he changed the rhythm of one voice in a chord to match the note
values of the other parts.

Example 2.10a   Greene, 'O God, thou art my God', in Birchall, *40 Select
                 Anthems*

Example 2.10b   Novello's adaptation of 'O God, thou art my God' in his
                 Cathedral Voluntaries

In his collections of eighteenth-century music, Vincent's editorial
alterations, in large part, are only slight alterations in phrasing, ornamentation, and voicing. These changes were made to accommodate the
technical abilities of his market. Thus, the simplified rhythmic pattern
for an ornament or an additional phrase marking could guide the musician through difficult passages. Indeed, Vincent's tinkering with
eighteenth-century scores reflects the original composer's own flexibility
to adapt to the different demands of performers and audience in his own
century.

Editions of Contemporary Music: the *Missa solemnis*

Vincent Novello not only acknowledged the sources for his editions of earlier music, he frequently supplied this information in his arrangements of contemporary works. Towards the end of the 1820s (*c.*1828) Vincent edited and published the Kyrie and Quoniam, in piano-vocal score, folio format, from Beethoven's *Missa solemnis*. An examination of Vincent's edition reveals only one set of page numbers each for the Kyrie and Quoniam and the absence of continuous pagination. The last page of the Kyrie (p. 13), ends on a recto and the verso is blank; that is, the next section is not begun, suggesting that a complete edition was not planned. At the beginning of the Kyrie and the Quoniam, the following citation, in the top right-hand corner of page 1, is included: 'Arranged by V. Novello, from the Full Score, published at Mainz, 1827'.[18] Vincent refers here to the first edition, published by Schott, in March or April 1827, which bears plate number 2346.[19]

It is of note that Vincent and Alfred participated in the first *complete* performance in Britain of the *Missa solemnis*: a private concert given on Christmas Eve, 1832, at the London home of the journalist Thomas Alsager (1779–1846), in which various members of the Novello family performed.[20] In addition to both father (organist) and son (solo bass), four other members of the family performed in the concert: Vincent's daughter Clara (solo soprano); daughter Mary Cowden Clarke (chorus alto); son and son-in-law, Edward Novello and Charles Cowden Clarke (chorus bass). The work was not performed publicly in England until 1839, when on 1 April, the Choral Harmonists, at their meeting at the London Tavern, presented the work; it was not repeated until 1 April 1844.[21] While the exact date of the first public performance of the complete work is peripheral to our discussion, information on the title page of the Novello folio piano-

---

[18]The following analysis of the *Missa solemnis* will refer to this piano-vocal edition by Novello. It appears that Novello's first complete edition was only published in 1846 to coincide with the Beethoven Commemorative Festival in Bonn.

[19]Georg Kinsky and H. Halm, eds, *Das Werk Beethoven: thematisch-bibliographisches Verzeichnis seiner sämtlichen vollendeten Kompositionen* (Munich: G. Henle Verlag, 1955), p. 364.

[20]For an account of Alsager and the Beethoven reception in London in the early nineteenth century see David B. Levy, 'Thomas Massa Alsager, Esq.: A Beethoven Advocate in London', *19th-Century Music* 9 (1985), pp. 119–27.

[21]Other works by Beethoven were performed and readily accepted in London during the composer's lifetime, however, and did not take as much time as the *Missa solemnis* to enter the canon. Nicholas Temperley notes that Beethoven's first three symphonies, at least, had their London premieres during the first ten years of the century. See 'Beethoven in London Concert Life, 1800–1850', *Music Review* 21 (1960), pp. 207–14. In addition, some of Beethoven's works were already published in small score, primarily for study, by

vocal edition under investigation suggests, nevertheless, that a concert did take place before 1839. The title page bears the line: 'As performed at the York Music Festivals' and the address: 'Printed for the Editor, No. 66, Great Queen Street, Lincoln's Inn Fields'. The second half of the 1820s was a period of much domestic movement for the Novello family, and, among other residences of that time, at one point, between 1826 and 1830, they lived at the Queen Street address. Moreover, Vincent's introduction to his *Collection of Haydn's Masses*, bearing the Queen Street address, is dated October 1828. If Vincent's application of that address on the Beethoven edition coincides with his actual time there, then it is possible that a performance of at least *part* of the work took place at the York Music Festival well before the Choral Harmonists presentation. The November 1828 issue of *The Harmonicon* offered a critique of that year's York Festival. On Friday, 29 September, the programme (as listed in the review) contained the chorus 'Quoniam tu solus' from the *Missa solemnis*. Vincent's note on the title page of his edition, 'as performed at the York Music Festival', may refer to this number only and not to the presentation of the entire piece.

British bafflement over the composition continued into the 1840s and is well documented in a report of the 1845 Beethoven festival in Bonn, organized to offset the cost of a monument to the composer. The September *Musical Times* made the following observation:

> The writer in the *Morning Chronicle* has excellently spoken of this wonderful composition in the following critique upon its performance at the Bonn festival: 'This Mass was generally regarded as an incomprehensible production, the depths of which (if they really were depths) it was impossible to fathom.' This opinion, I confess I adopted; but, however mistaken, it was conscientiously formed. Nobody in England tried to perform it; and an examination of the score was the only means of judging. As happened to many others, after pouring for hours over its ponderous pages, the only result was absolute bewilderment among its mazes – black despair succeeded brown study, and the hopeless task was laid aside. Such is the general case in England at this day where the 'Missa Solemnis' is as completely unknown as on the day it was published. The Germans, however, have mastered it; and the performance of the 10th August displayed it in all its grandeur and beauty.

One year later, as we learn from a review of the performance by the Philharmonic Society (published in *The Spectator* on 9 May and quoted in

---

the first decade. The first full scores of Beethoven's Symphonies Nos 1, 2, and 3 were published by the London firm Cianchettini and Sperati, in octavo form (*c.*10 × 7 in.). See Hans Lenneberg, 'Revising the History of the Miniature Score', *Notes* 45 (1988), pp. 258–61.

The Musical Times in June), at least one English audience remained confused and unappreciative:

> Beethoven's Mass in D, the grand attraction at this concert, corresponds in its kind to the Posthumous Quartets, which, through the diligent study and perfect execution of Sivori and his companions, have made so profound an impression lately;[22] not, however, without partial dissentiments among musicians of indisputable taste and liberality of feeling. To expect therefore that the enormous crowd which the fame of Beethoven's Mass collected received a due impression of it, would be absurd: a glance at the faces right and left during the performance was the test, and showed the 'pensive public' agonizing at an extraordinary rate with 'thoughts beyond the reaches of their souls.'[23]

Vincent's edition of the *Missa solemnis* differs from the 1827 Schott source in two respects: articulation and, to a lesser degree, dynamics. In large part, Vincent retained the more complex sets of dynamics found in the Schott score: the rapid sequence seen, for example, in the Quoniam tu solus Sanctus, bars 198–200: *sf–f–p–f–p–f*. Vincent did not modify these abrupt dynamic shifts to appease a more faint-hearted audience. Rather, he surely recognized that the excitement of the work lay in such dramatic gestures. Vincent also kept the additional moments of interest in the Kyrie II (bars 141–51), with the passage *f–p–f–p–ff–p* presented intact.

To a greater extent than dynamics, Vincent altered the articulation from the Schott edition, yet his version nonetheless still follows the general pattern of his source. When he did make changes, he more often included a slur. Thus, in bars 174–83 of the Kyrie, slurs were added for the intervals although the Schott edition does not have them. The addition of slurs was a small practical decision above all else. In the Schott score, the syllable on '-lei-' carries a slur at only one point (bar 182), although this may have followed Beethoven's manuscript. It is likely that Vincent believed the uniform presence of phrase markings would aid the performer or at least avoid confusion at bar 182. Vincent also added slurs over the octave leaps in the Quoniam, bars 95–7, again possibly to provide a sense of continuity for repeated words.

The above comparison has focused on the Schott full score Vincent cited as his source and his resulting piano-vocal reduction. Far from being an inaccurate rendition, Novello's piano-vocal reduction remains surprisingly compatible with the Schott version; indeed, the similarity to the German edition is an important factor as it may reflect Novello's wish to offer the

---

[22]Camillo Sivori, 1815–94, Italian violinist.

[23]Clara and Alfred Novello also participated in this concert: Clara as solo soprano and Alfred as solo bass.

market a publication which, most accurately, introduced the controversial *Missa solemnis*. In an analysis of Vincent's level of alteration within the work it appears that a standard policy was adopted: Vincent was more inclined to preserve the orginal dynamics, articulation, and phrasing than he was in the eighteenth-century editions discussed above. One reason may hinge on the differing degree of familiarity of the two works to the market, which purchased and performed Novello editions, made up primarily of amateurs and some professionals. Boyce's *Cathedral Music* and portions of Purcell's *Sacred Music* were already part of the repertoire in choral societies and church services and no doubt Vincent believed the pieces could sustain subtle interpretation and change. In turn, he may have felt a responsibility to introduce the little-understood Beethoven work in its original form rather than alter it too drastically for amateur use.

Editions from Spurious Sources: Mozart and Haydn

Some of the works Vincent arranged and published we now know to be spurious. Two of Vincent's largest early endeavours, the collected masses of Mozart and of Haydn, contain compositions which are most likely by other composers. A brief review of these editions offers a glimpse into the Victorian reception of the Mozart and Haydn repertoire: enthusiasm for both composers was such that often works were attributed on only little evidence (see below Edward Holmes's critique of 'Mozart's Twelfth Mass'). By examining the introductions to a selection of these editions, we can follow Vincent's decision-making process as he presents these spurious works to the Novello market. Which Novello editions are now considered spurious and what information led to mistaken identification?

Between 1819 and 1824, Vincent published his edition of masses he attributed to Mozart (see Table 2.3); the title page reads: 'Mozart's masses, with an accompaniment for the organ arranged from the full score by Vincent Novello'. Vincent's numbering of the volumes is slightly confusing and can be explained as follows. The complete edition of Mozart masses consisted of a total of eighteen numbers, with Nos 13 and 16 presented as two parts of the same work, the Mass in E flat: Kyrie and Gloria as No. 13 and No. 16 with the remainder of the service (see Table 2.3). Nos 1–15 were published for Vincent by W. Galloway between 1819 and 1820. Vincent published Nos 16–18 himself in 1824.[24] The Novello catalogue of October 1856 lists all eighteen Masses as still in print.

---

[24]Dates taken from Ludwig Köchel, ed., *Chronologisch-thematisches Verzeichnis sämtlicher Tonwerke Wolfgang Amade Mozart*, 6th edn (Wiesbaden: Breitkopf and Härtel, 1964), p. 811.

Table 2.3　Sources of Mozart works as listed by Vincent Novello in the Introduction to his edition of Mozart masses, Nos 1–15 (1820) and Nos 16–18 (1824)

No.	Title	K. no.	Source indicated by V. Novello
1	Mass in C	317	Breitkopf & Härtel
2	Mass in C	257	Breitkopf & Härtel
3	Mass in F	192 (186f)	Hoffmeister & Co.
4	Mass in C	258	'from a Score in MS'
5	Mass in C	220 (196b)	'from a Score in MS'
6	Mass in D	194 (186h)	'from a Score in MS'
7	Mass in B flat	Anh. 233.c.1.06	C. F. Peters
8	Mass in C (brevis)	Anh. 234 (Anh. C1.08)	M. Falter[a]
9	Mass in G (brevis)	Anh. 235 (Anh. C1.09)	M. Falter
10	Mass in B flat	275 (272b)	'from a Score in MS'
11	Mass in C	259	'from a Score in MS'
12	Mass in G	Anh. 232.c1.04	'from a Score in MS'
13	Mass in E flat (Mass continues with No. 16)	Anh. 186.C1.03	'from a Score in MS'[b]
14	Mass in C	337	'from a Score in MS'[c]
15	Requiem	626	Breitkopf & Härtel
16	Mass in E flat	Anh. 186.C1.03[d]	
17	Mass in C	Anh. 185.C1.01	
18	Mass in D	Anh. 237.c1.90[e]	

[a]Falter and Sohn: German firm of music publishers, founded 1796.
[b]Vincent adds a note to the source: 'From a manuscript score in the possession of The Revd. C. I. Latrobe.'
[c]Vincent adds a note to the source: 'From a manuscript score purchased by the Editor [V. Novello] from Messrs. Breitkopf and Härtel, Leipsic.'
[d]Mass No. 16 and No. 17 are noted by Vincent: 'From a very scarce ms score preserved at the Chapel of Moses de Aaron, Amsterdam.'
[e]For Mass No. 18, Vincent adds his source: 'From a German manuscript source in the possession of the Revd. C. I. Latrobe.'

There can be little doubt that Vincent was concerned with the authenticity of the works he published. In the introductions of two separate numbers of his 'Mozart Masses Collection', he questioned the origin of specific works. In the edition of Nos 1–15 (the introduction is dated September 1820), Vincent explained why one work in particular had been omitted:

> The Editor has also seen a short 'Requiem' in Manuscript, which has been attributed to Mozart; but it is so very unlike the usual elevation of his Style, and disfigured by so many inaccuracies in the Counterpoint, that considerable doubts have occurred as to its being genuine and as the Editor could not ascertain its authenticity in a satisfactory manner, he did not think himself justified in adding it to this Collection.

Yet both Vincent and his audience were apparently unsatisfied with this conclusion and further enquiry provided the following note in the introduction to the subsequent edition (dated March 1824):

> Several of the Subscribers having expressed a wish that the Short Requiem, alluded to in a former Number, should find a place in this Edition in order to render the Collection quite complete, the Editor has inserted it; and he had the less hesitation in complying with their wish, as he has lately met with a much more correct Copy than the one he had formerly examined, and consequently he has more reason for now believing it to be a genuine Composition of Mozart, although probably a very early production.

Novello's initial instinct, however, was correct and Köchel lists the Requiem as spurious (K. Anh. 237.c1.90).

Vincent found the Masses he would attribute to Mozart in both published and manuscript scores. In the 1819/20 publication (Nos 1–15), he sometimes listed the sources, a practice he would continue for the rest of the edition (Table 2.3 includes the attributions Vincent provided at the beginning of each Mass, and the respective Köchel numbers). According to Köchel, we now also recognize as spurious Novello's Masses Nos. 7, 8, 9, 12, 13, 16, 17, and 18.[25] The question of attribution for Novello's 'Twelfth Mass', in particular, is a fascinating case of mistaken identity. The origins of the work are unclear although in 1821 Simrock published a score of the Mass (plate no. 1815).[26] In 1826, writing in *Cäcilia*,[27] Ignaz Xaver von Seyfried

---

[25]Ibid., p. 811.

[26]H. C. Robbins Landon, 'Mozart fälschlich zugeschriebene Messen', *Mozart Jahrbuch* (1957), p. 87.

[27]*Cäcilia* 17 (1826), p. 77.

(1776–1841)[28] cast doubt on the authenticity of the Mass; in the same journal Simrock countered this the following year.[29] Simrock noted that he had obtained the manuscript from the Mainz music teacher and publisher Carl Zulehner. Köchel, however, believed the work was written by Zulehner himself. Despite such early doubts, other publishers accepted the Mass into the Mozart repertoire where it gained enormous favour throughout the nineteenth century.

The 'Twelfth Mass' became one of the most popular sacred works in the Victorian repertoire (see Chapter 3 for the record of demand and printing according to the Novello stockbook). The popularity of the work is attested to by Edward Holmes in his introduction, 'Critical Notice', to Novello's piano-vocal octavo edition (c.1850) (the text was an extract from Holmes's series of articles on Mozart's Masses published in *The Musical Times*):

> Notwithstanding all that has been said for and against the Twelfth Mass, its history in England is peculiar – for never has any work of the kind been so popular, its melodies almost rivaling in that respect those of the *Zauberflöte* or *Don Giovanni*. It has been translated from its original destination in the Catholic choir, to the theatre, the cathedral, the drawing-room. As the earliest ambition of the aspiring bass singer is to perform the Kyrie, its echoes have doubtless extended to many of the haunts of secular business; its melody, caught up, has been hummed unexpectedly in many a place where melody is rare, lightening for a while the burden of life.

It is of note that Holmes sensed within the Twelfth Mass a divergence from the more familiar Mozart style, yet it did not lead him to conclude that the work might be spurious:

> The origin of the Twelfth Mass seems to be indicated by Mozart in one of his letters from Mannheim in 1778, in which, speculating on the best means of getting an appointment at that place he writes: 'I intend to compose a new Grand Mass, and present it to the Elector.' The character of the music, destined for some important festival of the Church, displays him in this work not so much employing his own pen as imitating the Italian style, which was in vogue towards the close of the 18th century; yet as was his custom when adopting another style, blending and insinuating his own therewith in a manner which distinguishes him from all musicians.[30]

---

[28]Von Seyfried, an Austrian composer, conductor, writer, and teacher was reputedly a piano student of Mozart's. See Peter Branscombe, 'Ignaz (Xaver) Ritter von Seyfried', *The New Grove Dictionary of Music and Musicians*, 2nd edn, ed. Stanley Sadie and John Tyrrell (London: Macmillan, 2001), 23: p. 184; and Hugo Riemann, *Musik Lexikon*, 10th edn, ed. Alfred Einstein (Berlin: Max Hesses Verlag, 1922), pp. 1195–6.

[29]*Cäcilia* 21 (1827), p. 129.

[30]Edward Holmes, 'Critical Notice', *Mozart's Twelfth Mass* (London: Novello, [1850]), n.p.

Holmes then offers detailed programme notes, with music examples, of various sections of the Mass, and again observes the 'Italianate' style peculiar to the work:

> The Qui tollis, Adagio C minor, 3/4, is for solo voices and chorus, stringed instruments, oboes and bassoons. This solemn, grand, and ecclesiastical movement, is one of the finest in the Mass; and yet it is not so much in Mozart's own style as in that of the Italian church music of its period. Notwithstanding the elegance and expression of the solo parts, it contains certain passages of accompaniment marked by the peculiar taste of the age, and which by successive hearings have acquired an antique and formal character.

Holmes compares the style to that of other composers, but quickly dismisses any other possible attribution: 'Thus far might be the work of Jomelli; but at the second entrance of the chorus at "suscipe deprecationem," the harmonies become so impassioned and dramatic, that the true composer cannot be longer concealed.'

The publisher Robert Cocks and Co. also recognized the popularity of the Twelfth Mass and presented a piano-vocal edition as well (*c*.1854: the date of the introduction, by John Bishop, is 11 May 1854). The edition was part of Cocks's series Hand-Book for the Oratorios, with the title page: 'Mozart's Twelfth Service in G Major (with English words, written and adapted by William Ball), edited with an accompaniment for the piano forte, by John Bishop'. At mid-century, Cocks could be counted as one of the more active and successful firms, featuring numerous editions of sacred music in both octavo and folio piano-vocal arrangement of Handel, Mendelssohn, Haydn, and Mozart – clearly a rival to Novello's for the amateur market. To a large extent the Cocks catalogue was made up of editions and arrangements of works reprinted and reissued with added appendices or introductions under new series titles such as 'The People's Edition', 'The Students Edition', 'The Library Edition', and 'The Festival Edition'. An advertisement for Cocks's edition of *Messiah*, for example, lists the various editions available and the dates of first publication:

> 1st edition, in folio, The Centenary Edition (1841)

> 2nd edition, in Imperial Octavo, The Library Edition (1852) with a complete book of the words prefixed, and an Appendix containing 16 different settings of pieces in the Oratorio

> 3rd edition in Imperial Octavo, The People's Edition (1855), abridged from the 2nd edition by the omission of the appendix, with a book of the words prefixed

> 4th edition, The Student's Edition (1855) engraved from the 2nd edition with Appendix and a book of the words. Also a Memoir and fine Portrait of the Author

5th edition in large Octavo The Handbook Edition reprinted from the Third Edition

6th Edition in Foolscap Quarto, The Festival Edition

Beyond the fact that two contemporary firms erroneously published the Mass as part of Mozart's oeuvre, striking differences exist between the two editions and a comparison offers further insight into Vincent's editorial style. Concerning the text, the Novello edition follows the original Latin and supplies an almost direct English translation. The Cocks version also offers the sacred text but includes a completely new English version, 'written and adapted by William Ball', which takes the shape of a narrative in the guise of a prayer. The use of a different English text also affects the text setting in the Cocks edition and this will be discussed below. Aside from text variance, the primary difference between the two editions can be found in Bishop's Preface to the Cocks edition:

> In editing a series of the Masses of Haydn, Mozart, and Beethoven, I have arranged the accompaniment expressly for the Pianoforte, as the florid instrumental passages which so frequently occur in the scores appear to me scarcely suitable for performance on the Organ; and had all such passages been either omitted or greatly changed, a less faithful transcript of the orchestral portion of these works must have resulted.

English text of Mozart, *Twelfth Mass*
(Cocks edition 1854)

Praise to Thee, Jehovah
(Mozart's Mass, No. 12)

Kyrie
Praise to Thee, Jehovah, Lord of all creation!
Holiness, and blessing, and power, dwell with Thee for ever! None like to Thee hath dominion, O great Eternal, Father and Ruler Almighty!

Let Thy servants extol Thy mercies, and upraise to Thy glory their songs of praise and thanksgiving.

Gloria
Glorify His great and awful name, O all ye nations! Hallelujah! Sing unto Him, your heavenly Father! and you, ye creatures all, —ye of earth, and air, and the dwellers in the regions of the mighty waters, —in worship and in reverence come before Him, the Lord, your Maker!

Tell of the bounties His hand bestoweth on each and all in their season, —tell of his Wonders, —tell of His mercies, and make known His great loving-kindness from the beginning, even until now.

Though shadows and darkness are round about Him, Righteousness and Truth abide within His habitation, Honour and Majesty are throned beside Him, fearful are His judgments, there is yet for as the light or gladness, even the light of our salvation.

Heaven and Earth declare His triumphs; he giveth liberty to the captives, He healeth the wounds of the sorrowful, and breaketh the sword of the spoiler.

All created things proclaim Him, the ever Gracious, ever Holy, and ever Merciful, the life and breath of all that live.

To Thee, whom all adore,
Unending praise be given!
Glory for evermore!
Great King of Earth and Heaven!
Amen.

[Followed by text for Credo, Sanctus, Benedictus, and Agnus Dei.]

In contrast, the Novello octavo vocal edition was prepared for either piano or organ – and the various stops for the organ are often designated, for example at the beginning of the Benedictus with 'Choir stop Diap. and Dulciana'. The paths chosen by the two publishers reveal not only different accompaniments but also separate editorial philosophies.

A brief examination of the beginning of the Kyrie, for an example of text setting variances, and of the beginning of the Benedictus, a purely instrumental instance, clearly illustrates two different editorial styles at work. The Preface to the Cocks edition, as noted above, stresses that the piano is particularly suitable as ornamental passages from the full score can more easily be executed on piano than on organ. Vincent also may have been aware of this. For example, in bars 68ff. of the Benedictus (Example 2.11, p. 75 Novello edition and Example 2.12, p. 107 Cocks edition) the florid line of the right-hand accompaniment found in the Cocks version does not appear in the Novello edition, which instead employs a steady, crotchet rhythm. Similarly, at points throughout the score, the Novello edition uses one single dotted minim chord per bar, while the Cocks edition presents repeated quavers (the Kyrie, bars 39–40: Example 2.13, Novello edition; Example 2.14, Cocks edition). Some amateur musicians may have found the Cocks edition more challenging and perhaps more musically interesting and the Novello version, under the restrictions of the dual purpose for organ and piano, somewhat limited.

By the mid-1850s, organ performance and technique had improved as instruments with pedals became more commonplace than earlier in the century (see above) and the Novello edition may not have offered adequate opportunity for showmanship. Yet twenty years earlier, Vincent's

Example 2.11   Novello's edition of the Benedictus from Mozart, 'Twelfth Mass', bars 59–73

Example 2.11 continued

arrangements were faulted for being too elaborate and difficult.[31] In a publication review of Novello's *Select Organ Pieces* ('from the masses, motets, and other sacred works of Mozart, Haydn, Beethoven, Cherubini, and Palestrina, and other classical composers of the German and Italian schools, arranged by Vincent Novello'), in the July 1833 issue of *The Harmonicon*, his keyboard reductions were found to be still too complex:

> We are not among those who think that the Masses, etc. of Haydn
> and Mozart are, taken altogether, equal to their secular works; many
> of them, we are persuaded, would never have been published by the
> consent of the composers, but parts of them make very good organ
> pieces. These Mr. Novello has culled and, with his well-known abil-
> ity, converted them to a very useful purpose. He certainly calculates
> his adaptations for superior organists, and is not sparing of notes.
> Sometimes there will be found too many, by second-rate performers;
> and we take the liberty to mention to Mr. Novello that in the coun-
> try, nay even in the metropolis, are several respectable organists,
> very well qualified to do the duty of parish churches, who think his
> arrangements too much crowded for ordinary players, and too full
> of harmony for country congregations.

---

[31]For a survey of the state of the instrument in Britain during the early nineteenth century see Andrew McCrea, 'British Organ Music after 1800', in Nicholas Thistlethwaite and Geoffrey Webber, *The Cambridge Companion to the Organ* (Cambridge: Cambridge University Press, 1998), pp. 279–98.

Example 2.12   Cocks's edition of the Benedictus from Mozart, 'Twelfth Mass', bars 61–71

Example 2.13   Novello's edition of the Kyrie from Mozart, 'Twelfth Mass', bars 37–41

Example 2.14   Cocks's edition of the Kyrie from Mozart, 'Twelfth Mass', bars 36–40

Why, then, had Vincent 'tamed' this Mozart Mass, smoothed out the motivic and rhythmic edges and thereby lost that quality of tension and excitement? In an analysis of the Victorian view of Mozart, William Gatens suspects that the composer's sacred works may have been too reminiscent of his operatic style for Victorian comfort: 'With a few exceptions, like the "Ave verum Corpus" and parts of the *Requiem*, Mozart's church music was stylistically unacceptable to most Anglican ears. To them, the florid Austrian tradition of the choral mass seemed operatic, ostentatious, and frivolous.'[32] This mid-century sentiment may have been a key element in Vincent's editorial framework: he not only provided an edition suitable to *both* pianists and organists (capturing an even larger audience than the Cocks publication), he also arranged the score to satisfy a more specific aesthetic expectation. Indeed, there can be little doubt that Vincent prepared his edition with the Victorian audience in mind. These parameters of sacred music are reflected by J. A. Latrobe writing in 1831 in *The Music of the Church*:

> Sacred music, as a medium of divine communication, ought to possess a character of its own – so distinct from the music of the concert room, as in no respect to recall vain and idle association. The same marked contrast should be visible in the style of performance. Any attempt to assimilate the service of Jehovah to the amusement of the theatre, is in effect to associate God and Mammon. It is to make the Holy One pander to human iniquity – it is to point the weapons of His warfare against His servants – it is to fill the vessels of the temple with the wine of a Belshazzar's banquet – it is, in the expressive language of the scripture, 'to bring the hire of a whore, and the price of a dog into the house of the Lord our God'.[33]

Within Novello's *Collected Edition of Haydn's Masses*, the issue of authenticity can also briefly be examined. Vincent published the edition in organ-vocal score and folio size during the first part of the 1820s. The title page reads: 'Haydn's Masses with an Accompaniment for the Organ. Arranged from the full score and respectfully inscribed by permission to his serene Highness The Prince Esterhazy by Vincent Novello. Organist to the Portuguese Embassy in London ... Published by W. Galloway ... No. 21, Wigmore Street, Cavendish Square ...'. Galloway held premises at the Wigmore Street address from *c*.1819 to 1828.[34]

---

[32]William J. Gatens, *Victorian Cathedral Music in Theory and Practice* (Cambridge: Cambridge University Press, 1986), p. 86.

[33]J. A. Latrobe, *The Music of the Church* (London, 1831), p. 134, quoted in Gatens, *Victorian Cathedral Music*, pp. 60–61.

[34]Charles Humphries and William C. Smith, *Music Publishing in the British Isles: from the Beginning until the Middle of the Nineteenth Century*, 2nd edn (Oxford: Basil Blackwell, 1970), p. 152.

During the same decade another issue of Vincent's edition was published by Galloway in a larger folio size.

Beyond the fourteen actual settings known to be by Haydn, another 167 have been incorrectly attributed to the composer.[35] Among the sixteen masses published by Vincent Novello under Haydn's name, four are now considered doubtful: Novello's No. 9 (Hoboken XXII:C1); No. 10 (Hoboken XXII:C1); No. 13 (Hoboken XXII:C2); and No. 14 (Hoboken XXII:D1).[36] Although no other composer can be named for XXII:C1 and XXII:c1, MacIntyre regards these two settings of questionable authenticity[37] and No. 13 (XXII:C2) has been assigned either to Monsching or, more likely, to Johann Baptist Vanhal.[38] MacIntyre pinpoints these spurious attributions to two causes: mistaken identification and intentional renaming. In eighteenth-century manuscript preparation it was common practice to mark only the wrapper or cover of a work, while the individual vocal and instrumental parts inside remained without the composer's name. At a later stage, an incorrect name was often added to each part, either through error or artifice, and such mistakes then formed a tradition of performance and acceptance. A well-known composer such as Haydn had his name included on many works not his own.

As with many other of Vincent's editions, for his publication of the Haydn Masses he provided attributions (see Table 2.4). It is of note that the source for one spurious work (No. 10) was, as with a number of the Mozart works, C. I. Latrobe; Vincent also received the manuscripts for Nos 7, 8, and 11 from him. Nos 13 and 14, both attributed 'from a MS score in the possession of the Editor', are spurious but unfortunately it is not possible to uncover Vincent's own sources.

One small example suggests that Vincent was as concerned with authenticity in his Haydn edition as he was with the Mozart collection, discussed above. At the end of the Kyrie for Haydn's Mass No. 7, Vincent printed the note: 'In the edition of this Mass published at Bonn by Simrock, there is another movement inserted here, but it is not the Composition of Haydn; it is by Jommelli, and forms part of the Kyrie in his Requiem Mass.' (Novello is referring to Jommelli's Requiem in E flat, published in 1764.) As we have also seen with the instance of the 'Short Requiem' by Mozart (Novello's Mass No. 18, K. Anh. 237.C1.90), when

---

[35]See Bruce G. MacIntyre, 'Haydn's Doubtful and Spurious Masses: An Attribution Update', *Haydn-Studien* 5 (1982), pp. 42–54. MacIntyre identified the spurious works on both stylistic and textual grounds, through an analysis of incipits from the eighteenth-century mass repertoire. See p. 43, n. 7.

[36]Ibid., pp. 42–54.

[37]Ibid., pp. 44, n. 9.

[38]Ibid., pp. 45.

Table 2.4 Sources as listed by Vincent Novello in the Introduction to *Collected Edition of Haydn's Masses*

Novello No.	Hoboken No.	Source as per V. Novello
1	XXII:10	'from the score published by Breitkopf and Härtel'
2	XXII:9	Breitkopf and Härtel
3	XXII:11	Breitkopf and Härtel
4	XXII: Nr. 13	Breitkopf and Härtel
5	XXII:5	Breitkopf and Härtel
6	XXII:14	Breitkopf and Härtel
7	XXII:6	'From a MS score in Haydn's own handwriting. In the possession of the Revd. C. I. Latrobe'
8	XXII:7[a]	'From a MS score in Haydn's own handwriting. In the possession of the Revd. C. I. Latrobe'
9*	XXII:C1	'From MS score in the possession of the editor'
10*	XXII:c1	'From a MS score in the possession of the Revd. C. I. Latrobe'
11	XXII:1	'From a MS score in the possession of the Revd. C. I. Latrobe'
12	XXII:4	'From a MS score formerly belonging to Dr Burney, now in the possession of the Editor'
13*	XXII:C2	'From a MS score in the possession of the Editor'
14*	XXII:D1	'From a MS score in the possession of the Editor'
15	XXII:8	'From the score published by Breitkopf and Härtel'
16	XXII: Nr. 12	'From a MS score, purchased by the Editor of Mr Edmund Harris, Professor, Bath'

*= spurious
[a]Anthony van Hoboken, *Joseph Haydn: thematisch-bibliographisches Werkverzeichnis*, vol. 3 (Mainz: B Schotts Söhne, 1978), 85 cites this mass as Novello's No. 15.

Vincent grappled with questions of authenticity he often published his doubts and conclusions as notes or introductions. Although performers of the Novello edition were most likely unfamiliar with the Jommelli music, Vincent apparently found it his editorial responsibility to reveal some of the steps leading to his final publication. He also understood the promotional advantages of publishing his methods and presenting himself as a relatively concerned and insightful editor.

From an evaluation of Vincent's editorial practices – his piano-vocal arrangements of Handel and Beethoven and of earlier sacred music – we may further understand Novello's publishing policies. In preparing his editions, Vincent had to consider the primary questions of suitability and demand. For example, where would the edition be performed? Was the conductor familiar with full scores or would a reduction, with cue notes, be more accessible? Could the organist or pianist perform from unrealized figured bass or should an arrangement be provided? Are the original dynamics appropriate? Such questions of technical ability, musical experience, and artistic sophistication influenced Vincent's presentation of editions. In a discussion of early attempts at editing during the first half of the nineteenth century, Philip Brett notes: 'The methods of evaluating the sources and achieving a text have not, however, been a matter of overriding concern to musical editors, at least not until comparatively recent times. Far more important has been the question of how the edition presents its information.'[39] Examples of this editorial approach can be seen in Vincent's efforts to prepare scores, which 'afford an opportunity for their performance', as noted in the Preliminary Remarks to Novello's collection of Haydn masses. The inclusion of a realized figured bass in some editions or an innovative combination of typeface sizes for notation in others were the features which attracted the market – any historical considerations were a secondary matter. Indeed, the mid-nineteenth-century Novello editions remain important today for what they tell us about Victorian musical life and performance practice – the expectations, aesthetics, requirements, and demands – rather than what they reveal about the composer's intentions.

We now come full circle, returning to the remark by Paul Henry Lang quoted at the beginning of the chapter. Lang dismisses the Novello editions as 'so lacking in elementary care that they cannot be considered in any scholarly, critical analysis' (see n. 1). Within Lang's observation lies the modern view that editions must exist as historical

---

[39]Philip Brett, 'Text, Context, and the Early Music Editor', in Nicholas Kenyon, ed., *Authenticity and Early Music: A Symposium* (Oxford: Oxford University Press, 1988), p. 87.

documents, accurate and pristine records of the music in its precise form. Yet an edition cannot offer an objective presentation; rather, it will be a combination of the aesthetic, social, and historical influences inherent in the period in which it is made.

In Chapter 1 we examined the overall social and economic environment in which Vincent and Alfred Novello published. In this chapter's analysis of the firm's editing style, through specific examples of editions, we have noted how these cultural factors are translated into the presentation of the editions themselves. In the following chapter we will gauge the financial success of Vincent's editorial decisions through the firm's records of supply and demand as reflected in their stockbooks.

CHAPTER THREE

The Novello Stockbook, 1858–1869: A Chronicle of Publishing Activity*

The relationship between composer and publisher reflects the delicate balance between art and business. For the composer, the publisher is sometimes friend and confidant, more often adversary. For the publisher, the composer may be an artistic charge or a financial liability. Their symbiotic relationship has been examined, in large part, from the viewpoint of the composer. Almost completely unexplored, however, is the publisher's role in the dissemination of a work. How have publishers struck a balance between their perception of the market and the actual demand? To appreciate such financial stargazing, we must locate and analyse the business documents that chronicle a firm's practices. In the absence of such records, publishers are judged by the insufficient data supplied by correspondence and catalogue advertisements. The lack of primary source material has critically limited studies of music publishers and their relationship to society. Without quantitative data, it is almost impossible to gauge either a publisher's anticipation of the demand for a particular work or the reality of the demand. Such records are quite rare,[1] and have not often been evaluated in financial terms.

One document now offers the opportunity to examine music publishing from the economic viewpoint of printing and disseminating editions. The private records of Novello's include a stockbook that records the printing and removal from the warehouse of the firm's editions during

---

*A version of this chapter was published in *Notes* 44 (1987), pp. 240–51.

[1] One collection of a nineteenth-century music publisher's records is described in James J. Fuld, 'The Ricordi "Libroni"', in Rudolf Elvers, ed., *Festschrift Albi Rosenthal* (Tutzing: Hans Schneider, 1984), pp. 139–45; another, the *Druckbuch* of Schott, has been employed for dating and other information in John Deathridge, Martin Geck, and Egon Voss, eds, *Verzeichnis der musikalischen Werke Richard Wagners und ihrer Quellen* (Mainz: B. Schotts Söhne, 1986).

the period 1858–69[2] (see Appendix 4 for a partial transcription). This is
the earliest of Novello's surviving nineteenth-century stockbooks. The
title page reads: 'Stockbook, J. Alfred Novello's Printing Office, Dean's
Yard, Dean Street, Soho, 1858', with the record beginning in November
of that year. The pages contain entries made under six printed headings
(Figure 3.1). A number of entries in the stockbook include a note, 'To
new book', indicating that additional records from this period existed,
although these now appear to have been either lost or destroyed. The
stockbook under discussion records in large part Novello's editions of
sacred music. A glance at the firm's 1863 catalogue reveals the publication of secular works as well. If other stockbooks from the years under
investigation could be located, a more complete picture of production
and demand for Novello's publications would be possible.

By 1858, the Novello firm was already an established music publisher
in England, having in the previous decade initiated its Cheap Classics
series, Octavo editions, and the publication of its journal *The Musical
Times* (see Chapter 5). As noted in Chapter 1, during the late 1850s and
early 1860s, Alfred Novello made preparations to transmit control of the
firm to his protégé, Henry Littleton, who would assume complete ownership of the house in 1866. While the following analysis focuses primarily
on the period of Alfred Novello's tenure, stockbook information to the
close of the record in 1869 is also considered.

Publishing Policy: Compositions, Format, Quantity

When Alfred Novello published an edition, his perception of market
demand determined his decisions not only concerning the compositions
to print, but also the format, number of copies, and months of the year
in which these pieces would be issued. Novello's simplest decision
surely concerned when to publish. (The factor of timing is discussed in
greater detail in Chapter 4.) A large portion of the Novello catalogue
was given over to sacred works, many of them in performance editions
for choral groups. Not surprisingly, preparation for the Christmas holi-
day period began months ahead, making October to December the time

[2]The stockbook was kindly made available to me by the staff of Novello and Company;
Margaret Pace and the late Bernard Axcell were particularly helpful. I would also like to
thank Michael Hurd, who was generous with both his time and information concerning the
Novello archives. A large portion of these archives has now been placed on permanent loan
at the British Library – see Michael Hurd, 'The Novello Archives', *The Musical Times* 126
(1986), pp. 687–8. The stockbook evaluated here is now part of the British Library
Novello Business Archive, Deposit 1996/09 Part E.

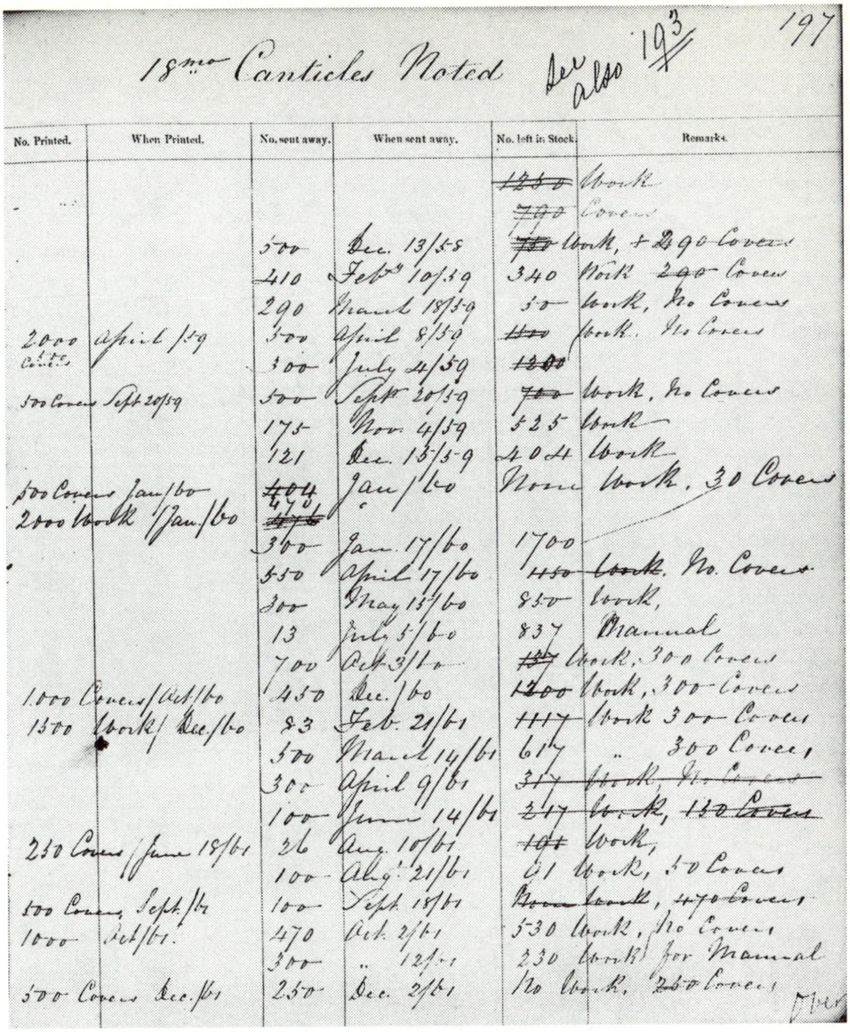

18mo Canticles Noted — See also 193 — 197

No. Printed.	When Printed.	No. sent away.	When sent away.	No. left in Stock.	Remarks.
				~~1250~~	Work
				~~700~~	Covers
		500	Dec. 13/58	~~750~~	Work, + 290 Covers
		410	Feby 10/59	340	Work ~~290~~ Covers
		290	March 18/59	50	Work, No Covers
2000 [illegible]	April /59	300	April 8/59	~~1100~~	Work. No Covers
		300	July 4/59	~~1200~~	
500 Covers	Sept 20/59	500	Sept 20/59	~~700~~	Work, No Covers
		175	Nov. 4/59	525	Work
		121	Dec. 15/59	404	Work
500 Covers	Jan/60	~~404~~	Jan/60	None	Work, 30 Covers
2000 Work	Jan/60	~~470~~			
		300	Jan. 17/60	1700	
		550	April 17/60	~~450~~	~~Work~~. No Covers
		300	May 15/60	850	Work,
		13	July 5/60	837	Manual
		700	Oct 3/60	~~137~~	Work, 300 Covers
1000 Covers	Oct/60	450	Dec./60	~~1200~~	Work, 300 Covers
1500 Work	Dec/60	83	Feb. 21/61	~~1117~~	Work 300 Covers
		500	March 14/61	617	" 300 Covers
		300	April 9/61	~~317~~	~~Work, No Covers~~
		100	June 14/61	~~217~~	~~Work~~, ~~130 Covers~~
250 Covers	June 18/61	26	Aug. 10/61	~~101~~	Work,
		100	Aug. 21/61	01	Work, 50 Covers
500 Covers	Sept/61	100	Sept. 18/61	~~None~~	~~Work~~, 470 Covers
1000	Oct/61	470	Oct. 2/61	530	Work, No Covers
		300	" 12/61	230	Work for Manual
500 Covers	Dec/61	250	Dec. 2/61	No Work,	~~250~~ Covers

Over

Figure 3.1 Page from the Novello stockbook: Novello Business Archive, Deposit 1996/09 Part E

of greatest printing activity. In 1859, for example, all the printing of three choral editions occurred in the final quarter of the year, as did the larger of two printings of a fourth choral edition, 'Mozart's Twelfth Mass' (Table 3.1).[3]

[3]See Chapter 2 for a discussion of spurious works.

No. Printed.	When Printed.	No. sent away.	When sent away.	No. left in Stock.	Remarks.	

Figure 3.1   continued

The musical format (full score, piano-vocal score, or parts) and the publishing format (folio, octavo, or 'pocket') also required decisions. All Novello octavo publications of the period and many of the folio editions are in piano-vocal score (the musical format presumed when none is indicated). From 1844 on, Novello published octavo editions of vocal works, initially as performance supplements to *The Musical Times* (see Chapter 5 for the relationship between the journal and this editorial format). By 1858, a popular composition such as *Messiah* could be purchased in folio, octavo, or pocket piano-vocal score, as well as in separate instrumental parts. Studying the print runs of *Messiah* in the various formats reveals a correlation between function and demand. During May 1859,

Table 3.1   Printing schedule and quantity by month for selected
Novello editions, 1859

Printing months 1859	Number printed (octavo edition unless otherwise stated)
Alexander's Feast	
1. January–March	0
2. April–June	0
3. July–September	0
4. October–December	1,500-wk
Mozart's 'Twelfth Mass'	
1. January–March	1,000-cv
2. April–June	3,000-wk; 1,000-cv
3. July–September	0
4. October–December	4,000-wk; 2,000-cv
Boyce–Arnold *Cathedral Music*	
1. January–March	0
2. April–June	0
3. July–September	0
4. October–December	1,500-wk; 1,000-cv
Messiah (folio)	
1. January–March	0
2. April–June	0
3. July–September	0
4. October–December	500-wk

wk = work
cv = covers

for example, 6,000 copies of the octavo edition and 7,500 copies of the
pocket version were produced, followed in November by a small run of
500 in the folio size. Such apportioning of print-run quantity reflects the
practical use of each of the formats. Until the 1840s, Novello published
primarily in folio editions, whose large dimensions, while luxurious in
presentation, were cumbersome for performance. With the mid-century
growth of choral societies and their demand for appropriate performance editions, octavo became the format of choice. It is, then, not
surprising that a November 1859 supply of 600 *Messiah* folios (500
newly printed and 100 still in stock), did not near depletion until February 1864, when 22 remained. The demand for editions of the individual
vocal parts also diminished: annual impressions averaged only 500. This

may suggest that performers preferred the convenience of a complete score (in piano-vocal reduction) rather than a single part.

One of Alfred's primary decisions concerned the kinds of compositions he chose to publish. The majority of the works recorded in the stockbook are sacred, reflecting, in fact, Novello's dedication to this repertoire. The annual print runs for 1859–61 of selected compositions, as revealed by the stockbook, are (predictably) largest for the octavo and pocket editions of *Messiah* (see Table 3.2). *Messiah*'s popularity in Victorian England is well known, and the work was never in greater demand than during the Handel Centennial Festival at the Crystal Palace in 1859. Indeed, Novello was appointed by the Crystal Palace Company as publisher for the Festival of all scores to be used by both performers and audience.[4]

Table 3.2   Annual print run by editorial format for selected Novello editions

	Messiah	Creation	St Paul	Judas Maccabeus
Folio	500 (1859)	—	—	—
Vocal parts	500 (1863)	500 (1862)	500 (1867)	500 (c.1863)
Octavo	17,000 (11/1858–12/1859)	5,000 (1859)	3,000 (1859)	6,500 (1859)
'Small (pocket) edition'	7,500 (11/1858–12/1859)	—	—	—

The size of the print runs for some other compositions reveals Novello's perception of the public demand for editions of sacred music (see Table 3.3). Handel's *Samson* was reprinted more often, and in larger print runs, than either *Solomon* or *Saul*. Of two Mendelssohn Psalms, the 95th received larger and more frequent printings than the 42nd. The practical collections of chants and anthems were reprinted at a rate

---

[4]'J. Alfred Novello informs the Public that he was again entrusted by the Sacred Harmonic Society to print the Musical Copies necessary for the performers at the Commemoration, and by the Directors of the Crystal Palace Company to provide the Vocal Score octavo Hand-Books for the use of the audience. He was also authorized to print the whole of the Music for the Wednesday's Selection in the order of its Performance, which was published uniform with his complete editions of Handel's *Messiah* and *Israel in Egypt*' (*The Musical Times*, 1 August 1859, p. 101).

Table 3.3   Print runs by year for selected Novello editions

	1859*	1860	1861 (or later)
INDIVIDUAL WORKS			
Handel, *Messiah*	17,000	6,000	6,000
Handel, *Messiah* (pocket edn)	7,500	0	5,000
Handel, *Samson*	3,000†	750	2,000
Handel, *Saul*	1,000	0	0
Handel, *Solomon*	1,000	0	1,000
Mendelssohn, Psalm 42	1,000	0	1,000
Mendelssohn, Psalm 95	1,000	1,000	1,000 (June 1863)
Mozart's 'Twelfth Mass'	7,000	0	4,000
COLLECTIONS			
Bird's [Byrd's] *Chants*	1,000	1,000	2,000
Boyce/Arnold, *Cathedral Music*	1,500	0	1,500 (Feb. 1862)
Dr Monk's Anglican Chants	¥	1,000	1,000 (Aug. 1862)
Kent's Anthems	1,000	0	1,500
Westminster Chants	¥	1,000	1,000
EDUCATIONAL WORKS			
Berlioz, *Treatise on Modern Instrumentation and Orchestration*	500	0	500 (Aug. 1865)
Marx, *General Musical Instruction*	1,000	0	500 (July 1863)
S. Novello, *Voice and Vocal Art*	¥	¥	1,000 (Dec. 1863)

*Nov. 1858–Dec. 1859.
†Feb. 1858–Dec. 1859.
¥No figures recorded; records may have been kept in other, concurrent stockbooks.

similar to that for the Handel oratorios, suggesting a comparable level of popularity and use. When the market for a particular work was suspected of becoming saturated, Novello reduced its print run. Thus, all 3,000 copies of *Samson* printed in two lots of 1,500 each between February 1858 and December 1859 had been removed from the warehouse by April 1860. Novello reprinted the work again, but in a cautiously small run of only 750 copies. When that supply ran out in February 1861, an optimistic run of 2,000 copies was immediately produced, 500 of which were quickly removed from the warehouse. This example demonstrates Novello's response to the ebb and flow of supply and demand – a rhythm that clearly required both sensitivity to the market and flexibility of production.

Compared to performance editions of music, reprints of volumes in Novello's Library for the Diffusion of Musical Knowledge appeared at a much slower rate. The series, announced in 1852,[5] was dedicated to the publication of music histories, treatises, and instrumental and vocal instructors. The infrequency and small size of printings of *Dr. Marx's General Musical Instruction* (translated from Adolph Marx's *Allgemeine Musiklehre*), Berlioz's *Treatise on Modern Instrumentation and Orchestration*, and Sabilla Novello's *Voice and Vocal Art* reflect the public's use of these works: as separate books in a series, they were usually bought one at a time, unlike oratorio and anthem editions which were normally purchased in multiple copies for a performance.

Alfred Novello recognized two vital elements of publishing: context and timing. Not only were choice of composition, format, and size of print run considered, but the date of printing as well as the overall balance of production in any one year were taken into account. Indeed, a prediction of the market could result in profit only if it made use of these factors. Such decisions, then, affected both publisher and composition, and yoked them, merchant and article, together financially.

Novello's Printing Methods

In light of Novello's sizeable catalogue and press runs, it is important to examine how the firm produced such relatively large numbers of publications in such short periods of time. Novello's increasing rate of production was aided by technological advancements in printing, transportation, and artificial energy – innovations that filtered through to all areas of industrialized society.[6] Alfred Novello was personally involved in the development and economics of printing technology. He designed two fonts, Pearl Nonpareil and Gem Gregorian, specifically for the firm; the latter font would come to be associated with the octavo editions and with *The Musical Times*.[7] In February 1847 he opened a

---

[5]Hurd, *Vincent Novello*, p. 62. See the additional discussion of this group of publications in Chapter 1.

[6]For a discussion of nineteenth-century technology and its influence on printing and publishing see J. A. Sutherland, *Victorian Novelists and Publishers* (Chicago: University of Chicago Press, 1976), p. 63.

[7]Joseph Bennett, ed., *A Short History of Cheap Music* (London: Novello, 1887), pp. 37–9.

printing office to serve both his own publishing requirements and those of other individuals and firms.[8] He announced the new facilities in a pamphlet, which also outlined the contemporary methods of music printing and their relative benefits according to print-run size.[9] Novello noted that 'the probable number of *copies* to be sold must decide whether it be more advisable to produce the work on Engraved Pewter Plates, or by Moveable Music Types'. When 'hundreds' of copies were needed, Novello found engraving sufficient, while print runs in the thousands required movable type.[10]

The firm also employed stereotyping: an August 1863 sales catalogue, in offering *The Musical Times*, recommends that 'the Work be ordered to be supplied at the time it appears, as only the music pages are stereotyped, and after the sale of the first impression, the advertisements and the notice of musical matters cannot be obtained'. A similar notice appears in issues of *The Musical Times* that date from the 1850s; and an 1898 inventory of the firm includes '91,869 stereos in octavo and quarto size and 48,002 in smaller sizes'.[11]

While the stockbook indicates print runs and schedules, a more complete picture of Novello's production arrangements depends on identifying the type and number of printing presses available in-house and on determining whether outside printers were also employed. The 1898 inventory cited above includes four hand-operated platen printing presses: a Crown Broadside Imperial Press by Cope and Sherwin (dated 1836), a Folio Albion Press by Hopkinson and Cope (1844), a Platen Galley Proving Press by Essen [*sic*][12] (1844), and a Columbian Press by George Clymer (1845). All of these are Albion presses except for the Columbian.[13] A brief discussion of the capabilities of the Columbian and

---

[8]The majority of Novello's entries in Stationers' Hall from the period 1830–69 represent printing jobs undertaken for outside publication in cases where some semblance of copyright protection was desired by the client. The Novello entries for 1830–42 were made available at Stationers' Hall, London and those for 1843–69 at the Public Record Office, Kew.

[9]Alfred Novello, *Some Accounts of the Methods of Musick Printing, with Specimens of the Various Sizes of Moveable Types; and of Other Matters* (London: Novello, 1847).

[10]Laurence Swinyard, ed., *A Century and a Half in Soho* (London: Novello, 1961), pp. 73–4.

[11]Hurd, *Vincent Novello*, pp. 143–4. For additional studies of stereotyping see George A. Kubler, *A New History of Stereotyping* (New York: George A. Kubler, 1941); and Hans Lenneberg, 'The Haunted Bibliographer', *Notes* 40 (1984), pp. 239–48.

[12]Probably John Esson, a printer's engineer and valuer who sold many presses under his own name; see James Moran, *Printing Presses: History and Development from the 15th Century to Modern Times* (London: Faber and Faber, 1973), p. 99.

[13]Hurd, *Vincent Novello*, pp. 145–6.

Albion presses, coupled with production data from the stockbook, will help clarify Novello's in-house printing structure.

The Columbian was one of the earliest nineteenth-century presses to be manufactured in great numbers. This iron hand-press, invented by George Clymer (1754–1834), was sold throughout New England, yet the heavy cast-iron frame proved impractical for transporting westward. Clymer thus decided to explore a possible European market; in May 1817 he sailed for London and by November had patented his press in England. The innovation of Clymer's press lay in its method of combining various levers, thereby demanding less of the operator's strength and energy. Through this new system 250 impressions could be produced in one hour. Yet many printers still found the Columbian inefficient, expressing sentiments such as the following: 'No press can possibly produce better work than the *Columbian*; yet we do not consider them so well adapted for light jobs as they are for heavier work; neither are they so expeditious as some others; the *Bar* is too far from the hand; from the quantity of levers, the *Bar* can never come down or return so quick, as where the power is gained by a simple motion.'[14]

The other type of press noted in the Novello inventory, and an alternative to the Columbian, was the Albion, invented about 1820 by Richard Cope. The advantages of the Albion over the Columbian were threefold: 'a simplified mechanism, lighter weight, and a quicker and shorter pull'.[15] An illustration of the Albion's printing capacity is found in an advertisement for the 'Self-inking Albion Press, invented by D. Napier', a press based on Cope's design. The manufacturer claimed that 'at the rate of five sheets per minute by two men at the *Common Press*, one man with this Press will print six'.[16]

Although Alfred Novello employed such presses from the beginning of his printing endeavours, when he assumed management from his father, by mid-century the production demands of the firm could not be met by the limited means of hand-operated equipment and by in-house printers alone. The stockbook indicates that Novello also employed outside printers: the names of Saville (also written 'Savill') and Kenny, two London printing firms, appear frequently in the 'Number Printed' column.[17] Also,

---

[14]Quoted in Jacob Kainen, *George Clymer and the Columbian Press* (New York: The Typophiles, 1950), p. 56, n. 43.

[15]Ibid., pp. 34–5.

[16]Moran, *Printing Presses*, p. 90.

[17]Both Saville and Kenny have been identified as letterpress printers; see Philip A. H. Brown, *London Publishers and Printers c.1800–1870* (London: The British Library, 1982), pp. 105, 170; and William B. Todd, *A Directory of Printers and Others in Allied Trades: London and Vicinity, 1800–1840* (London: Printing Historical Society, 1972), p. 169.

the names of at least two additional outside firms are found in the Novello editions themselves. Sawyer and Son (later Richard Sawyer and Son), acknowledged in the 1832 edition of *Purcell's Sacred Music*, presumably enjoyed an early relationship with Novello's. The phrase 'R. and E. Williamson', stamped on some Novello editions, probably refers to Richard Williamson of Lambeth, who is listed as owning a press as early as 1812.[18] That an outside printer should be used by Novello's in 1832 is not surprising: documentation from that decade indicates that the in-house work force was indeed limited. The size of Novello's printing staff in the 1830s is recorded in a statement taken by the firm's legal counsel in preparation for a case against the musician and editor Edward Taylor.[19] The testimony chronicles Taylor's public accusation that copies of his arrangement of Spohr's *The Last Judgment* were secretly printed and sold by Alfred Novello. Two revealing interviews with Novello employees shed considerable light on the firm's printing capacity. One witness, a Mr Pearman, testified that he was the only music printer employed by the firm during the early 1830s – a statement confirmed by Novello's foreman, Frederick Hehl (see Chapter 4 for a more detailed account and Appendix 6 for a transcription of the statement). The practice of contracting with outside firms to share the workload continued – as the names in the stockbook suggest – throughout the following decades, and if the records of these firms are uncovered, future studies may be able to define the financial and administrative arrangements that such relationships entailed.

Balance of Supply and Demand

How successfully did Alfred Novello predict the market for his editions? Was the firm able to strike a balance between the number of copies printed and their rate of depletion? And what compositions and editions were removed from Novello's warehouse in the greatest number? The stockbook provides answers to all these questions. The firm took from its warehouse only as many copies of a work as were needed at any particular time. Depletion of the stock was erratic: for example, 4,122 octavo-edition copies of *Judas Maccabeus* were taken during 1859, but November alone accounted for 1,205 of these (in two unequal lots of

---

[18]Ibid., p. 213.

[19]The document is part of the Novello Cowden Clarke Collection, located in the Brotherton Library, Leeds University. I wish to thank Mr D. Cox, University Librarian and Keeper of the Cowden Clarke Collection, and Mr C. Sheppard for their assistance in allowing me to examine the records.

205 and 1,000 copies). Such figures not only show us the number of copies actually distributed for potential sale, they also suggest the relative popularity of the various composers, compositions, editions, and formats in the publisher's catalogue (see Table 3.3). In the case of *Messiah*, for example, the formats most quickly distributed were the octavo and pocket piano-vocal scores: a supply of 6,000 octavo copies printed in November 1859 was depleted in ten months, and a print run of 7,500 pocket editions produced in May 1859 had been entirely removed by April 1861. The folio edition and individual vocal parts left the warehouse at a slower pace: as noted above, the November 1859 stock of 600 folio copies served the firm's needs for over four years, and 500 copies of a separate bass vocal part printed in December 1863 lasted for three years. This pattern, not surprisingly, reflects the growth of choral societies and their increasing demand for published music in inexpensive piano-vocal editions.

The burgeoning choral-society market also determined Novello's emphasis on oratorios and other large sacred works: the firm's most rapid rate of reprinting is found within these genres (see Table 3.4). Like *Messiah*, Haydn's *Creation* showed a vigorous turnover: 2,500 octavo copies printed in November 1858 were entirely removed from the warehouse within five months. Novello also found great success with two Mendelssohn oratorios: the 2,000 copies of *Elijah*, printed in January 1860, were gone by April (with a reprinting in the latter month exhausted by August), and nearly all 1,500 octavo copies of *St Paul* printed in October 1859 were shipped within ten months of that date.[20]

Rossini was, like Mendelssohn, one of the few living Continental composers in Novello's list at mid-century. The choice of a Rossini work, the Stabat Mater (1841 version), was characteristic of Novello's emphasis on sacred music. The firm first published its edition during the 1840s, before the period covered by the stockbook. Although listed as a co-publisher in the Troupenas first edition, which was issued shortly after the January 1842 premiere in Paris, Novello did not use the Troupenas

---

[20]Novello's editions of Mendelssohn were well received, as the following publication review illustrates: 'In the case of Mr. Novello's miniature editions of classical works, both the sacred and secular, perseverance and success seem to re-act upon each other. His prolonged industry and care have created a large demand for these publications, and that demand has very properly stimulated an increased supply. *The Hymn of Praise* or *Lobgesang* of Mendelssohn is certainly a work which the enlightened amateur would wish to see disseminated ... A form and size convenient for the desk or the hand, a clear and easily readable typography, both of notes and of words ... a careful transcription of the vocal score, and a masterly compression of the accompaniments' (*The Dramatic and Musical Review* 9 [1850], pp. 261–2).

Table 3.4   Printing and depletion activity from the Novello stockbook[a]

Amount printed	Date printed	Date impression depleted[b]
Handel, *Messiah*:		
6,000	11/1859	9/22/1860
6,000	12/1860	12/11/1861
Handel, *Messiah* (pocket edition)		
7,500	5/1859	4/4/1861
5,000	10/1861	5/29/1862
Handel, *Messiah* (folio)		
500	11/1859	2/2/64 (22 remaining)
Handel, *Messiah* (parts)		
500-bass	c.12/1863	11/2/1866
Haydn, *Creation*		
2,500	11/1858	4/18/1859
5,000	4/1859	8/6/1860
4,000	8/1860	2/26/1861
Mendelssohn, *Elijah*		
2,000	1/1860	4/1860
2,000	4/1860	8/1860
Mendelssohn, *St Paul*		
1,500	10/1859	8/13/1860
Handel, *Judas Maccabeus*:		
3,000	3/1859	11/2/1859
3,500	11/1859	10/30/1860
Handel, *Judas Maccabeus* (parts)		
500-SATB	c.6/1863	11/1866
Dr Monk's Anglican Chants		
1,000	10/60	3/22/62
1,000	8/62	11/3/63
Westminster Chants		
1,000	8/60	11/6/61 (200 remaining)
1,000	12/61 (250 in stock)	1/16/63
1,000	4/63	10(31?)/63
Boyce/Arnold, *Cathedral Music*		
1,500	11/59	7/27/61
1,500	2/62	10/29/63

[a]Assumes octavo piano vocal score unless otherwise stated.
[b]Date style: month/day/year.

plates for its own edition.[21] (It is of note that the renowned soprano Clara Novello, Vincent's daughter, sang the first Italian performance in Bologna in March of that year.) Because no stockbook record appears to exist for the years 1841–57, we cannot reconstruct the Stabat Mater's early production history at Novello's. But we know that in some span of time between April 1859 and July 1863, four separate printings yielded a total of 9,000 copies – a figure that testifies to the work's continuing popularity two decades after its premiere.

Compared to the editions of oratorios and large-scale sacred works, Novello's so-called 'practical' editions, such as *Kent's Anthems*, Boyce's *Cathedral Music*, and *Westminster Chants*, left the warehouse at a slower rate. For example, Mendelssohn's *St Paul*, Handel's *Samson*, and Boyce's *Cathedral Music*, were all issued in print runs of 1,500 during one two-month period, October–November 1859. The supply of *Samson* was exhausted by April 1860 and that of *St Paul* by August, but copies of *Cathedral Music* remained in stock until July 1861. Similar comparisons – involving equivalent quantities and dates – offer similar results, suggesting a more limited demand for the anthem and church-choir collections than for the piano-vocal oratorio editions. Not surprisingly, Novello's educational publications, musical instruction books, and histories present, as noted above, the slowest depletion rate (see Table 3.2). Thus, the various kinds of Novello publications, according to listings in the stockbook, can be divided into three categories, in descending order of demand: (1) complete sacred compositions: oratorios, masses, and requiems, with the most desirable being the octavo piano-vocal scores of Handel and Mendelssohn oratorios; (2) practical sacred works: anthems, chants, and services; and (3) educational works.

An additional insight into the editorial and printing decisions Novello's made can be found in a printed transcript of a speech given on 4 May 1885 by W. H. Cummings, editor and founder of the Purcell Society, with Henry Littleton, Alfred's successor, in the audience.[22] The

---

[21]The title page of the Troupenas edition lists two other firms besides Novello – Ricordi and Schott – indicating that all three had co-licensing agreements with the Parisian company. (A similar arrangement appears to have been made for the full score: the title page of the Schott edition [published *c*.1842, plate number 6588] also lists Troupenas, Ricordi, and Novello as co-publishers.) The Troupenas edition contains 77 pages and bears the plate number T. 1106; the Novello edition, by comparison, contains 69 pages and bears the plate number 1071. Ricordi and Schott also prepared separate plates, according to Philip Gossett, who kindly supplied the information regarding the Troupenas edition.

[22]A copy of the transcript is located in the St Bride's Printing Library, London. The transcript appears to have been printed privately, perhaps for circulation among those attending the speech. The following quotes are taken from that copy.

speech surveyed the history of music printing although the series of comments after the speech made by Cummings, Littleton, and other members of the audience, including Ebenezer Prout, are especially valuable as they illustrate some of the firm's printing decisions suggested in the stockbooks. Cummings's closing remarks criticized the design and layout of the generic octavo edition, and, to Henry Littleton, focused squarely on Novello's in particular:

> But let us speak of the best type printed music. Here we find good paper, well-formed lines and notes, but all so minute and crowded that it requires a serious effort to identify and grasp the picture which has to be conveyed to the brain through the eye. The notes are small, but the words are smaller; and when you come to a recitative – in which, of course, the words form the more important element – you will find, for the sake of saving a little space, that the type setter has used a smaller letter than usual. I speak from painful experience when I say that these small type copies are productive of headache, eyeache, and neuralgia. Just think what the octavo type editions were first intended for. They were meant to be used as hand-books by the audience for following the music at public performances of oratorios. But latterly they have taken another position; they are used by singers, pianoforte players, and conductors – often there is no choice, for no folio editions are obtainable.

Littleton's reply and examples are especially illuminating. He offers two instances when folio and octavo editions were available simultaneously with the expected outcome that the octavo editions sold at a faster and greater rate:

> Mr Cumming's later statements appear to be very like a libel on our popular octavo editions, which have always been accepted as specimens of neatness and cheapness. It is impossible to have printed music with large notes and large words without materially adding to the size of the publications, and consequently adding to the price. The public have now become so accustomed to buying an oratorio for 2/-, or even 1/-, that it is useless to publish editions at a much higher price ... To test the matter in a smaller way, an Easter Anthem, which was issued two or three years ago in *The Musical Times*, was also printed in the folio size, and two months after Easter had passed, I found that sixteen copies of the folio edition had been sold against a very large number of the octavo. It is of no use blaming the publisher for printing in a small size if the public will not buy the larger size when it is to be had.

Littleton also mentioned his plans to redesign the octavo type size for future reprints:

> I should add that I have some octavo editions with which I am not satisfied, such as *Saul* and *Solomon*, but I have so much new work that I have not yet had time to reprint them. I began a new edition of

Solomon a year and a half ago, and on asking the other day how
much was done of it, I found only twenty pages were done. There is
certainly no excuse for some of this smaller type, and, as fast as I
can, I am going to reprint the whole of these works, whether they are
particularly saleable or not.

Alfred Novello also experimented with a new, larger design although the
extra length and expense forced him to abandon the revisions, as Littleton recalls: 'Mr. Novello tried once to [increase the type size in octavo
editions] and he issued a specimen page of *Jephtha* in large type, but the
book would have taken double the number of pages; only two scores
could be got on each page in the choruses, and there would not have
been more than two-thirds as much in the width.'

The Novello stockbook allows us to glimpse the decision-making process that maintained a financial balance for one mid-nineteenth-century
music publisher. Alfred Novello's perception of the market is suggested
in the recorded print runs of his firm: the fulfilment of expectation and
the frustration of misjudgement can, with caution, be assessed from the
sales histories of his editions. We have focused on Novello's choices of
composers and compositions, editorial formats, publication dates, and
print-run sizes, and the fiscal consequences each of these choices
entailed. No comparison with the production levels of other firms has
been attempted.[23]

Regrettably, much useful information is absent from the stockbook,
which tells us nothing, for example, about shipping and distribution:
what were the destinations of copies removed from the warehouse?
How many copies were purchased by individuals and how many by

---

[23]To place Novello's print runs in perspective, comparable records of houses that
published similar works would have to be studied. Yet even if such documents were
located, comparisons would have to be approached with caution: genre, publishing
format, musical format, market demand, time-period, and geographical area must all be
carefully taken into account before conclusions are drawn regarding print runs and
production rates. For example, the relatively low print-run figures for opera piano-vocal
scores and piano works rested in large part on the small number of copies required for
performance of these works, when compared to the hundred or more needed by one
choral society presenting a Handel oratorio. Thus, any study of printing records that
compares the production of oratorio scores with that of opera piano-vocal scores should
proceed with caution. Comparisons between Novello's stockbook and Ricordi's *Libroni*
or Schott's *Druckbuch*, for example (see n. 1) must take many factors into account,
including the socio-economic and aesthetic worlds of the amateur musician in England
and on the Continent.

organizations?[24] A series of documents has recently come to light which can help to answer the question of distribution.[25] These records, named Commission Books by the British Library archivists, list a selected number of Novello editions, when copies were printed, the quantity, and the destination from the warehouse. The Commission Books span over 130 years, from 1840 to 1974, with the information most relevant to a study of Novello's early years found in volume 1 (Add. MS 69516, with entries from 1840 to 1869). Unfortunately, large shipments sent from the warehouse have not been noted in the book, that is, quantities most likely ordered by choral societies or their suppliers destined for the large cities where festivals were held, such as Birmingham, Manchester or Leeds. Rather, the book lists only relatively small removals from the warehouse and the total sent out for sale is probably larger than the records reflect. Some of the entries list the term 'Self' which may indicate copies sent to the Novello showroom for sale. A detailed analysis of the Commission Books would reveal particular patterns and further insights into the firm's printing and distribution practice and this work should be pursued in future studies.

Initial examination, however, suggests some standard publishing practices of the firm which are of note. Appendix 5 is a partial transcription of entries from the Commission Book, volume 1. Of particular interest is the entry for the edition of *The Evening Service*, by 'J. Wells'. The entry begins on 28 August 1852 with 250 copies printed. On 31 August, along with 200 copies allocated to 'Self', nine different newspapers and journals each received one copy. The periodicals listed read almost like a rota of the most popular fine arts journals of the day (*The Musical World*, *The Illustrated London News*, *The Athenaeum*, *The Atlas*, and *The Spectator*) as well as some

---

[24]The question of distribution and dissemination is complex. Hans Lenneberg has pointed out, for instance, that the relatively small print-run and reprint figures for Schlesinger's first piano-vocal edition of *Robert le diable* (published soon after the work's premiere in the Paris season of 1831/32) are deceptive, since the limited number of copies that were produced actually achieved wide circulation through music lending libraries; see Lenneberg, 'Music Publishing and Dissemination in the Early 19th Century: Some Vignettes', *The Journal of Musicology* 2 (1983), pp. 174–83; and Lenneberg, 'Early Circulating Libraries and the Dissemination of Music', *Library Quarterly* 52 (1982), pp. 122–30.

[25]The Novello Business Archive, Add. MS 69516-69532, was acquired and catalogued by the British Library in 1990. I am grateful to Chris Banks for notifying me of the acquisition and making the records available. The archive is comprised of the last pieces of Novello's records which were uncovered while dismantling the firm's printing headquarters in Borough Green, Kent, before they were relocated to a new site.

of the major newspapers (*The Examiner*, *The Advertiser*, and *The Daily News*). Copies of the edition were most likely sent to announce publication and perhaps to garner a notice or critique in the music or 'recently published' columns. The list of mainstream periodicals receiving advance copies suggests Novello's perception of *The Evening Service* as a popular work which might attract the attention of a general audience. Yet it would be incorrect to imagine that Novello's routinely sent review copies of each new publication to the daily and popular press. A glimpse at the distribution list for the edition *Sacred Music for Schools*, by J. Tilleack, indicates a more specialized publicity campaign. Thus, on 5 March 1852, copies were sent to *The Educator*, *The Educational Record*, and *Paper for Schoolmasters*, and later, in July, one copy went to the Inspector for Schools. Although it is not surprising that the appropriate periodicals alone should receive review copies of specific new publications, the Commission Books offer the first evidence of such publicity and marketing strategies and illuminate another aspect of Novello's business practices.

Alfred Novello knew his audience well; his publications sold briskly among amateur musicians and choral society members, who required performance editions, in multiple copies, of oratorios and sacred works. To a great extent, then, Novello's print runs were a product of this expanding market. When Alfred completed the sale of his firm in 1866 to Henry Littleton, he turned over a financially sound and prospering company that would continue to make an important contribution to the musical education of Victorian society.

CHAPTER FOUR

Contemporary Issues of the Victorian Music Publisher

In the industrial climate of England at mid-century, the growing complexity of business and society was often redressed by an almost equally intricate series of laws and regulations. Yet in addition to the protection intended by these new rules, a music publisher might also find them restrictive and counterproductive. Thus, to publish music in Victorian England often demanded a mastery of the legal labyrinth to ensure that compositions were sucessfully acquired, protected, printed, and distributed. How Alfred Novello published and prospered in this environment is revealed in an examination of the business methods he practised daily. We can chart Novello's methods by following his publishing procedures in chronological fashion. These functioned largely on a five-step basis: defining demand; selecting a work; purchasing it; protecting the copyright; and publishing within the strictures of the myriad taxes and duties levied on printed matter. By tracing the publication of editions through these stages, we may form a picture of Novello's participation in music publishing and Alfred's contribution to the industry. While examination of contemporary documents, journals, and ephemera to uncover and interpret the practices of a music publisher are a relatively new part of musicological investigation, this kind of methodology has been undertaken for some time in literary history and studies. Such recent works include Alexis Weedon, *Victorian Publishing: The Economics of Book Production for a Mass Market, 1830–1916* (forthcoming). Weedon explores the social, economic, and industrial environment of book publishing and employs a number of different approaches as examples for future analyses of publishers' histories. Robert L. Patten's major work, *Charles Dickens and his Publishers* is an example of publishing history explored from the standpoint of the writer and his relationship with the industry.[1]

---

[1]Robert L. Patten, *Charles Dickens and his Publishers* (Oxford: Clarendon Press, 1978).

Definition of the Market and Demand

Novello's initial task was to define and satisfy the market. His assess-
ment most likely included a study of the stockbook records (see
Chapter 3 for an analysis of one of these documents). He could also
gain a sense of taste and preference through direct messages to his
market, which he achieved in occasional 'communications' published
in *The Musical Times*. After the disappointing reception of *Novello's
Part-Song Book*, Alfred published an advertisement in the 1 October
1855 issue, requesting suggestions from his readers. The ingratiating
plea reflects an attempt to contact his audience:

> To choral, vocal, and glee societies. It is a curious part of my long
> experience to find that after twenty-five years I feel more and more
> doubtful in deciding what will suit popular taste. The most signal
> instance of this is, I think, presented by the book I printed a short
> time since, called 'Novello's Part-Song Book'; a work, which has not
> yet had the sale and success which I expected, and which it deserves,
> from the expense, labour, and attention bestowed on its production.
>   The details are as follows – I secured a very good editor, Mr. E. G.
> Monk – one who took an interest in the work, far beyond the liberal
> salary that was fixed for the labours, and I may say that it was a
> labour of love with him. He obtained contributions from some of
> the first composers and Poets of the day. Original poems by Mrs.
> Newton Crosland, R. Monkton Milnes ... were set to music by Sir
> Henry Bishop, Jules Benedict, G. A. McFarren, W. C. McFarren, Dr.
> Rimbault, E. G. Monk ... many of whom appear to have been happy
> in their compositions.
>   There were given seven prizes, of eight guineas each, offered for
> original Part-Songs; and the selection was made from above 200
> competitors; Mr. E. G. Monk (the editor), Mr. John Hullah, and
> Mr. Edward Holmes, acting as umpires ...
>   In publishing this carefully collected material, I applied my print-
> ing experience to produce it in the most convenient forms (quarto
> vocal score and separate vocal parts) ... Now, what I have to ask is,
> that my good friends in the Societies to whom this is addressed will
> consider what I have left undone – what they would advise me still
> to do – or what change (if any) they would propose in the Part-Song
> Book, to make so valuable a collection of carefully selected new
> partsongs a useful contribution to the vocal societies of the day.

In addition to the open solicitation of advice, Alfred also seemed particularly fond of taking more formal polls. In 1849 he purchased the
plates and copyrights of the dissolved firm Coventry and Hollier. Alfred
subsequently had new editions prepared from a number of the sacred
works in the catalogue, using modern clefs and realized organ accompaniments. To gauge the success of his revised editions, in the March 1854
issue of *The Musical Times*, Alfred petitioned his readers: 'It is requested

that Subscribers will be so good as send their names as early as convenient to 69, Dean Street, that from the number it may be decided whether
the re-engraving of these simple works is generally desired and further
works be prepared.'

Yet it would be misleading to suggest that Alfred did not hold his own
views of the market; his specific and surprisingly candid opinions are
reflected in a letter to Mendelssohn of 29 May 1840: 'We are going to do
St. Paul at Exeter Hall on the 17th and 26th of June. It has been done
lately at Bristol and they are about doing it at Bath and Liverpool. The
English indeed I hope are beginning to understand it which it is a work of
some labour to make them do, any thing that is good.' In his postscript
he adds the further observation: 'My own opinion is decidedly to repeat
St. Paul at Birmingham as nothing in England is a greater criterion of
popularity with the public than the frequent repetition of the same
piece.'[2]

Acquisition Methods

Through the combination of financial experience and personal viewpoint,
Alfred formed his picture of the market and thus proceeded to fulfil
demand. At mid-century, a large portion of the Novello catalogue represented the repertoire of earlier centuries – music often readily available
through Vincent's efforts as collector and editor. To acquire contemporary
compositions, however, was a more diplomatic procedure, frequently
involving contact with composers and other publishers. For such works,
Alfred often employed two methods: selecting particular pieces or suggesting future projects.[3] Alfred's correspondence with Mendelssohn, for
example, is sprinkled with the publisher's recommendations for new
enterprises. In his letter of 28 October 1839, Alfred writes: 'Pray tell me

---

[2]Letter in the Deneke Collection, Bodleian Library. Ms M. Deneke Mendelssohn, shelf
number Ms. M.D.M.d.37, fol. 164. All the following numbers with the Ms.M.D.M.d. catalogue number refer to the Deneke Collection, with shelf markings cited in Margaret Crum,
Catalogue of the Mendelssohn Papers in the Bodleian Library, Oxford (Oxford: Oxford
University Press, 1980), vol. 1.

[3]Alfred's acquisition policies cannot be completely observed, however. Extant copies of
his correspondence with composers are rare and the largest source, located in the Deneke
Collection, is limited to exchanges between Alfred Novello and Mendelssohn. Yet this
correspondence reveals the policies for an especially popular composer; what is lacking is a
record of editorial management of the less successful ones. For additional information on
Mendelssohn and the Novellos, see Peter Ward Jones, 'Mendelssohn and his English
Publishers', in R. Larry Todd, ed., *Mendelssohn Studies* (Cambridge: Cambridge University
Press, 1992), pp. 240–55.

what you would think of an oratorio founded on the life of St Peter. I think I could get one very well selected from the Bible – but I suppose you would prefer writing to German than English words. This, however, you might still do as you could find the corresponding passages in your German version, supposing you liked the subject.'[4] In the same letter Alfred further proposed a concerto for the English conductor and composer, Charles Salaman (1814–1901): 'My friend, Mr. Salaman, who is a very promising pianist in London has requested me to you to know what terms you would write him a concerto for the pianoforte, with orchestra. He wishes to have it for his exclusive use for two seasons, say 1840 and 1841, after which you will be at liberty to sell it in any country except England, for which latter country he would wish to keep the copyright. Salaman is an influential professor and would introduce the concerto well if you would write one for him. Pray let me know of this as early as you can by post.'[5] Yet the concerto did not arrive, and on 18 February Alfred wrote Mendelssohn: 'Mr. Salaman wished to have had the concerto particularly for this season as he says that he should have a greater possibility of playing [it] at the Philharmonic concerts, but he has given up the idea of having it, and is sorry that I troubled you on the subject.'[6]

Coupled with suggestions for works, Alfred also proposed performances of his editions. Timing was essential: a concert scheduled soon before publication promised a fresh and enthusiastic public. The financial implications are reflected in Alfred's letter to Mendelssohn of 12 December 1837:

> To write first on business. I very much fear some misfortune has come to your concerto, as from the accounts I receive, it must have been more than a month on the road and still no sign of its arrival. On receipt of this, write me word exactly when it went off, through whom, and to whom it would come in London, as I must make enquiries of the steam offices, etc.
>
> The delay has already been a great loss to me as three concerts have passed where Wm. Auder [?] could have played it for me with great good effect viz.: at Woodford, at Exeter, and Bath, indeed, I fear more, after he gets it, it will take some time to practise it, and indeed, unless I get it very soon, the arrangement for which the extra price was paid, will be frustrated.[7]

---

[4]Ms. M.D.M.d.36, fol. 105. It does not appear that the oratorio was ever written.
[5]Ibid.
[6]Ms. M.D.M.d.37, fol. 63.
[7]Ms. M.D.M.d.32, fol. 155. Alfred probably refers to the Piano Concerto, Op. 40, completed on 5 August 1837 and published by Novello in 1838. Completion and publishing dates, unless otherwise noted, follow Karl-Heinz Koehler and Eveline Bartlitz, 'Mendelssohn', in Stanley Sadie, ed., *The New Grove Dictionary of Music and Musicians* (London: Macmillan, 1980), 12: pp. 134–59.

The manuscript was finally received and Novello prepared for publication. On 30 January 1838, he wrote to Mendelssohn: 'You would hear from my mother of the arrival of the long delayed concerto, and since its arrival I have taken the greatest care to make all the alterations you directed in the wind instrumental parts, and we are going to put it to the best possible proof, namely to play it through with all the band.'[8] On 6 March Alfred could finally write of the performance: 'Last evening your concerto was played at the Philharmonic Society and was amazingly well received, and everyone pronounced it a chef d'oeuvre. I will put it in the engraver's hands immediately and as soon as engraved I will send you the proofs.'[9]

Similarly, Alfred also desired a performance of *St Paul* to coincide with publication: 'I should feel very much obliged if you would [hurry] Breitkopf and Härtel with your Paulus as I wish to get it performed at the Gloucester Musical Festival and it will take us some time to translate print and get it into practice. Pray therefore tell them to send me a copy manuscript or other.'[10]

During the early years of Alfred's direction of the firm, Vincent also acquired compositions and made recommendations to composers. In an almost paternal role, the elder Novello had introduced Mendelssohn to the firm. Their first correspondence indicates that Vincent had originally approached Mendelssohn with suggestions for future compositions. On 22 August 1832, the composer wrote to Vincent:

> I have to beg your pardon that the first letter I write to you is to be a letter of business, but if it was not for that I should not venture to give you the trouble of reading so bad an English as mine is. – I do not try to repeat to you the thanks for all your kindness because I am not able to express it as I wish to do and as I feel it.
>
> I want today to ask whether you still remember your writing to me once that you wished me to compose an evening and morning service for publication in your country? I could not then fix the time when I was to do it as it was the first thing in that style I was to compose, but as soon as I got quiet here, I tried to begin the Te deum in the style of your cathedral music and it is now finished. Although it is not entirely as I wish it to be and though I hope the following pieces will be better, I do not think it unworth being published and I accordingly want to ask you whether you are still of the opinion which you expressed to me in your kind note and whether I am to go on with the composition of the Jubilate and to send it to you, when it is finished. You asked me also for my terms; but I am really at a loss to fix them, as I never published any compositions of the kind in

---

[8]Ms.M.D.M.d.33, fol. 31.

[9]Ms.M.D.M.d.34, fol. 104.

[10]Letter dated 15 May 1838. Ms.M.D.M.d.34, fol. 119.

your country; you would oblige me particularly if you would tell me
your opinion on this subject or if you do not like this let me know
how you like to pay other composers in that style that I may fix my
terms accordingly.[11]

In a similar manner, the following year Vincent acquired an organ
fugue from the composer. Writing from Berlin, Mendelssohn informed
Vincent that the work was completed: [19 March 1833] 'The organ
fugue which you requested to [have] is finished and I am exceedingly
anxious to know whether you will [approve] of it or not, for till now I
like it very much myself. But that may [go] away before I give it to you,
and as I have often experienced it, particularly as it is just finished and as
I like everything during my writing it and perceive the faults only after
some time, when I grow colder.'[12] In May, Vincent received the manuscript (see Figure 4.1):

> As Mr. Attwood tells me that he does not intend going to St. Pauls
> next Sunday I fear I shall have no opportunity before my return from
> the Rhineland of playing to you the organ fugue which I wrote for
> you at Berlin, and I beg therefore you will accept it as it is, although
> I have not yet tried it on the organ and do not know whether it is not
> too great a trifle to be offered to you. As I liked it when I wrote it,
> and on that account I hope you will excuse the wants in it and my
> sending you instead of a copy in better writing, the original, with all
> its alterations, cuttings, etc. I intended to finish here the Praeludium,
> which I have begun for this fugue but could not yet find time for it,
> and beg you will excuse its coming some weeks late and being then
> instead of a Prae- a Postludium.[13]

---

[11]BL Add. MS 11730, fols 129–30. The work was published, without opus number, in
1832 as Te deum in A, for solo voices, chorus, and organ. Mendelssohn appears to have
experienced difficulties in composing the work. Writing to Moscheles from Berlin on 10
August 1832 he remarked: 'I am working on the Morning Service for Novello, but it does
not flow naturally; so far alot of counterpoint and canons, and nothing more.' See *Letters
of Felix Mendelssohn to Ignaz and Charlotte Moscheles*, trans. and ed. Felix Moscheles
(London, 1888), pp. 30–31.

[12]BL Add. MS 11730, fol. 131.

[13]BL Add. MS 14396, fols 31–2. The manuscript contains Mendelssohn's note: 'Written
for V. Novello by Felix Mendelssohn. Berlin. d. 29 March 1833.' The music is located in
fols 33–4. Figure 4.1 is Mendelssohn's manuscript of the fugue which was published in vol.
5 of William Little's edition of Mendelssohn's *Complete Organ Works* (Novello, 1990).
Mendelssohn also later revised it to become the third fugue of the Op. 37 Preludes and
Fugues. I am grateful to Peter Ward Jones for this and additional information related to
Mendelssohn. The manuscript was given to the British Museum, along with others from his
collection, by Vincent Novello in a donation made on 27 July 1843. See A. Hyatt King, *A
Mozart Legacy: Aspects of the British Library Collections* (London: The British Library,
1984).

Figure 4.1 Manuscript by Mendelssohn of organ fugue written for Vincent Novello, 29 March 1833, BL Add. MS 14396, fols 33–4

Figure 4.1 continued

Figure 4.1   continued

Mendelssohn's *Songs Without Words*, Book 1 (initially published by Novello's as *Original Melodies for the Pianoforte*) was also acquired through Vincent's arbitration. In his letter of 1 July 1832, Charles Klingeman wrote to the firm (probably to Vincent) that the work could be published:

> I have to apologize for sending so late an answer to your kind note concerning our friend Mr. Mendelssohn's Piano-forte Melodies – but I had previously to enquire at Mr. [Ignaz] Moscheles as all I knew about them was my recollecting Mr. Mendelssohn say[ing] how you had offered him your assistance in publishing them, in a truly friendly way – and that he had left the manuscript at Mr. Moscheles'. That Gentleman tells me that it is indeed Mr. Mendelssohn's intention to avail himself of Mr. Novello's [probably Alfred's] assistance in committing to him the principal sale of those compositions. As soon as they are ready for publication you will hear about it from Mr. Moscheles under whose care Mr. Mendelssohn left the whole.[14]

Beyond the arrangement of 'principal sale', this letter, in conjunction with Vincent's further correspondence, suggests a new date for the initial publication in London of *Songs Without Words*, Book 1. Published sources have dated the edition as 1830,[15] yet Klingeman promises to contact Novello 'as soon as they [the 'piano-forte melodies'] are ready for publication'. In his letter of 22 August 1832, mentioned above, Mendelssohn's remarks further suggest recent publication: 'I have still to thank you for the kindness you showed me in having my Piano-forte melodies sold at your house; I think they must be published already.'[16] According to information received 'from the books of that eminent firm [Novello's]', Felix Moscheles also placed publication in 1832.[17] This later date is further corroborated by manuscript evidence. Christa Jost notes that an autograph copy of Book 1 (probably the *Stichvorlage*, located in the Huntington Library, HM 1019), bears the date 20 July 1832 (with a previously written '10' crossed out).[18]

Vincent Novello had contacts with other Continental composers as well. His acquaintances, and often his subsequent friendships, allowed

---

[14]BL Add. MS 11730 and a copy in the Deneke Collection Ms. M.D.M.c.18, fol. 98. For further information on publication of the Songs Without Words, see Peter Ward Jones, 'Mendelssohn and his English Publishers', in R. Larry Todd, ed., *Mendelssohn Studies* (Cambridge: Cambridge University Press, 1992), pp. 240–43.

[15]Carl Dahlhaus, ed. *Das Problem Mendelssohn* (Regensburg: Bosse Verlag, 1974); and Koehler and Bartlitz, 'Mendelssohn'.

[16]BL Add. MS 11730. fol. 129.

[17]Moscheles, *Letters of Mendelssohn to Moscheles*, p. 65. The recordbook examined by Felix Moscheles in the 1880s now appears either lost or destroyed.

[18]See Christa Jost, *Mendelssohns Lieder Ohne Wörte*, Frankfurter Beiträge zur Musikwissenschaft, 14 (Tutzing: Hans Schneider Verlag, 1988).

him to obtain music for the firm. In November 1847, Vincent received a letter from 'Madame Berlioz' (the singer Marie Recio; Berlioz and she would not marry until 1854), probably in reply to his request for possible publications.[19] Her letter was housed along with a collection of numerous autographs and musical fragments in Vincent's autograph book, begun during his period at 4 Craven Hill, Bayswater.[20] In her letter, Recio lists the arrangements available for purchase. Vincent adds a note at the bottom of her letter: 'The annexed list of Berlioz compositions that have been arranged as Duetts for the Piano-forte in his own handwriting. Given to me from Madme Berlioz by Wm. Shield November 1847.'[21] The following works were on offer:

> Overture a [sic] 4 mains de Berlioz
> 1o Du.   Waverley: chez Richault
> 2o Du.   Roi Lear: Boulevant poisomier 16
> 3o Du.   Francs juges
> 4o Du.   Carnaval Romain: chez Brandy [Brandus] rue Richelieu
> Symphonie fantastique arrange a [sic] 2 mains par Liszt: chez Brandy

Novello catalogues and advertisements examined do not list any of the above Berlioz works and they do not seem to have been published by the firm during this period.

The presence of contemporary Continental composers in the Novello catalogue was in large part the product of Vincent's acquaintance with

---

[19]The communication took place during Berlioz's visit to England, between November 1847 and July 1848. He had been brought to London by Louis Jullien to conduct the premiere season at Drury Lane Theatre; yet what had promised to be a lucrative and promising enterprise was bankrupt within the first few months and subsequently abandoned.

[20]Formerly BM Novello Loan $769C Loan 93/23. The autograph book, an oblong black leather-bound book, 5½ × 9½ in., contains a leather-stamped notice on the inside front cover: 'J. Robinson to V. Novello Esqr.'. Robinson, an organist at York, was the music teacher of Clara Novello and Alfred. Vincent has also added the note: 'This collection of Musical autographs, etc. belongs to Vincent Novello, 4 Craven Hill, Bayswater.' In addition to signatures from the familiar friends and colleagues of Vincent's musical circle, autographs are also found of Malibran, Mozart's widow and son (obtained during his journey to Salzburg in 1829), and the artist Constable. The Novello Collection Loan $769C was presented to the British Library in 1987 on loan by the firm's owners, Granada. In June 1989 the loan was removed from the British Library by Granada Group PLC and sold at auction. (For a detailed description of the autograph book and its contents see the auction catalogue for the Novello collection, Phillips, London, 14 June 1989.)

[21]The editorial history surrounding these arrangements is complicated: piano four-hand arrangements were made and published that were not by Berlioz. It is rather curious that Recio would refer to editions on offer as 'in his own handwriting' although this may have been simply to attract attention to the works. To trace the background of each work would be beyond the scope of the present study; for details of the arrangements, the published editions, and dates see D. Kern Holoman, *Catalogue of the Works of Hector Berlioz* (Kassel, Basel, London, New York: Bärenreiter, 1987).

the composers. We have seen how he inaugurated and fostered a relationship with Mendelssohn which resulted in one of the major
contributors to the firm's catalogue. (The popularity of Novello's Mendelssohn editions can be seen in the evaluation of the stockbook, Chapter
3.) During the 1830s and 1840s, another Continental composer, Sigis-
mund Neukomm, became part of the Novello list. His reception in
England is of note for although his works became part of the choral society repertoire, critical response to his compositions was not entirely
favourable. To take two performance reviews as examples, Neukomm is
regarded as a serviceable composer, but not in the same category as
Mendelssohn or even Spohr. The May 1845 issue of *The Musical Times*
reprints, from *The Musical World*, a review of Neukomm's oratorio
David. The reviewer notes:

> This oratorio was composed for the Birmingham Festival and first
> performed in 1834. Its success was but equivocal. It has remained
> unnoticed for eleven years, and, but for the Sacred Harmonic Soci-
> ety, would most likely have sunk into oblivion. Since Handel, only
> one writer has given to the world a chef d'oeuvre in this department
> of musical composition. The writer is Mendelssohn ... Haydn's *Cre-
> ation* ... is not up to the standard ... Bach's *Passion* is much more
> talked about than known; and our acquaintance with the score leads
> us to be wary of the enthusiasm of its wholesale admirers, who place
> it far above the finest works of Handel. Beethoven's *Mount of
> Olives* is essentially dramatic, and, moreover, too brief to admit of
> its being classed among the great oratorios ... To speak of the Chev-
> alier Neukomm in such company were absurd. He has few
> pretensions to merge from the ranks of composers, albeit a tolerably
> good specimen of the ordinary average talent of modern Germany.

One year later, the May 1846 issue of *The Musical Times* carried an
equally unenthusiastic review of Neukomm's *Easter Morning Cantata*:

> We were sorry to find at the last meeting of this society [the Choral
> Harmonists], on 13th April, that they had gone from their estab-
> lished rule of commencing with a mass, with orchestral
> accompaniments, and that this innovation was made to give place to
> a very weak composition by Neukomm. The *Dramatic and Musical
> Review*, speaking of the work at this meeting, says, 'The first con-
> sisted of Neukomm's cantata, "Easter Morning" – a production
> appropriate enough in its subject for the present period but rarely
> reaching the grandeur and impressiveness of the higher order of
> sacred music ...' The second part made amends, consisting of a most
> judicious and admirably-executed selection from, Mozart's 'Clem-
> enza di Tito'.

It is of note that, despite harsh critical reception (even within his own
house journal), Vincent fostered and published Neukomm's compositions. The answer may be found in the musical accessibility of the

works. Although not regarded as an equal to Mendelssohn, Neukomm was performed by choral societies, suggesting a style within the technical grasp of the amateur musician. Vincent no doubt appreciated the dichotomy between critical reception and musical accessibility, yet, recognizing profit in the amateur market, published Neukomm nonetheless. Some of the Neukomm editions clearly maintained demand, as the August 1863 Novello catalogue, almost twenty years after the reviews, still offered an edition of *David* as well as various sacred compositions.

The source for some of the Neukomm editions was Vincent's private library, as shown in a note in Vincent's hand in the front cover of one of his manuscript collections of the composer's music: 'All the above pieces have been published: (1839) [*sic*]. They are copied from the original MSS kindly lent me by the Chevalier Neukomm for my own private library – and they must not be engraved or published without the permission of the composer. – Vincent Novello.'[22] The manuscript collection is bound, with a blocked front, 'Neukomm's MSS V. Novello 1839' and includes the compositions 'L'Orgue Grand Choeurs, sans accompagnement (g minor)'; 'I am the Resurrection' Funeral Anthem 4 voices (in F); 'In thee O Lord, do I put my Trust' Anthem for 4 voices. A letter to Vincent from Neukomm (in a highly eccentric French) is attached to the book and indicates the circumstances in which the compositions were obtained:

> Vous avez desire, Monsieur, pour voir le catalogue des mes ouvrages, qui, parle fait, devenu, un veritable journal de voyage. Le voici je vous priera de vouloir bien me le renvoyer, sans foute, ce soir, attend que je gartira demain matins. Si Mr votre fils veut publier les messes que je vous ai montrez hiers, je lui cederais mes droits d'auteur pour 30 Guineas s'il les prendes des [?] on a raison de12 Guineas chaques separated ...[23] [*sic*]

Following the active and frequently successful selection techniques practised by both father and son, attention then turned to the purchase of compositions. Correspondence between Mendelssohn and the firm alone reveals diverse contractual arrangements often based on the need to balance aesthetic with financial criteria. Not surprisingly, Novello hoped to obtain works at the lowest price possible and more than once pleaded the case of an ignorant English audience to secure a modest honorarium. In his letter to Mendelssohn of 26 June 1840, Alfred wrote:

---

[22]BL Add. MS 65433, vol. 52.
[23]BL Add. MS 65433, vol. 52.

> We are very anxious to have your new oratorio[24] and Mr. Moore
> tells me he shall write by today's post. I hope you will ask me some-
> thing moderate for the copyright as the yet untaught taste of the
> English public does not allow me to give as good a price as I could
> wish for such works – but of all things pray let us have the work as
> soon as [possible as] there is now so very little time to get it trans-
> lated with any justice.[25]

At other points as well, Alfred bargained for fees to lie in proportion
to demand: 'For the Psalm let the price be what you say, fifteen pounds,
but when I named the price it was rather with a view to the somewhat
limited sale of these sorts of works.'[26] On the pretext of limited demand,
Alfred also solicited additional compositions as part of the set fee. Writing on 2 July 1838, he enquired: 'I should be pleased to have the Andante
and Rondo at the price you name, £20, but perhaps you would do me the
favour to include the Violin Quartet and Sonata for Piano-forte and
Violin in that sum for although (as you say) they are not a style of music
for an English publication to sink money in in the way of copyright, yet I
would engrave them if you would enable me to publish on the same day
as the German publisher.'[27] In at least one instance, domestic demand
was held as excuse for rejection. On 18 February 1840, Novello
informed Mendelssohn: 'In answer to yours of the 21st January just
received, I am sorry to decline the purchase of your trio[28] which I suppose is for stringed instruments, but I fear such a work would command
a very small sale amongst our ignorant public.'[29]

---

[24]Although Alfred refers to the work as an 'oratorio', he may have in mind either Psalm
114, Op. 51, finished on 9 August 1839 or *Lobgesang*, Op. 52, both published in 1841
with Breitkopf and Härtel.

[25]Ms.M.D.M.d.37, fol. 215.

[26]Letter dated 6 March 1838. Ms.M.D.M.d.34, fol. 104.

[27]Ms. M.D.M.d.34, fol. 3. The 'Violin Quartet' is probably a reference to the String
Quartets, Op. 44, with numbers 1–3 published in 1838 by Breitkopf and Härtel although
not by Novello. The 'Violin Sonata' is likely that in F (without opus number), completed 15
June 1838 and first published in 1953, ed. Yehudi Menuhin (see Koehler and Bartlitz,
'Mendelssohn').

Alfred recognized the benefits of simultaneous publication and wished to take advantage of them in his negotiation with Mendelssohn. As Jeffrey Kallberg has shown,
publishers were required to publish on the same day to secure copyright protection in more
than one country. Such an arrangement promised equal status for the composition and
(theoretically) protected the work in both locations from piracy. See Kallberg, 'Chopin in
the Marketplace: Aspects of the International Music Publishing Industry in the First Half of
the Nineteenth Century', *Notes* 39: pp. 535–69, 795–824.

[28]Alfred may be referring to the Piano Trio, No. 1 in D, Op. 49, completed 23
September 1839 and published in 1840 by Breitkopf and Härtel.

[29]Ms.M.D.M.d.37, fol. 63.

At points, Alfred also requested small fees, omitting altogether the cloak of apology or plea of limited market demand. In his letter of 6 March 1838, he writes: 'I think I would venture to print your service if you would let me have it *very cheap*;'[30] or simply: 'I should have much pleasure in publishing your new Psalm ... I would rather you had named a price, but as you have left it to me, I would say ten pounds.'[31] Yet the negotiation of fees did not always play a central role. When Alfred found other firms involved, he seized the opportunity to participate. On 14 August 1841 he wrote to Mendelssohn: 'Mr. Kistner of Leipzig writes me that you have at last determined upon the publication of your 95th Psalm which you sold to me some two years since. I shall of course be most pleased to have it on the terms which you then mentioned – £15.'[32]

In addition to negotiations with foreign composers, Alfred also purchased compositions from sources closer to home – from his father. A glance at the Novello catalogue reveals the editorial contribution made by Vincent – not only did he bring composers to the list, he further prepared or supervised many of the editions himself (see Chapter 2 for an examination of his editorial techniques). In presenting his editions for publication, it is surprising to find that he also received remuneration for the work and the copyright. Thus, on 23 June 1849, Vincent wrote to his son:

> I have now quite finished my collection of Psalm Tunes: there are 150 of *my own*, and 250 harmonised from three composers: but they had better be kept separate, and published as two distinct and complete works. As to terms, I shall be satisfied with whatever you think *a fair price* [sic] for the copyright of two such carefully written works, each tune in which consists of 4 voices with a separate accompaniment and I shall be the more pleased if you fix a *literal price*, as *whatever* is paid for these 2 works of mine, I shall immediately remit to your mother in Italy.
>
> The sooner they are placed in hand the better, as I should like to correct the proofs (together with my 'Collection of Chants') before I leave England this autumn, instead of you having the trouble of sending them over to me on the Continent.
>
> I shall leave *the mode* of publication entirely to your own judgement and decision; to bring them forward as companion works to

---

[30]Ms.M.D.M.d.34, fol. 104.

[31]Ms.M.D.M.d.33, fol. 31, dated 30 January 1838. Novello probably refers to Psalm 42, Op. 42, completed 22 December 1837 and co-published in 1838 with Breitkopf and Härtel.

[32]Ms.M.D.M.d.40, fol. 35. The 95th Psalm was completed in 1838 and revised July 1841; it was published by Novello and Kistner later that year.

the Surrey Chapel Music, or in any other way that you may consider
most profitable to yourself.[33]

An examination of Novello catalogues does not reveal editions which
exactly fit the description offered in Vincent's note, but the resulting
publication may have been *Novello's Congregational Music*, 'being
the Surrey Chapel Music and Supplement bound in one volume'. The
supplement is described in the October 1856 catalogue as: 'Supplement to Novello's Surrey Chapel Music and 169 Psalms, containing
58 psalms and Hymn Tunes and seven Pieces, together with proper
indexes and titles, for binding the Supplement and Surrey Chapel
Music in one volume, forming altogether Novello's Congregational
Music.' An eight-page catalogue, dated 1 March 1849, lists the *Surrey
Chapel Music* and *Novello's 169 Psalm and Hymn Tunes from the
Surrey Chapel Music* but does not mention a supplement; the collection of pieces mentioned by Vincent may have formed a part of this
addition.

What is especially noteworthy is that Vincent offers the editions to his
son for a price to be agreed upon – although it would have been thought
that a standing arrangement, to cover all Vincent's editions, might have
been employed. The letter suggests that Alfred may have purchased each
edition and its copyright on an individual basis, as he would from any
other composer. One clue to this arrangement may lie in the relationship
between father and son at this time. By the 1840s, communication
between Vincent and Alfred had developed a professional and detached
tone, with Vincent moving away from his own firm occasionally to publish with other houses. Vincent's participation with Novello's had taken
a more advisory definition and he was now almost completely severed
from any financial or business decisions. In 1848 Vincent's wife, Mary,
had retired to Nice and her husband would follow in 1849.[34]

The process of selecting and purchasing compositions was interwoven
with the strands of market demand and the musical environment. This
combination required a knowledge of public taste, composers' reper-
toires, concert schedules, and foreign publishing practices. Through
these strands ran the common thread of timing. From his 'communications' to *Musical Times* readers, Alfred gauged market demand and the

---

[33]BL Novello Collection Add. MS 65462, vol. 81. The edition of *Surrey Chapel Music*
is probably that advertised in a March 1849 catalogue as: 'A new edition of the large score,
with organ part, forming one of the best and cheapest selections of pieces, chants, psalm
and hymn tunes, extant. The whole of the harmonies are revised and corrected with a separate organ part by V. Novello.' The edition was available in vocal score, '18mo size' or in
separate vocal parts.

[34]Hurd, *Vincent Novello*, pp. 33ff.

urgency for particular editions. Timing was also a feature if publication dates could coincide with performances. The advantages of simultaneous publication also made schedules a critical issue. Thus, the pairing of demand with timing served as the decisive factor for Alfred's selection and purchasing policies. Once a composition had been accepted, however, the next step was to secure its protection.

Copyright Law: Protection and Co-publication

As we have seen above, Novello's selected and purchased compositions largely on the basis of demand, availability, and timing. At best, Alfred hoped for a fresh work, recently performed, and reasonably priced. When he obtained such a prize, he knew it must be protected both from piracy and from the abuses of ambiguous copyright law. His vigil demanded familiarity with foreign publishers, domestic performances, the timing of co-publications and competitive bargaining.

Before examining Alfred's activities concerning copyright enforcement, we may briefly review the state of legal protection for publishers, in both music and literature, from the 1830s to the 1850s. During this period the urgent need for copyright protection can be gauged in the creation of no less than five copyright acts and five customs acts passed by Parliament. It is of note that the acts passed for the protection of books were also valid for musical works as well as for encyclopedias, newspapers, engravings, patents, and dramatic performances.[35] In 1838 the international copyright act passed Parliament (1 & 2 Vict. c. 59, 1838) which provided protection and the priviledge of copyright to authors publishing outside Britain; the premise was that foreign countries would, in turn, provide reciprocal cover to British authors. It was hoped that this symbiotic arrangement, for Britain, France, and Prussia, would ensure that pirated editions were not imported and sold. Yet the three governments could not agree on details, and the act was never enforced. It remained until 1842 for an amendment (5 & 6 Vict. c. 45, 1842) to be drawn up which solidified copyright protection. The main point of this act was the mandatory deposit of one copy of every British publication in the British Museum (other copyright libraries were added to the list at a later date). In addition, it was prohibited to print, without consent, any

---

[35]The following discussion is based on information from Simon Nowell-Smith, *International Copyright Law and the Publisher in the Reign of Queen Victoria* (Oxford: Clarendon Press, 1968). A full examination of the 1842 Copyright Act can be found in Catherine Seville, *Literary Copyright Reform in Early Victorian England: The Framing of the 1842 Copyright Act* (Cambridge: Cambridge University Press, 1999).

work under copyright protection or to import and sell material first published and copyright in Britain (this included editions reprinted outside 'the British dominions'). The 1842 act was especially vital as it sought to tighten the law preventing piracy.[36]

In 1844 the act of 7 & 8 Vict. c. 12 (which also replaced 1 & 2 Vict. c. 59, 1838) was introduced. It was hoped that this law would now provide appropriate protection to both English and Continental countries in a mutual arrangement. The proviso was that the work must first be published and registered in the author's own country, with copies deposited in the assigned government office (such as Stationers' Hall) and copyright libraries. Between 1850 and 1887 (the year of the Berne convention of copyright), Britain made additional agreements with Germany, France, Belgium, Spain, and some of the Italian States (the States of Sardinia in 1861, for example). Yet even in these protected areas, piracy was not eradicated. Nowell-Smith notes that the majority of important cases concerning international copyright infringement during the mid-nineteenth century involved music publishers.[37]

Well versed in the copyright laws of the day, Alfred quoted them vigorously when necessary. In the advertisement section of *The Musical Times*, for the 1 December 1849 issue, Alfred placed a notice which left no doubt that copyright protection was strictly enforced at Novello's:

> CAUTION
> J. Alfred Novello has extended the above arrangement to the various Copyright adaptations, and to the Poetry of original Works – of which the Words as well as the Music are his copyright; and he takes the opportunity of cautioning all those interested in Festivals and other public performances against reprinting and selling any of his copyrights as Books of Words. The Act 5th and 6th Victoria, c.45, provided protection for all such Works. The penalty is set forth in the 15th clause.
>
> And in the 2nd clause is described what shall be understood by the word 'book': 'II. And it be enacted, That in the construction of this act, the word "book" shall be construed to mean and include every volume, part or division of a volume, pamphlet, sheet of letter-press, sheet of music, map, chart, or plan, separately published.'
>
> J.A.N. will be ready either to supply the required books, or to give the necessary written permission for the purposes of a Festival, on payment of a fair amount to be agreed upon.

His scrupulous vigil is not surprising in light of possible choral society and festival performances of his editions. As the size of such groups were large and ever-increasing, with numbers of performers amounting

---

[36]Nowell-Smith, *International Copyright Law*, pp. 23–5 for details regarding the 1842 act.
[37]Ibid., p. 33.

to hundreds for a single performance, the financial implications were considerable.

By the mid-1830s, Alfred's battle against copyright infringement had already become a standard part of his editorial practices and over the course of his career he would enter the courts at least twice to regain his musical property. In autumn 1836, Alfred was involved in a legal suit which not only concerned copyright but, further, questioned his character and business ethics. In Chapter 3, mention was made of the document, similar to a deposition, prepared by Alfred's legal counsel against the accusations brought by Edward Taylor (see Appendix 6 for a complete transcription).[38] We may now examine this record more closely for it reveals the arguments of a case defending copyright protection. As a musician and editor, Taylor was known for his English editions of Spohr (*The Last Judgment* from *Die letzten Dinge*), Mozart (Requiem), and Haydn (*Jahreszeiten*). Taylor affiliated himself with Spohr, promoting his concerts and music throughout England, and many believed the composer suffered from the association. In 1843, *The Morning Post* reported the poor attendance at a concert organized by Taylor: 'It was pretty well known that Edward Taylor was the director of the arrangements. This fact kept away a large number who would not, like some of the elder professors we recognized in the room, distinguish a German Spohr from a Norwich Taylor.'[39]

The title page to Taylor's edition of *The Last Judgment* indicates that he, and not Novello's, held the copyright for the English version printed by the firm: 'The Last Judgment, an oratorio by Louis Spohr. Translated from the original German, adapted to English words, Edward Taylor. London: published by Edward Taylor.' In producing and selling the edition for Taylor, Novello's was accused of 'defrauding' the editor by printing more copies than recorded and later pocketing the extra profit. From the deposition we also learn that Taylor 'was confident many more copies of *The Last Judgment* had been printed than he (Mr. Taylor) had any knowledge of. That he, Mr. Taylor, was the more convinced of this from having met with copies in the country not containing the letter press ...'. (The term 'letterpress', in printing technology, refers to the movable-type method, which Alfred employed for a number of his

---

[38]Located in the Cowden Clarke Collection, the Brotherton Library, Leeds University.

[39]Clive Brown, *Louis Spohr: A Critical Biography* (Cambridge: Cambridge University Press, 1984), p. 278.

editions;[40] the use of the term by Taylor indicates the title page, quoted above.) As a consequence of the discovered, non-copyright edition, Taylor felt moved to publicly claim that 'Alfred Novello is a thief' and 'a person wholly unfit to be trusted'. Besides interviews with Taylor's associates, statements were also taken from three members of the Novello staff: Charles Cowden Clarke (Alfred's brother-in-law and, according to the deposition, 'keeper of the ledger since 1831'), 'Mr. Pearman (printer)', and 'Mr. Frederick Hehl (foreman)'. Pearman is defined as 'the only music Printer employed by Mr. Novello since the publication of The Last Judgment in April/31, he having the care of the plates in Dean Street'. (See Chapter 3 concerning Novello's printing limitations and the employment of outside firms.)

Beyond the case itself, the document records Novello's alleged practices to print, distribute, and sell music for which he did not hold the copyright. It appears that Alfred housed the plates, printed the main text, and sent the sheets to Taylor's brother where his own title page was added and the entire volume bound together. The deposition notes:

> The Last Judgment [presumably the sheets of music printed by Novello's] was always sent to Mr. Richard Taylor, in Fleet Street (brother of Edward Taylor) in order that he should add the letter press and Board [bind] the work. Mr. Edward Taylor always kept the Engraved Title of the Christian's Prayer [also printed by Novello's] which was engraved by his own Engraver and printed by his own printer and was added to the work, when sent to Fleet Street, with the letter press and sewed by his brother Richard. These precautions, altho' they ought [to] have satisfied Mr. Ed. Taylor gave Mr. A. Novello no cause to suppose his integrity was doubted, as the reason given was that Mr. Ed. Taylor's brother would do that part of the work very cheaply being a Printer.

Such arrangements could not have been entirely to Alfred's satisfaction: a large percentage of control, and profit, eluded him, while the management and printing of plates consumed both time and effort. Unfortunately, any original contracts between Alfred Novello and

---

[40]Alfred advertised the firm's printing facilities in The Musical Times and in his catalogues. His notice in a March 1850 catalogue states: 'Letter Press Printing in every variety. J. Alfred Novello would respectfully announce, that having a carefully organised Printing Office, he is enabled to execute orders for every variety of letter-press printing; and he trusts he may safely point to the various works published by him during the last four years as favourable specimens in that department; all these – the Cheap Oratorios and other moveable-type works, their covers, the large posting and other announcement bills, the "Musical Times", his catalogues, etc. having been the produce of his own press.'

Taylor are no longer extant, yet such documentation would offer valuable insights into this 'non-copyright' scheme.[41]

The security of the copyright laws, even at mid-century, continued to be undermined by interpretation, and, once again, Alfred found he was forced to turn to the courts. In 1850, the conductor of the Liverpool Philharmonic, William Sudlow published Julius Benedict's 'The Wreath' which had appeared in Novello's *Part-Song Book*. The piece was copied onto lithographic stone and distributed, without charge, to the approximately 250 members of the Liverpool Philharmonic Society for a performance.

The course of the case can be traced through the itemized invoice of legal fees presented to Alfred by his solicitor.[42] Under the heading 'As to the piracy of your copyright by the Philharmonic Society of Liverpool' we can see that in December 1850 Alfred believed there had been a breach of copyright and he sought confirmation, through legal counsel. Sudlow was notified of Novello's legal action and turned to his own solicitors a few weeks later. A partial transcription of the invoice indicates Alfred's clear desire for retribution:

> December 18. Perusing correspondence between you [Alfred Novello] and Mr Sudlow, the Secretary of the Philharmonic Society, as to the printing by that body of music which the copyright was vested in you and attendances on you thereon you instructed us to have the question tried and we were to consider whether it could be brought before the Court at once by special case and we were to take the opinion of Mr Rott and someone to be recommended by him at the Common Law Bar. 13 4 [presumably the fee: 13 shillings and 4 pence]

> 1850 December 20. ... Writing to Mr Sudlow, the Secretary of the Society, that we were instructed to take proceedings and proposing a special case for the opinion of the Courts of Common Law 5 [5 shillings]

> December 26. Mr Sudlow having referred us to Messrs Horsham as the Solrs [solicitors] of the Society writing to them and proposing to raise the question by special case. 5

[...]

---

[41]Novello's went on to publish other Spohr editions – employing a variety of translators and editors: the *Vocal Mass* arranged by Charles Severn; *Sacred Cantata*, 'God Thou Art Great', Op. 98, translated by Morley Chubb; and an octave piano-vocal edition of *The Last Judgment* (*c*.1854), arranged by Vincent Novello and translated by 'Miss Emily Gregg and R. G. Loraine', with the curious introduction (perhaps in reaction to the Taylor experience): 'The present Translation of Spohr's "Die letzten Dinge" was completed when that work first appeared in Germany, and before the publication of any other adaptation. It was made for the use of a small circle of friends.'

[42]The invoice is located in the Novello Business Archive, BL Add. MS 69594.

> 1852. May 7. Attending court-argument concluded – judgement given in your favour.

The following month, Alfred published the proceedings of the case in the June 1852 issue of *The Musical Times*. This published report illustrates the interpretation of the copyright law, 5 & 6 Victoria, 15th section, c. 45, within the practical context of litigation and therefore quotation of the proceedings at some length is of interest.

> For the plaintiff [Alfred Novello], Mr. Phipson contended that the point was one of considerable importance, for if the defendant [Sudlow] should succeed, the Copyright Act, instead of being a great boon, would be one of the most inefficient Acts that had passed. The question turned on the construction of the 15th sec. of the 5th and 6th Victoria, c. 45 which provided that if any person should 'print, or cause to be printed, either for sale or exportation, any book in which there should be subsisting copyright, without the consent in writing of the proprietor thereof, or shall import for sale or hire any such book so having been unlawfully printed from parts beyond the sea, or knowing such book to have been so unlawfully printed or imported, shall sell, publish, or expose to sale or hire, or cause to be sold ... such offender shall be liable to a special action on the case.' The interpretation clause defined the word 'book' to mean 'music' and the word 'copyright' to mean 'the sole and exclusive liberty of printing, or otherwise multiplying copies of any subject ...' This was an enactment for the benefit of authors and publishers, and gave them a clear and well-defined right. The question was, did this 15th section curtail the common law right of action for an infringement of copyright? It was submitted that it did not, and that the plaintiff had a right of action independently of the statute ('Miller v. Tayler', 4 Burr.). If under this section it was no infringement of the Act to print and give away copies, Mr. Dickens's new work, *Bleak House*, might be copied the day after it was issued, and reprints of it be given away for nothing.

Sudlow's defence argued, however, that such a ruling would severely curtail any musical instruction whatsoever: 'if the plaintiff's argument were to prevail, it would extend to give an action in the minutest case, for instance of copying out a piece of music for a pupil to play or the like, or by a young lady for her music book.' Nonetheless, following the interpretation of the Act that copyrighted material could not be duplicated either for profit or donation, the court ruled in favour of Novello's: 'The act of the defendant in multiplying copies of [Novello's] work, without his consent, though for gratuitous circulation, is a violation of that right. Judgment for the plaintiff.' While the case involved a relatively small printing, the incident nonetheless spurred Alfred to print periodically his 'copyright caution' in *The Musical Times*; an example is found in the 1 May 1859 issue:

J. Alfred Novello has been made aware, from various sources, of the great extent to which his copyright works are copied and otherwise multiplied, for the purpose of being used or hired by Choral Societies. Without entering upon the injustice which such conduct is to the best interests of the musical public, those who thus trespass in ignorance of the law are reminded of the decision in the case of Novello v. Sudlow, which was fully reported in *The Musical Times*, No. 97, of June, 1852. It is here reprinted in the hope that its perusal will have the effect of putting an end to illegal and unjust copying.

At least one publication found such surveillance too restrictive. With Novello's as their model, *The Athenaeum* presented their view of current copyright protection in the column 'Musical and Dramatic Gossip':

It might have been thought that the question of musical copyright was intricate enough – sufficiently clogged with difficulties, exceptions, and everything that complicates a simple business transaction; but here is a new point raised by the proprietors of Novello's Part-Song Book, which we will allow them to describe in the words of their own advertisement on the first page of the November number of that publication:

'It has come to the Knowledge of the Proprietors of Novello's Part-Song Book, that their copyrights have been multiplied by musical societies and others who have made manuscript and, sometimes, printed copies for the use of their singers instead of using the copyright editions. Legal steps have been taken to defend their rights against such transgressors as have yet been discovered, and the proceedings will be published when they have reached a more advanced stage; but in the meantime the present caution is given to deter others from committing similar practices.

'The Proprietors, therefore, give this public notice to such as may be ignorant of the law, that by such multiplication of copies, trespassers render themselves liable to the penalties provided by the Act of the 5th and 6th Victoria, chapter 45 (generally known as the Copyright Act). In the second section of the Act, "Copyright", is defined to mean "the sole and exclusive liberty of printing or otherwise multiplying copies of any subject to which the word is applied in that Act." On a trial for Literary Piracy, Lord Ellenborough said – "The test by which we must decide whether or not a party has infringed on the copyright of another is, not by inquiring what was the intention of the trespassing party, but whether the work of the party complaining has been so copied that the copy may by any possibility supersede the original work."'

The case specifying not only 'musical Societies' but 'others who have made manuscript copies,' assumes a stringency of prevention which will place every *Miss Marblen* written music book at the mercy of an informer. Can this be the law? We cannot but think that the body of

musical publishers – or failing them, some barrister in lack of a special subject – would do well to see if some settlement of the question
at once less rigorous than the presented one could not be arranged.
Nothing can be worse than matters as they now stand.[43]

An additional case of copyright infringement against Novello's should
also be mentioned. In February 1851, Alfred's solicitors again went to
court, this time to defend the publisher against the journal *The Pianista*
which had published Mendelssohn's *Songs Without Words* (the book
number is not given). An invoice from Alfred's solicitors, similar to the
one for the Sudlow case, details the proceedings:[44]

> 1851 As to the piracy of your copyright by Mr James in *The Pianista*
> February 4. Attending you as to some music the copyright of which
> was vested in you having been pirated in *The Pianista*, a periodical
> publication and advising. 6/8
>
> February 5. Attending you further conferring thereon we advised a
> general notice to the trade but were first to consult counsel on the
> subject. 6/8
>
> [...]
>
> March 24. Attending court motion made and argued and injunction
> ordered to be continued on the condition that you should bring an
> action at law within ten days unless you and the Defendant con-
> sented to abide the result of the pending decision in the Exchequer
> Court. 13/4
>
> March 25. Attending you conferring and advising as to the propriety
> of an offer to compromise and you authorized us to propose that if
> the Defendant would give up the plates of the printed music and
> undertake not to have fresh ones made you would not proceed and
> would pay your own costs.

It is of note that Alfred and his solicitors wished to propose an offer of
conciliation which would allow the case to be dropped without damages.
It is not recorded whether the offer was accepted although the case
passed in Novello's favour. Moreover, Alfred was willing to halt proceedings if *The Pianista* destroyed the plates and, further, he would not
seek compensation for the infringment. Alfred's priorities were to stop
breach of copyright rather than to obtain financial reward from it.

Contrary to Novello's attentiveness to copyright protection and
enforcement, however, it is surprising to discover that he rarely registered his publications, despite the notice, 'Entered Stationers' Hall'
frequently printed on the title pages. During the period 1830–64 the

---

[43]*The Athenaeum* (14 December 1852), pp. 1318–19.
[44]BL Add. MS 69594.

majority of entries reflect printing jobs for outside publications.[45] A typical Stationers' Hall entry by Novello's, for 28 June 1854, reads: 'Sacred Cantata "Millennial Glory" with accompaniment for the flute. J. Alfred Novello, 69 Dean Street, Soho, and 24, Poultry-London. William John, 21, Upper King Street, Southsea, Portsmouth, Hampshire, 1853.' (Although a composer is not named, presumably it is the copyright holder, William Johns.) Other firms were more fastidious, however, and the Stationers' record includes numerous registrations by Cocks and Co., D'Almaine, Wessel, and Boosey. Thus, a standard practice of registration was not followed by all music publishers. Alan Tyson notes that numerous music publications bear the words 'Entered at Stationers' Hall' but an entry record cannot be found. Many publishers believed that these words hopefully would deter any piracy attempts, and, by avoiding official registration, the mandatory free copies did not have to be donated to the Stationers' Hall depository. In turn, instances can also be seen where the phrase is not printed on the title page, but a record of registration can be found.[46] The Commission Books (located in the British Library, Novello Business Archive, and discussed in Chapter 3) occasionally note Stationers' Hall or the British Museum as recipients of pieces in the lists of copies sent out upon publication, although these institutions are not included in every entry.

If there existed any lapse in domestic enforcement, Alfred was nonetheless scrupulous in copyright arrangements with foreign publishers. Writing to Mendelssohn on 28 October 1839, he cautioned: 'In your letter of 17 October you say your Psalm is published but I suppose you mean that it is ready for publication for should it be really published in Germany you are aware that you have no longer any power to sell the copyright anywhere else.'[47] Yet it is unlikely that Mendelssohn was confused by copyright law: he held quite definite views which he expressed to Simrock in a letter from Leipzig, dated 31 March 1841, regarding his *Three Sacred Songs*: 'Der Tag der engl. Herausgabe ist der 15te April; es wird nicht möglich sein das Stuck bis dahin in Deutschland *erscheinen* zu lassen; aber es ist damit ja wohl eine blosse

[45]The Novello entries for 1830–42 were examined at Stationers' Hall, London and at the Public Record Office, Kew, for 1843–64.

[46]Alan Tyson, *The Authentic English Editions of Beethoven* (London: Faber and Faber, 1963), pp. 131–43.

[47]Ms.M.D.M.d.36, fol. 105. Of the works finished in 1839, the letter may refer to Psalm 114, op. 51, completed 9 August 1839; less likely is Psalm 5, 'Lord Hear the Voice', in autograph, completed 26 February 1839, or Psalm 31, 'Defend me, O Lord', in autograph, completed one day later.

Förmlichkeit, und es kann ja wohl Keiner dem eigentlichen *Erscheinen* nachrechnen.'[48]

The regard for simultaneous publication underscores an almost practical difference between composer and publisher. While Mendelssohn may have found attempts at synchronized publication futile, Alfred, nevertheless, laboured to meet the dates appointed by foreign firms. Thus, he informed Mendelssohn (27 November 1840): 'I have ordered the piece to be entered on the 2nd December, the day appointed by Messrs. Breitkopf and Härtel.'[49] One incentive for such precise timing was as protection in case a publication matter ever came to court. In such an instance, correspondence and a clear record of effort to obtain simultaneous publication would indicate a publisher's good and well-meant intentions.

In addition to simultaneous press dates, arrangements with Continental firms also concerned translation of vocal works, preparation of title pages, and selection of opus numbers. Mendelssohn's correspondence suggests he frequently served as mediator between his publishers, coordinating and organizing details for forthcoming editions. In a letter to Breitkopf and Härtel, Mendelssohn requests (29 March 1838): 'Der Psalm[50] kann hoffentlich recht bald gestochen werden, und sobald der Clavierauszug fertig ist (der wohl zuerst vorgenommen werden muss) bitte ich Sie ihn verabredetermassen nach London an Hrn. Novello zu schicken und den Tag der Herausgabe zu bestimmen, auch den engl. Text für die Part. zu verlangen.'[51] As final preparations were made, in June Mendelssohn wrote again to Breitkopf (Berlin, 11 June 1838): 'Jedoch würde ich Sie bitten ihm [Alfred Novello] deshalb noch einmal zu schreiben, und ihm zugleich den Tag der Herausgabe und die Opuszahl des Psalms anzugeben.'[52] In the same letter, he added the postscript: 'Hr. Novello sagt mir, das Concert [probably Op. 40] sei dem Erscheinen nahe, oder schon erschienen. Sie bemerken ihm wohl noch einmal, dass er nicht vergisst Ihre Firma auf dem engl. Titel mitzustechen, wenn Sie ihm wegen des Psalms schreiben.'[53]

While Mendelssohn often supervised the finer details of publication, Alfred nonetheless participated in the larger issue of translation,

---

[48]Rudolf Elvers, ed. *Felix Mendelssohn Bartholdy: Briefe an deutsche Verleger* (Wiesbaden: Breitkopf and Härtel, 1968), pp. 228–9.

[49]Ms.M.D.M.d.38, fol. 147.

[50]Probably Psalm 42 completed 22 December 1837 and published in 1838.

[51]Elvers, *Mendelssohn*, p. 70.

[52]Ibid., p. 72.

[53]Ibid., p. 73.

frequently offering alterations or suggestions for the text. Writing on 23 April 1841, Alfred noted:

> I am working hard to get the translation quite what you will like and have made many changes which I feel sure you will like – they are not quite complete but the piano arrangements which I have got today will be of much assistance. It certainly is of the utmost importance to do away with the stiffness which attends a [first?] translation. I have great hopes that I shall send it for your approval next week.[54]

Seven days later, Alfred sent the changes:

> [30 April] I send you on the other side the alterations we have made in the adaptation to the English words. Our friend Mr. Klingeman approves them all but those enclosed in red which we have promised to meet again about tomorrow afternoon – but indeed you are unreasonable in expecting us to be so very sudden in adaptations of this difficult nature which require many times to return again and again to the expression to get rid of the stiffness and not sacrifice the music – and I did not feel at all sure of the adaptation until we had a good opportunity of playing it over with the accompaniment. This I received on the 23rd April and I hope you will be good enough to fix with Messrs. Breitkopf and Härtel for the *29th May* for the day of publication before which day it cannot possibily be ready. They ought to calculate better than to fix an earlier day. The translation they [want] they already have with the exception of the alterations on the other side. I will write to you again on Tuesday about the red ink passages if we decide.[55]

Alfred appears to have taken particular care concerning both the tone and rhythm of the translations. For his edition of the 95th Psalm, he wrote to Mendelssohn (5 November 1841):

> I send for your approval a part of the translation of the 95th Psalm which we are engraving but still if you wish any change we can make it if you write immediately. The tenor [part?] I am working away at and hope to send you the adaptation by next Tuesday's post. If you refer to what we call the prayer book version of the Psalm in English you will find that we are very close to the original ... I hope you will understand the places where two syllables are used for one ... Mr. Kistner wants the English version as soon as you approve.[56]

By mid-century, the protection of musical property and, in turn, the definition of copyright reached a level where music publishers found it necessary, as a matter of common businesss practice, to confront the issue, often in court. The extent to which a publisher found it necessary

---

[54]Ms.M.D.M.d.39, fol. 199.
[55]Ms.M.D.M.d.39, fol. 211.
[56]Ms.M.D.M.d.40, fol. 152.

publicly to declare his legal rights and protect his editions can be seen in Alfred's cases against Taylor and against Sudlow as well as in his frequent announcements in *The Musical Times*. In addition to the published statements and legal battles, Novello's also prepared editions and established policies which helped to keep piracy at bay. Novello's edition of the Revd J. A. Baxter's sacred works, is described in the 1863 catalogue as:

> Te deum, Jubilate, Magnificat, and other parts of the Morning and Evening Prayer, with the words divided for chanting. Over the words are placed blank music staffs, on which any appropriate chant may be written. Price 6d. An abatement will be made to choirs requiring large numbers.

The offer of a discount for large purchases is a critical publishing policy, and Alfred also applied it to other editions where a choral market was anticipated. It was clearly advantageous to provide an attractive price, achieve the bulk sale, and thereby obviate any temptation otherwise for choral groups to copy out additional parts. In addition, Novello's frequently prepared editions with a special editorial format, typeface size, and design which were heralded as beneficial to the performer in a way that manuscript (that is, pirated) versions were not. The octavo edition is an example. In advertisements for the octavo edition, they are described: 'Novello's [octavo] editions were also the first type of works which had the *words* (or text) of a proportionate size to the *music*, so that both could be conveniently read at the same distance from the eye.' Thus, through the more subtle means of design and production of special editions, through the occasional offer of special rates, by public reminders of the copyright law, and, when necessary, in the courts, Alfred Novello protected his editions and included this activity as one of his major publishing practices and concerns.

The 'Taxes on Knowledge' and the Printing Duties

The attraction of newspapers and periodicals for the Victorian middle class cannot be underestimated. Publishers and authors alike recognized the profit to be made, for example, in the serialization of novels and the growing appetite for self-education and information spawned an increasing number of new publications.[57] Yet both audience and publisher had to contend with a myriad of newspaper taxes which forced prices higher and limited readership. The first newspaper tax

---

[57]See Patten, *Charles Dickens*.

was established in the Act of June 1712. The original regulation required that any publication defined as a newspaper must obtain a licence by paying the tax – the newspaper was then stamped and thus legally available for sale. In addition, taxes were also applied to the advertisements in the newspaper.[58] If the taxes were not paid, the fines could be damaging: purchase of an unstamped newspaper might cost an individual a £20 fee, non-payment by the publisher would incur a £100 fine, and imprisonment was also a possible punishment for evasion.[59] For an active publisher, payments could amount to vast sums and the existence of such regulations financially hobbled the industry at every turn. Enlightened editors frequently devoted their pages to a call for abolishment. *The Dramatic and Musical Review* was one such forum, and the August, 1849 issue summarized the central argument:

> We have received a circular from the secretary of a society called 'The Newspaper-Stamp Abolition Society,' the object of which is to obtain the exemption of the press from taxation. The pressure of taxes now, in a general point of view, is most excessive. While the means of meeting it are daily becoming more limited, the burthen of taxation is increasing, and the expense of government is more overwhelming. How, it may reasonably be asked, is the loss of the amount of revenue at present received from the newspaper stamps and advertisement duty to be replaced in the event of their abolition? What tax do you propose in its stead that will fall lighter upon the people? None, we answer; we propose no new impost: we ask for a general reduction in the expenditure of the country. We ask for a revision of all salaries paid by the government – an equalization of labour and of renumeration. We ask that those offices to which no duties are attached shall be abolished.[60]

The clamour for repeal was not unwarranted; the costs to a newspaper could be crippling. In the same article, the following figures were presented as an example of annual charges for 'a paper, independently of their own private taxes – income, land, and assessed':

> The duty on paper, which yearly amounts to: £745, 795 9s 4d
> The duty on advertisements: £153,016 19s 0d
> The penny stamp on newspapers: £360,273 13s 7d
>
> Total: £1,259,086 1s 11d[61]

As Treasurer for the 'Association for Promoting the Repeal of the Taxes on Knowledge', Alfred actively participated in the movement and

---

[58]Pauline Gregg, *A Social and Economic History of Britain, 1760–1965*, 5th edn rev. (London: George G. Harrap, 1965), pp. 267ff.

[59]Ibid., p. 268.

[60]*The Dramatic and Musical Review* (August 1849), p. 209.

[61]Ibid., p. 210.

printed the organization's newsletter, *The Gazette of the Association for Promoting the Repeal of the Taxes on Knowledge*, at his press in 69 Dean Street.[62] He apparently also provided financial support when needed – the 12 November 1856 issue of *The Gazette* notes that 'The Treasurer', although owed almost £200, had advanced the Association a further £27 12*s*. 4*d*. to the organization. The sentiment of the Association was embodied in the definition of 'excise', borrowed from *Johnson's Dictionary* and printed on the masthead of each issue: 'Excise – A hateful tax levied upon commodities, and adjudged, not by the common judges of property, but by wretches hired by those to whom excise is paid.'

The implications of these taxes ranged beyond publishing expenses, however. Authors also feared they would not be paid an adequate fee for contributions once duty costs had been extracted from newspaper budgets. The 12 November *Gazette* voiced these worries: 'We have repeatedly shown, by figures, that in a time when books and newspapers sell by thousands of copies, a tax of three halfpence in the pound will often abstract the author's salary from the price of a publication, and thus render it worthless.'[63] Moreover, if professional writers found themselves unable to survive the diminished wages, it was feared that the path would be open to partisan opportunists willing to accept the lower pay for a public platform. The ramifications of an uncontested taxation system were regarded as a serious threat to independent journalism well beyond the anxiety of balanced accounts. The Association gathered supporters from London as well as from other areas of England – especially the business and manufacturing centres of Birmingham, Manchester, Bristol, and Norwich. A glance at the List of Subscribers at the back of a *Gazette* issue also reveals the participation by politicians – at least twenty-six were Members of Parliament, including the president of the Association, T. Milner Gibson.

Apart from his duties for the Association, Alfred also fought for repeal both in the government and in the pages of *The Musical Times*, frequently informing his readers of the expenses incurred by his journal:

---

[62]A copy of the 12 November 1856 issue of *The Gazette* is located in the Cowden Clarke Collection.

[63]*The Gazette of the Association for Promoting the Repeal of the Taxes on Knowledge* (12 November 1856): p. 2.

[December, 1852]

Taxes on Knowledge
The Direct Taxes* in this number of *The Musical Times*:
£5 5 4
Brought forward since January: £62 17 6

[Total:]   £68 2 10

*See details in former numbers – but it must not be forgotten that this heavy Tax is on our humble three-half-penny periodical.

Alfred's notice follows one of the tactics of the repeal campaign: to inform readers of the costs passed on to them by the inclusion of the tax duty on the price. It was hoped that public sympathy and perhaps protest would result and help the cause.

Alfred's devotion also placed him before the government, and in April 1850, he requisitioned the House of Commons to revoke the duties. In the May issue of *The Musical Times*, he published his statement:

Taxes on Knowledge. To the Hon. the House of Commons, the Petition of J. Alfred Novello, Music Seller, London, presented by T. Milner Gibson, Esq., M.P., April 8, 1850. Sheweth – That the petitioner is engaged in publishing music and that he has especially turned his attention to supply the best works at the small price required by the present increasing desire to cultivate the better class of music; and that in the prosecution of this object he has found the several Acts which regulate the Advertisement Duties, the Newspaper Stamp Act, and the Excise Duty on paper, have each offered serious impediments.

It has been found the most convenient mode to publish his popular series of cheap oratorios in numbers containing 16 pages of music, to be ready at an ascertained time, and to keep these sheets clean they are stitched in a coloured wrapper; but the fact of having a date in the wrapper subjects the catalogue of this publication to advertisement duty, although books published with a catalogue bound with them are not liable; and if for the better arrangement of the catalogue, dividing rules are used between the works enumerated, then separate duties are charged. Musical works so printed have not any temporary or periodical character in their contents beyond the date to which they are ready for sale. The advertisement duty thus acts as a heavy tax on these useful and popular works and in the case of *Novello's Cathedral Choir Book* (containing a mere reprint of Church Services), the duty was one of the main causes which stopped the work, for the Stamp Office insisted on the duty being levied, after representation was made of its small scale.

That your petitioner is also publisher of a small monthly sheet called *The Musical Times*, consisting of a piece of music, a brief chronicle of passing musical events, and musical advertisements, price 1½d or stamped, 2½d. The stamped edition is for the facility of sending through the Post; but in order to obtain that convenience he

has been subjected to the Newspaper Act, which requires every proprietor not only to give security for the payment of the
advertisement duty, but also to enter into recognizance to Her Majesty the Queen, by himself and others, to the amount of £1200., that
he shall not insert a libel in *The Musical Times*, an offence which the
nature of the work renders scarcely possible, and for which offence
there are remedies, should the offence be committed. There are also
heavy penalties enacted for the failure to deliver at the Stamp Office
copies of all works called periodicals or newspapers.

That the Excise Duty on paper is directly a very heavy percentage
upon cheap musical publications, by enhancing the cost of the works
themselves; but is also indirectly so, by increasing the cost of the catalogues necessary to make them known.

Your petitioner therefore prays, that the Excise tax upon papers,
the tax upon advertisements, and the Stamp tax upon newspapers
may be abolished, leaving the proper Authorities to fix a small
charge for the transmission of newspapers by the Post. And your
petitioner will ever pray.

Yet four years later, Alfred found the situation still unresolved and
exacerbated by the correspondence he now received from the government. In May 1854, Alfred was sent a letter from the national tax
office; it was promptly published and turned to good use as a platform
for the continuing struggle:

The 'Musical Times' Threatened with Government's Prosecution

Inland Revenue, London, 8 May, 1854

Mr. J. A. Novello

Sir – I am directed by the Commissioners of this Board to communi-
cate with you respecting a paper entitled *The Musical Times*, printed
and published by you, some unstamped copies of which have been
brought under their observation. As this paper contains news as well
as principally advertisements, and is published at intervals of less
than 26 days, it is a newspaper liable to stamp duty, and for every
copy printed upon unstamped paper a penalty has been incurred. I
shall be happy to submit to the Board any explanation you may
think proper to offer upon the subject.

J. Timm, Solicitor of Inland Revenue

Directly beneath the letter Alfred publicly replied, declaring his intention to continue current practices without alteration:

The above letter will clearly shew that no publication, however humble, can escape the repressive influence of the stamp laws, if by good
management and usefulness it obtain[s] an extensive circulation.

The object of Mr. Timm's communication is to prevent *The Musical Times* from appearing so often as once a fortnight, and he also
objects that too much musical information is given in the form he

calls advertisement. We feel pretty sure that we are on the safe side of the legal nets spread to catch publishers who make their publications too popular; but our being even threatened will serve to indicate how many are the trammels which these Taxes on Knowledge oppose to prevent periodicals from being rendered as useful as they might be, so soon as printing and publishing were relieved of the heavy Excise on paper, and the vexatious securities, penalties, and anomalies of the compulsory Stamp.

Either through the vigilant efforts of the Association or the increasing evidence of impracticality, between 1853 and 1861, one by one, the 'taxes on knowledge' fell: in 1853 the advertisement duty was repealed; 1855, the compulsory newspaper stamp duty disappeared; and in 1861 the paper duty was abolished. In the minutes of the ninth annual meeting of the Association, reported in the 1 March 1860 issue of *The Musical Times*, complete repeal was anticipated:

> It was no less than eleven years since this Association was first formed. Its success had been marked by the Repeal of the Stamp Duty on Newspapers, the Abolition of the Advertisement Duty, and several minor grievances – events which had exercised a vast influence on the diffusion of news and general knowledge throughout this country. These were triumphs, and they were now on the eve of obtaining the repeal of the last of the Taxes on Knowledge – the Duty upon Paper ... After the condemnation of this tax by the House of Commons, it was evident that the duty could no longer be maintained, and that it was only kept on owing to the loss revenue would sustain. Mr. Gladstone, in his excellent Budget, has had the courage to overcome this difficulty, and he was deserving of every praise for his enlightened conduct.

The fight for repeal of the stamp duty and various taxes united publishers of both music and literature, as well as authors and composers. Even Charles Dickens, who had initially held an ambivalent view toward the cause (for him the stamp duty would offer 'some protection to the public against the rash and hasty launching of blackguard newspapers')[64] by 1851, as 'part owner' of the journal *Household Words*, entered the fray for abolition. It is of note that, at the height of conflict and confrontation with national institutions and the government, publishers such as Alfred Novello were willing to place their own professional security at risk to uphold a firmly held ideal. Alfred did not shy away from the conflict nor did he tacitly accept the established rules for publishing and printing journals. Despite the threat of heavy fines and perhaps the loss of the firm, he fought the legal system. Alfred supported the repeal not only for the benefit of music

---

[64]Patten, *Charles Dickens*, p. 222, n. 16.

publishers but also on behalf of journalists, authors, literary publishers, and printers in all ranges of the profession. Coupled with his concern for adequate copyright law, Alfred Novello played an active and influential role in the life of Victorian publishing.

When Alfred Novello began publishing in 1830, the marketplace was rapidly assimilating the demands and innovations of the Industrial Revolution. The technological advancements reflected in more efficient printing presses and expanding railway lines meant greater quantities of information reached a larger audience at a faster rate. The byproduct of such growth and prosperity, however, appeared in the laws and regulations created to manage this new level of communication. For music publishers in mid-century England, such restrictions affected the printing duties, copyright laws, and co-publication arrangements addressed daily in business practices.

Alfred led his firm through the labyrinth of contemporary publishing with an enterprising yet prudent spirit. While he eagerly sought the most recent sacred works of a popular composer such as Mendelssohn, he nonetheless kept abreast of audience demand and co-publication restrictions in his editorial decisions. He joined ranks with his fellow publishers and printers to oppose the 'Taxes on Knowledge' and recognized that such levies fettered the industry in books as well as in music. For his own editions, Alfred fiercely protected his copyright sanctions and informed both domestic and foreign markets of his legal entitlements.

By the middle of the nineteenth century, music publishing was no longer the provenance of shopkeepers and instrument makers, nor the occupation of the individual scholar printing the occasional edition; as in the rest of the commercial world, the Victorian entrepreneur also entered music publishing. Alfred Novello turned this burgeoning financial environment to his advantage and from his father's original private venture he constructed a flourishing business.

CHAPTER FIVE

The Musical Times as a Reflection of Novello's Editorial Policies

One of the clearest pictures of a publisher's house style and policy is often reflected in the pages of its journal. For Novello's, their periodical, *The Musical Times* (hereafter referred to as *MT*), proved to be a logical and successful extension of the firm's editorial policies. *MT* provided the pages to advertise and announce Novello's own publications and, through the music supplements at the back of each issue, samples of the house editions, either short, complete pieces or portions of larger ones, were provided. *MT* was not, however, the first journal published by the firm. On 18 March 1836 Alfred, in partnership with his brother-in-law, Charles Cowden Clarke, launched the first issue of *The Musical World* (hereafter *MW*). The different editorial style of *MT* and *MW* is striking and the two periodicals will be discussed and compared below.

During the period under investigation in this study, *MT* maintained a highly selective view of the musical scene of mid-century England. While the journal offered comprehensive coverage of choral society activities and advances in music education, such issues as recently composed works, the activities of current composers, and performances received scant mention. For this reason, Novello's portrayal of English musical life bears closer examination: their edited viewpoint – not only what was included but what was left out – further reveals the firm's market and its demands. The pages of *MT* reflected the repertoire, musical events, and genres which were of interest to the Novello purchaser; in turn, an analysis of the house journal offers a more closely defined image of this publisher's audience. Of course, the role of the house organ is to promote the repertoire and publications they produce and it would be a mistake to expect an entirely objective picture of musical life to emerge. At bottom, a house journal was another opportunity for self-promotion. In speaking of Novello's, Dave Russell reminds us of the role of the music publisher:

> Care must be taken not to misinterpret [Novello's] motives or to overstate its role as a propagator of musical activity. Existing histories give too much emphasis to the philanthropic aspect of music publishing. Alfred Novello and Henry Littleton *were* anxious to give music to the less affluent because they believed in its value as a bringer of solace, happiness and moral regeneration. They were also

part of a highly competitive industry and were seeking to develop and exploit markets and to make money.[1]

The beginning of the nineteenth century saw the expansion of the 'puff' or self-promotion by an advertiser in the columns of an editorial or by a publisher in reviews of his editions. The possibility that a journal also served as an advertisement must be taken into account and may, in part, explain the editorial choices made for the pages of *MT*. Thomas Macaulay, later Lord Macaulay (1800–59), notes that 'The publisher [of books] is often the publisher of some periodical work. In this periodical work the first flourish of the trumpets is sounded. The peal is then echoed, and reechoed by all the other periodical works over which the publisher or the author, or the author's coterie, may have any influence.'[2] To what degree, then, *MT* chose to 'puff' or promote Novello editions and to what extent the editorial biases reflect the view of the Novello market must be addressed in an examination of the firm. To answer these questions, this chapter will analyse the editorial nature of *MT* in comparison with other similar English music and fine arts journals. It will be seen that Novello's focused on a limited facet of Victorian musical life while other publications embraced a wider viewpoint. These differences and the motives behind them will help us further to define Novello's publishing policies.

Origins of *The Musical Times*

Although the origins of *MT* have been discussed in other sources, a brief outline here will illustrate many of the journal's editorial policies.[3] *MT* had its roots in an earlier periodical, *The National Singing Class Circular*, later enlarged and retitled *Mainzer's Musical Times and Singing Class Circular* (see below). The founder of these journals, Joseph Mainzer (1801–51) began his career as a priest but subsequently

---

[1]Dave Russell, *Popular Music in England, 1840–1914: A Social History* (Manchester: Manchester University Press, 1987), p. 135.

[2]From Thomas Macaulay, in his unfinished five-volume history of England, quoted in Michael Harris and Alan Lee, eds, *The Press in English Society from the Seventeenth to Nineteenth Centuries* (London: Associated University Presses, 1987), p. 157.

[3]Percy Scholes, *The Mirror of Music: 1844–1944*, 2 vols (Oxford: Oxford University Press, 1947, repr. 1970). Joseph Bennett, *A Short History of Cheap Music, as Exemplified in the Records of the House of Novello, Ewer & Co* (London and New York: Novello, Ewer and Co., 1887); Bennett, 'Our Year of Jubilee', *The Musical Times* 35 (1894), pp. 9–11; Laurence Swinyard, ed., *A Century and a Half in Soho*; Nicholas Temperley, 'MT and Musical Journalism, 1844', *The Musical Times* 110 (1969), pp. 583–6; Michael Hurd, *Vincent Novello – and Company* (London: Novello, 1981).

changed his profession to become a music educator and singing teacher. Through his work, Mainzer brought music education and singing to the general public and he is acknowledged as an important participant in the development of the choral movement in Britain and on the Continent.

Mainzer began his system of singing instruction in 1835 in Paris, with a series of classes, given without charge. Soon Mainzer's technique came to the attention of English musicians, largely through reports from Paris by H. F. Chorley. As music critic to *The Athenaeum*, Chorley noted: 'I was present at one of the meetings of M. Mainzer's singing classes of workmen and artisans, at a room in the Place de l'Estrapade. This gentleman's success should encourage all those who wish to diffuse a musical taste among the humbler orders.'[4] Through Chorley's reports, Mainzer's technique caught the interest of English singers and music teachers, including that of John Hullah (1812–84). By 1839, Hullah and Chorley had formed at least a professional friendship through their mutual admiration for Mainzer and his system, and that year they travelled to Paris to observe the technique at work.[5] Through growing English interest in his singing system and the need to leave Paris for political reasons, Mainzer travelled to London and in May 1841 founded his own set of classes.

In November 1841, as part of his educational programme, Mainzer began to publish *The National Singing Class Circular* which he expanded in July 1842 as *Mainzer's Musical Times and Singing Class Circular*. Mainzer promoted his sight-singing technique – based on the Continental 'fixed-do' sol-fa system – by training and appointing other instructors to conduct classes outside London. Interest from the provinces was a key to Mainzer's success and early issues of both his journals illustrate the numerous requests from other cities such as Bristol, Manchester, and Leeds for classes and instructors.[6]

An examination of *Mainzer's Musical Times* shows the kind of audience Mainzer cultivated and which Novello later inherited and

---

[4]Henry Fothergill Chorley, 'Foreign Correspondence', *The Athenaeum* 527 (2 December 1837), p. 881 and quoted in Bernarr Rainbow, 'The Rise of Popular Music Education in Nineteenth-Century England', *Victorian Studies* (Autumn 1986), pp. 25–49. For a full account of Chorley see Robert Terrell Bledsoe, *Henry Fothergill Chorley: Victorian Journalist* (Aldershot: Ashgate, 1998).

[5]Rainbow, 'The Rise of Popular Music Education', p. 30.

[6]See Scholes, *The Mirror of Music*, 1: pp. 3–10; and Bernarr Rainbow, 'Joseph Mainzer', in Stanley Sadie, ed., *The New Grove Dictionary of Music and Musicians*, 11: pp. 539–40. See also Bernarr Rainbow, 'Joseph Mainzer', *The New Grove Dictionary of Music and Musicians*, 2nd edn ed. Stanley Sadie and John Tyrrell (London: Macmillan, 2001), 15: p. 642.

nurtured.[7] The title page of volume 1 of *Mainzer's Musical Times* (15 July 1842) indicates his intended market: 'Mainzer's Musical Times and Singing Class Circular; a journal of literature, criticism and intelligence connected with the art, and the advocate of popular musical instruction.' The introduction, in the same volume, emphasizes the need for such a journal: 'Unfortunately, in the present state of English musical literature, the means of acquiring that general knowledge of Music, the desire for which grows with its growth as a practical art, are very scantily supplied: and the present Journal is intended as an endeavour – an earnest one at all events – to supply the desideratum.'[8] Mainzer grounded his journal primarily on the developments of amateur vocal music, concentrating especially on the educational contribution made by his method. Not surprisingly, his journal carried such columns as 'Popular Musical Instruction' (with the subsections 'Metropolitan Progress' and 'Provincial Progress'). The impact made by Mainzer and his educational system cannot be overestimated. Even by the 1840s, music education was only gradually gaining acceptance as a legitimate part of the curricula both in elementary schools and at universities. Mainzer thus provided an opportunity and filled a demand for musical instruction which was otherwise difficult to obtain. Mainzer was not alone, however, in recognizing this deficiency. In 1840, Hullah adapted the French singing system, the Orphéon technique, and presented it to English audiences. Hullah's system, like Mainzer's, also became popular for amateur singing groups, and many of Hullah's students travelled across the country teaching its techniques. The third leader in musical instruction was John Curwen (1816–80). Through his work as a Congregationalist minister he found that the singing of his parish was hampered by their inability to comprehend and perform from regular notation. Curwen became acquainted with the well-known music teacher, Sarah Glover, and she subsequently produced *Scheme to Render Psalmody Congregational* (1835) which then formed the foundation for Curwen's sight-singing technique.

No doubt Alfred Novello recognized the influence of these educational movements on the growth of the amateur market. The instruction received by the amateur in the Mainzer, Hullah, or Curwen technique could then be applied in singing groups, choral societies, and organizations such as the Mechanics' Institutes (see Chapter 1). In turn, growing participation in amateur singing created a demand for technically accessible performance editions.

---

[7]Because copies of Mainzer's two journals are scarce (see Imogen Fellinger, *Verzeichnis der Musikzeitschriften des 19. Jahrhunderts* [Regensburg: Bosse Verlag, 1968]), I include excerpts to illustrate his editorial style.

[8]*Mainzer's Musical Times* 1 (July 1842), p. 215.

Unfortunately, documentation concerning the transition of *MT* from Mainzer to Novello does not appear to have survived, although Mainzer's decision in 1844 to settle in Edinburgh may have induced him to sell the ownership of his journal. In addition, Novello also became the distributor of Mainzer's publications. The September 1846 issue of *MT* advertises the Mainzer repertoire sold by Novello's and suggests the musical preferences of this singing-class audience. Announced under the heading 'Mainzer's Musical Works', Novello's offered:

> Singing for the Million
> Musical Grammar
> Fifty Melodies for Children
> Psalm and Hymn Tune Book, for use in Congregations and classes
> Sonatas for the Pianoforte, by Beethoven, with the Fingerings
> Sonatas by Mozart
> Elementary Studies, or First Exercises, by Bartini
> Studies by Bertini
> Mainzer's Choruses
> Mainzer's Musical Times. Old Series, 320 pages of Letterpress and 9 valuable Musical Compositions, wrappers
> Ditto, with the Second Series, 13 numbers, containing 16 additional Compositions
> Prayer of the Israelites, from Rossini's Opera, 'Moses in Egitto'
> Address on Singing, as a powerful auxiliary in the moral and religious education of the people
> Essays on Music. An address to Mainzer on inviting him to Leven, with account of Demonstrations at Loch Lomond and Burns' Monument
> A Sketch of the Life and Labours of Joseph Mainzer, translated from the French

In Mainzer's last issue (vol. 13, 1 May 1844), he informed his readers of the impending change:

> We beg to refer our friends to the last page of the present number, from which they will see that on June 1st will be commenced a new series of *The Musical Times*, under a new proprietary and management.
>
> In commencing the present series, we stated our main objective to be the furtherance of Mr. Mainzer's plans for rendering music essentially and practically a popular science, by bringing within the reach of all, compositions of a superior character and an improving tendency. We flatter ourselves that to a considerable extent, *The Musical Times* has achieved this object, and proved an efficient aid in the accomplishment of the great ends contemplated in the singing movement. The need of approbation which our selections of music have received from professors and pupils, and their extensive circulation in all parts of the country, are evidences of their utility in ministering to the rational enjoyment, and moral and intellectual improvement of thousands, to whom but recently music was almost inaccessible.

> With a publication limited in its size, as this necessarily has been by
> its merely nominal price, it is obviously impossible to accomplish very
> great results within a short period. We have, in many instances, felt the
> difficulty which our contracted limits have presented to the carrying
> out of our wishes, and to the publication of musical compositions
> which might have proved highly acceptable and useful. In the altera-
> tion as proposed to be introduced by the new proprietors these
> difficulties will be in part obviated. The space devoted to the music
> will be extended and thereby composition of greater value will be pre-
> sented. The literary portion of the new paper will, we feel confident, be
> so conducted as to meet with the approval of the friends and subscrib-
> ers to the present publication.

At the close of this issue, Alfred Novello outlined his goals for the new
journal and the audience he wished to attract.

> It is intended by the new proprietors to improve, in a certain degree,
> the character of the work, which may now be considered as estab-
> lished in public favour.
>   The music of the chorus will, in future, occupy at least *three*
> pages; and the greatest care will be exercised in its selection.
>   The literary department will be superintended with an assiduous
> desire to combine interesting intelligence of the current month;
> reports of important musical performances, and a brief chronicle of
> minor events as they transpire; especially with a view to what may
> be interesting to Choral Societies and Singing Classes, including the
> announcement of all publications expressly adapted to their use.

Embedded in Alfred's statement lies the fundamental change he hoped to
implement in the transformation from Mainzer's periodical to the new
house organ. While Mainzer primarily used his journal to promote his
singing system, classes, and related publications, Novello intended to
fashion it into a proper musical periodical with more broad-based interests. Thus, the activities of choral societies and singing classes, outside
the Mainzer circle, would be discussed and publications featuring other
systems would be reviewed. Yet it is of note that, while on the one hand
Alfred hoped to eradicate, or in any case, play down, the 'puff' of the
Mainzerian method in future pages of *MT*, it would be replaced by his
own promotion of the Novello view of musical activities, substituting
one subjective view of Victorian musical life for another.

Contemporary Music Journals and Fine Arts Periodicals

While Alfred Novello may have envisaged a journal beyond the interests
of choral societies and the amateur, he no doubt recognized the demands
of his market. *MT* thus offered a portion of musical life which particularly suited the audience Novello's had already nurtured for its

publications. An examination of the choices of genres and composers made by *MT* reveals not only the preferences of this audience but, further, offers one profile of Victorian taste and aesthetics. If we compare *MT* to other contemporary music journals and fine arts periodicals, some of which also presented music supplements and catered to the amateur, striking divisions become clear.

In the following survey of five representative publications, it is surprising to discover an exciting and rapidly developing cultural environment barely hinted at by *MT*. The periodicals to be examined, and their audiences, are *The Musical Herald* (1846–7; that is, one year), *The Musical Examiner* (subtitled *An Impartial Weekly Record of Music and Musical Events* (1842–4; two years), *The Musical World* (*A Weekly Record of Musical Science, Literature and Intelligence*) (the period under review begins after Alfred sold the journal in 1837), *The Dramatic and Musical Review* (1842–52), and *The Athenaeum: Journal of Literature, Science, the Fine Arts, Music and Drama* (1827–1921). All of these journals carried small columns for the reports of recent concerts and events: *The Musical World* with 'Miscellaneous' and 'Foreign Intelligence', *The Musical Examiner*, in its early issues, with 'Foreign Intelligence', *The Musical Herald* with 'Musical Varieties', *The Dramatic and Musical Review* with 'Intelligence, Miscellanea, etc.', and *The Athenaeum* under 'Music and the Drama'. Each of these periodicals offers information on the three main features missing from *MT*: musical activities outside England, opera, and instrumental music. By mid-century, amateur interests ranged from brass bands and music halls to opera from the Continent, and almost every faction of musical life was represented by a journal. One of the most popular forms of entertainment even had its own periodical – *The Music Hall Gazette* – which used its pages to promote an image of decency and middle-class patronage.[9] Each journal had to seek its own audience amid the wide choice offered the amateur, and the success or failure to find that correct level of demand would decide publication.

How did these five journals differ from *MT* and did they successfully define and locate the amateur Victorian musician? *The Musical Herald* was founded in 1846 and lasted for only two volumes, closing in 1847 with its 1 May issue. Its choice of articles and reviews reveals a mixture of national musical news and information from the Continent. In the 10 April 1847 issue, an article from *The Spectator* is reprinted, calling for English music publishers to follow their French and German colleagues

---

[9]Peter Bailey, *Leisure and Class in Victorian England: Rational Recreation and the Contest for Control, 1830–1885* (London, New York: Methuen, 1987), p. 162.

and publish more operas: 'A new opera, in this country, is never published as an entire work; an emphatic indication of the state of our
musical stage ... In England we have no such thing; and, in the present
state of our musical stage, it does not matter; for this stage produced
nothing that can serve as a study to the composer, or that can give pleasure to the amateur who is conversant with the higher forms of the art.'
The underlying message here, and elsewhere in *The Musical Herald*, is
that the amateur might become interested in Continental music and
eager to learn if opportunities were provided. Yet such affinity with the
Continental approach to music publishing may not have found sympathy
with the amateur reader, as the limited life of the journal suggests. In the
final issue, the closing remarks by the editor lament the poor reception of
their educational effort:

> In commencing this undertaking, it was supposed that the love of
> music had sufficiently increased in this country to support a periodi-
> cal issued at the lowest possible price.
>
> The success attending the first twelve numbers was such as to
> induce us to consider that we had not been mistaken; but subsequent
> experience has proved that the time is not yet arrived for the multi-
> tude fully to appreciate the art in its most beautiful forms.
>
> Our object was to refine and exalt the mind, by presenting none
> but choice specimens of the most esteemed composers. The Press and
> the Profession have unanimously acknowledged that our intentions
> have been fairly carried out; and our efforts have been appreciated
> by a larger number of Subscribers than any publication of the kind
> previously issued. Still, however, the circulation is not sufficiently
> extensive to encourage our commencing another volume.
>
> We shall, therefore, reluctantly bring our labours to a close with
> the present number, and, with sincere thanks for the past, bid all our
> friends a grateful adieu.

The Musical Examiner survived briefly, from 1842 to 1844, and an
examination of its editorial policies may indicate why it failed to
appeal. *The Musical Examiner* placed atop its mast-head its 'motto':
'Fair Play to All Parties', yet a perusal of the volumes suggests quite the
opposite. Readers were often castigated for their naive tastes and musical ignorance. In a review from the 24 August 1844 issue, the
conductor and performers, as well as the English music public, are
criticized:

> The Italian vocalists, we repeat, are over-estimated, over-paid, con-
> ceited, and *ungrateful*, Signor Costa we shall, to the best of our
> ability, analyse and reduce *to his proper elements*, in an early
> number. Till then we reserve our reply to the charge of having
> underrated him. Other things we may include in our discussion of
> these matters – which we shall delay as little as practicable – since
> we are inclined to think a few candid remarks on 'the Italians' and

their doings, may be beneficial in undeceiving the English public, who have been too long hoodwinked by a silly and impudent *clique*.

A similar tone is taken in the review of a Bach suite in the 29 June issue of the same year. The positive public response was ignored and instead the critic found fault both with the composition and with the audience:

> The overture and *suite* of Bach must be regarded rather as a curiosity than as a specimen of musical beauty. The first and longest part is an elaborate and fugued movement in the style of some of the overtures of Handel, but more obscure and less effective ... The audience were evidently pleased with this composition, to judge from their repeated plaudits. To us, from the sameness of style, and the monotony of key – every movement being in D – it was on the whole (apart from historical interest) somewhat tedious.

It is not surprising that after two years of such education the amateur audience preferred less didactic journals.

The Musical World survived longer than either *The Herald* or *The Examiner*. Founded in 1836 by Alfred Novello and his brother-in-law, Charles Cowden-Clarke, the periodical was published until 1891. Novello sold the journal in 1837, however, and for the following comparison we will examine the period of the 1840s and 1850s. *The Musical World* as a Novello publication is discussed below; here we may briefly note that the journal's longevity was most likely due to its successful combination of criticism and reviews of Continental activities coupled with an interest in English musical life.

In addition to journals at mid-century which focused exclusively on music, there was great success with publications dedicated to the more encompassing area of fine arts. These periodicals contained articles, critiques, notices, and reviews of music, theatre, and art as well as occasional reports on engineering and science. While it is beyond the scope of this study to summarize the full range of fine arts journals, we can single out *The Dramatic and Musical Review* and *The Athenaeum* as examples which paid special attention to musical activities and aesthetics.

In a comparison of these periodicals to *MT* one striking difference predominates: all four focused, in part, on opera, an area almost ignored by Novello's journal. During the first half of the nineteenth century, the popularity of French and Italian contemporary opera in England was steadily increasing. This success is clearly illustrated with a brief review of the dates for London debuts in comparison to their Continental premieres:

Rossini
Guillaume Tell (1829; 1830 premiere in London)

Donizetti
Anna Bolena (1830; 1831 London)

Verdi
Ernani (1844; 1845 London)
I Masnadieri (commissioned for Her Majesty's – 1847 premiere)
Rigoletto (1851; 1853 London)[10]

Productions of French operas in London also soon followed their foreign debuts:

Meyerbeer
Robert le diable (1831; 1832 in English both at Covent Garden and Drury Lane)[11]
Le Prophète (1849 – both Paris and London)

The rapid succession of London premieres was possible in part from the existence of at least three major venues: Covent Garden (the Royal Italian Opera), Her Majesty's, and Drury Lane. While an examination of opera reception in nineteenth-century England is beyond the scope of this study, it is apparent that opera was an important contributor to English musical life, at least in the capital.

Throughout the pages of *The Musical Herald*, opera is a frequent topic. The 30 May 1846 issue contains a revealing lead article: 'Musical Entertainment at the Metropolis'. The article is a glimpse into the growth of the English opera audience at mid-century:

Thursday is the regular extra night [for performances at the Italian Opera]; it is made as attractive as possible, and, from the profusion of the entertainments, these nights have got the name of the 'long Thursdays.' They draw unprecedented crowds, and it was remarked last season, as a curious effect of railway conveyance, that numerous parties occupied the boxes who came all the way from Manchester, Liverpool, and other distant places.

In the same article, the English reception to Verdi is illustrated in the passing mention of the season's repertoire:

The musical novelties of this season have been two operas by Verdi, the favourite Italian composer of the day; – *Nino*, produced the first night of the season, and *I Lombardi* last week. The original title of *Nino* is *Nabucodonosar* (or *Nebuchadnezzar*); but scriptual subjects being in this country considered unfit for the stage, this objection was got rid of by changing the scene and subject. Both these pieces contain great beauties and have been very successful.

---

[10]Scholes, *The Mirror of Music*, 1: pp. 239–40.
[11]Ibid., p. 246.

While Verdi did indeed receive mention from English music journals, it was not always as favourable. Anticipating the Verdi reception in future London seasons, *The Athenaeum*, in 1844, printed a three-column discussion of his music, entitled 'Contemporary Musical Composers: Giuseppe Verdi', in the 31 August issue. Writing as the journal's critic, Chorley presents a certain amount of scepticism:[12]

> Recent occurences and appearances having called the attention of our English public to the modern style, or rather no-style, of Italian singing, it may be as well for the critic to see what is doing in the work of Italian vocal composition; and, since the name of Giuseppe Verdi has begun to circulate widely as the *maestro* most likely to become popular, we avail ourselves of such opportunities as perusal of his compositions here published affords us, to offer a word or two concerning his operas ...
>
> For new melody [in *I Lombardi, Ernani,* and *Nabuco*] we have searched in vain; nor have we even found any varieties of form, indicating an original fancy at work as characteristically as in one of Pacini's or Mercadante's, or Donizetti's, better *cavatinas*. All seems worn and hackneyed and unmeaning. The *andante mosso* to the 'gran scena', 'Lo vedremo', ('Ernani') has some pretension to richness of accompaniment; but the repetition of the same phrase, bar after bar, betrays intrinsic poverty of resource ... we cannot conclude these brief remarks – incomplete for obvious reasons, as a judgment – without saying, that flimsy as we fancy Sig. Verdi's science, and devoid as he seems to be of that fresh and sweet melody, which we shall never cease to relish and welcome, there is a certain aspiration in his works which deserves recognition, and may lead him to produce compositions which will command respect. At all extents, what we have *read* makes us curious to hear and see either 'I Lombardi' or 'Ernani' in Paris or London. 'Nabucodonosor' we suspect, is hardly presentable on this side of the water, on account of its story.

It is of interest that, two years after the performance and acceptance of Verdi's works in London, *The Athenaeum* maintained its sceptical stance:

> *The Verdi-Mania.* –We are led to pay more attention, to this newest of Italian *maestri* than his merits demand, from the circumstances that, bad or good, his Operas contain certain elements of popularity;

---

[12]Chorley's reaction to Verdi (his first published critique of the composer) is especially noteworthy as at that time Chorley had not yet heard any of the early operas ('At all extents, what we have *read* makes us curious to hear and see'). This point and Chorley's response, as critic of *The Athenaeum*, to Verdi over the years is detailed in Robert Bledsoe, 'Henry Fothergill Chorley and the Reception of Verdi's early Operas in England', in Nicholas Temperley, ed., *The Lost Chord: Essays on Victorian Music* (Bloomington, Ind.: Indiana University Press, 1989), pp. 119–42. For additional information on Chorley, see also Henry Fothergill Chorley, *Modern German Music*, 2 vols. New Introduction and Index by Hans Lenneberg (New York: Da Capo, 1973).

and the critic of stage music, however select and sober in his personal tastes, is not qualified for his office if he does not recognize a
success before the public as worthy of examination. A theatrical
audience is of necessity miscellaneous – made up of intelligences of
every order; and the conditions of triumph within its sphere necessarily embrace *effect* to a degree which would be a degrading
concession in music appealing to a more severe and select audience.
How long Sig. Verdi's reputation will last, seems to us very
questionable.

A comparison between *The Athenaeum*'s report and that of *The Musical Herald* the following spring, in May, is striking. While *The Herald*
offers a narrative report of the performances, with a small 'critical'
aside on the qualities of the operas, *The Athenaeum* does not provide
information specifically concerning forthcoming performances, but
uses the opportunity to bring forward again an aesthetic judgement.
MT, however, remained silent at this time, and when we do find mention of opera and Verdi, it is in a small announcement, relegated to the
'Brief Chronicle of the Last Fortnight' section, eleven years later in the
1 August 1855 issue:

> *Crystal Palace* – Signor Verdi arrived in London at the end of last
> week, accompanied by Madame Verdi, Monsieur Ricordi, of
> Milan, and Monsieur Escudier, of Paris. The celebrated composer
> has visited all the sights of London during the week, and on Thurs-
> day paid a visit to the Crystal Palace. He appeared greatly delighted
> with the magnificent building and grounds, and expressed his
> astonishment and pleasure in the most rapturous terms to those
> who accompanied him. Herr Schallehn having learned that the Ital-
> ian *maestro* was present, paid him a graceful compliment, in
> performing a selection from his latest operas, *Il Trovatore* and
> *Luisa Miller*. This little attention was duly appreciated by Signor
> Verdi, who complimented Herr Schallehn on the efficiency of his
> band.

In addition to lead articles and reviews, the birth of new operas was
frequently chronicled by a number of music journals in their smaller, regular columns. From the 10 October 1846 issue of *The Musical Herald*
early stirrings of *Le Prophète* are reported: 'Meyerbeer it is said, is composing a new opera, the hero of which is John of Leyden, the chief of the
Anabaptists.'[13] *The Musical World* would give three full pages to review
the premiere in their 18 April 1849 issue.

The Dramatic and Musical Review, like *MT*, also held the interests of
the amateur in high regard. Yet, in contrast, the editors of this fine arts
journal believed that their readers should be exposed to as wide a range

---

[13] *The Musical Herald* 1: p. 52.

of activities as possible. In an editorial essay from the 16 March 1850
issue, the progress of opera in London is included in the review of the
current musical environment:

> Since the projection of our work [from the publication of the first
> issue] another Sacred Harmonic Society has sprung into existence,
> and keeps its place; a second Italian Opera House,[14] in the teeth of
> many difficulties, maintained its ground; our concerts have
> increased, and, what is still better, the quality of the fare has been
> steadily advancing. Music now numbers its hearers by thousands
> instead of hundreds; and St. Martin's Hall is well filled by attentive
> listeners to classical music, under the direction of a native
> musician.

Operatic activities were frequently highlighted in *The Dramatic and
Musical Review* and the 16 March issue, mentioned above, also carried
an article assessing the forthcoming season.

> The commencement of the opera seasons gives the public an oppor-
> tunity of comparing the claims of the two establishments. The
> absence of Jenny Lind places them upon a more equal footing than
> formerly, for although we could not acquiesce in the public verdict
> as to the unrivalled excellence of that renowned artist, it cannot be
> denied that she held the reins of public opinion. The immense suc-
> cess of Madame Viardot Garcia, last season, has since been
> confirmed on the Continent ... The programme of Her Majesty's
> comprises in addition to the usual repertoire of operas – Mayer's
> *Medea*, Halevy's *La Tempesta*, Auber's *Le Prodigue*, Spohr's *Faust*,
> Gluck's *Iphigenie en Aulide*, etc. ... At the Royal Italian Opera, in
> addition to the varied repertoire of the theatre, *Der Freischütz*,
> Halevy's *Guido e Ginevra*, Donizetti's *Parisina*, Beethoven's *Fide-
> lio*, Gluck's *Iphigenia in Taurus*, Halevy's *La Juive*, Mercadante's
> *Il Bravo*, and Rossini's *Mose in Egitto* will be produced.

As well as opera, the instrumental repertoire was rapidly expanding.
Instrumentalists from the Continent performed extensively throughout
England; yet, as with opera, *MT* remained remarkably silent. This should
not suggest, however, that Novello's did not publish instrumental music.
But although the catalogue reveals an extensive choice of instrumental
music for the soloist or ensemble member, it was chosen from a closely
defined area of the repertoire. An examination of two Novello catalogues, from October 1856 and August 1863, reveals a focus on music
from earlier periods or, when contemporary music is represented, largely

---

[14]This is most likely a reference to the Royal Italian Opera, at Covent Garden, established in 1847, in rival to Her Majesty's Theatre in the Haymarket.

from English composers.[15] The October 1856 catalogue, for example, announced some of the instrumental editions available. Thus, the Continental composers most frequently published are Mozart, Haydn, Beethoven, and Bach. It is not surprising to find Bach among these accepted composers; in April 1854 the St Matthew Passion had its London debut, and portions of his repertoire were by 1856 becoming popular.[16] The appeal of Mozart, Haydn, and Beethoven can be observed through an analysis of the stockbook sales (see Chapter 3) in which the balance of demand and Novello's supply is analysed for a number of their editions. The instrumental genres published by Novello's are also of note for in large part they consist of ensemble arrangements for violin or cello and piano, trios, quartets, and quintets. All such editions would be attractive to amateur musicans wishing to play in groups. Novello's also published music for the pianist: sonatas, four-hand concertos with arrangements or full orchestral parts. Yet the piano selection nonetheless is limited to the circle of earlier composers or carefully selected contemporary ones.

A most revealing insight into the choice of contemporary instrumental composers published by the firm is seen in the catalogue entry for 'Dr. Gleitsmann Grand Sonata'. Beneath the catalogue announcement is a quote from a published review of the work from the February 1852 issue of *MT*. A portion of the quote presented in the catalogue notes that:

> The florid passages are principally arpeggios, and pertain more to the great style of Beethoven, than to the filigree work of the more modern composers ... There are passages of skips in the left hand, which are highly useful to master for the mechanical purposes of effective full playing ... Dr. Gleitsmann is, we believe, an amateur; but he appears to us in the light of so excellent a musician in the production, that we have the greatest curiosity to see his other works, and how far he is able to differ from himself. It is of the highest importance that the true classical school of pianoforte music should not fall into entire neglect; and of the high promise of this high work there can be no doubt.

It is of note that this publication review is included in the firm's sales catalogue. The description, and praise, of Gleitsmann's sonata describes a

---

[15]The October 1856 catalogue is located in the Pendlebury Library of Music, Faculty of Music, Cambridge University; the August 1863 catalogue is held in the collection of the Rowe Music Library, King's College, Cambridge. Publication catalogues for the early years issued by Novello's are relatively rare; additional publication listings can also be found in the endpapers of many of their octavo choral editions and at the end of scores in two- or four-page formats.

[16]For information on the English revival of interest in Bach see Temperley, *The Romantic Age*, pp. 498–9 and *passim*.

musically satisfying composition, in a familiar style, which will highlight as well as improve the performer's technique. Moreover, it is the work of an amateur, which clearly places the composer in Novello's sympathies. This small review, in fact, summarizes the audience Novello's wished to attract to its instrumental music. Beyond the description of one composition in the catalogue, however, the reviewer's critique encapsulates Novello's editorial policy for instrumental music. And, in turn, this policy and the market which initiated it is reflected in *MT*.

We have observed above that *MT*, unlike other music journals, did not focus on operatic activities. Where *MT* and its competitors did agree was on the waiting market for instrumental music. In an examination of published music reviews from *The Musical Herald*, for example, the critic finds amateur appeal one of the most important factors – a feature also singled out in the Gleitsmann Sonata critique quoted above. An example is found in the 2 January 1847 issue of *The Musical Herald*, for Thalberg's *Troisième nocturne pour le pianoforte*:

> Though we have always been the reverse of partisans of the school which Thalberg has formed, and of which he is the head, yet we willingly render justice to his great (and, in some respects, unrivalled) powers ... What we have desired of Thalberg is, that he should accommodate at least a portion of his published music to the wants and capacities, not of professional *virtuosi*, but of the best class of those who cultivate music as one of the accomplishments and charms of social life. Nobody knows better than himself that the most beautiful music is not necessarily the most difficult; and that, even in his own most brilliant compositions, the most exquisite passages are the most simple. Whenever, therefore we meet an entire piece from his pen, written in this style, it gives us a joy proportioned to its rarity. Such a piece is the *Nocturne* before us.

The Musical Herald believed in the promotion of new instrumental music, especially if it was within the reaches of the amateur musician. This combination allowed the journal to publish reviews of contemporary music yet remain within the confines of market demand. A similar example is found again in *The Musical Herald*, one year earlier, from the 1 August 1846 issue:

> The Paris journals announce the publication of twenty-four quintets, entitled 'Les Quatre Saissons' by Felicien David, the celebrated author of 'Desert'. 'We may predict,' says the *Gazette Musicale*, 'that these quintets will have great and legitimate success, for they have every requisite for pleasing ... besides these qualities, they have another, of great and general importance; they are of moderate difficulty and within the reach of amateur performers.'

MT tended to limit its involvement with contemporary instrumental music to the realm of the amateur. Activities and repertoire beyond those boundaries were given restricted coverage. An example is found in the *MT* announcement of Chopin's death, in which he is referred to simply as 'Chopin the Pianist'.[17] In contrast, *The Musical World* opened its 20 October 1849 issue with its announcement of the death of 'the celebrated pianist and composer' and on 10 November the journal provided an extensive report of the funeral, closing with a critique of his music, which in part included the observation: 'At any rate, it must be acknowledged that Chopin, by some means or other, was able to acquire the name of a musician at once profound and inventive, and, whatever may be our own opinion, we are not at present inclined to dispute his claims to be considered one of the most original, if not one of the most gifted and accomplished composers who have contributed to the *repertoire* of the pianoforte.'[18]

A brief examination of Chopin's English reception illustrates the editorial policies and styles of *MT* in comparison with the other music journals. The portrait of Chopin presented in *MT*, as fundamentally a performer, clearly distorts the composer's reputation in England. At his death in 1849 no less than five different publishers had produced first English editions of his works, although Novello's was not among them.[19] The firm of Christian Rudolph Wessel published almost all of Chopin's English editions and his relationship to the firm is well known. Yet Chopin also offered his English editions to Cocks and Co., Chappell, Cramer, Addison and Beale, Cramer and Beale, Cramer and Co., and Ewer among others. A list of the works and dates for these first editions indicates that Chopin had been actively publishing in England at least since 1834. In his article, Kallberg lists the dates of registration in France and England for these editions.[20] While we must observe Kallberg's caveat that registration in Stationers' Hall 'may not necessarily coincide with the dates of publication'[21] his information reveals an unbroken chain of registrations for copyright between 1834 and 1846. Clearly, Chopin was established as a composer in England and would not have been generally regarded solely as a pianist.

Novello's careful pruning of English musical life for the pages of *MT* also included attention to the journal's literary articles. In Alfred

---

[17]*MT* (November 1849) and also noted in Scholes.

[18]*MW* (10 November 1849), p. 706.

[19]The following information is taken from Jeffrey Kallberg, 'Chopin in the Marketplace: Aspects of the International Music Publishing Industry in the First Half of the Nineteenth Century', *Notes* 39 (1982–3), pp. 535–69; 795–824; and from Krystyna Kobylanska, *Frederic Chopin: thematisch-bibliographisches Werkverzeichnis* (Munich: Henle Verlag, 1979).

[20]Kallberg, 'Chopin in the Marketplace', p. 537.

[21]Ibid., p. 537.

Novello's correspondence we discover his concern that articles should never stray too far from the familiar grounds of amateur music-making. The author, critic, and close Novello family friend, Leigh Hunt, was counselled by Alfred to include more musical matters in his articles during his tenure as an *MT* contributor (December 1853 to November 1854). In one of the few extant letters regarding *MT* editorial matters, he writes to Hunt on 20 February 1854:

> I thought you would like a line to say your article reached me safely. I shall send it to you in proof [?] as usual and would ask you if you could add a paragraph or two in any part so as to connect the subject more immediately if possible – with music. You must not think me fidgety in asking this but much [advanced?] as the articles have been – I have been reminded in several notes how little they seem to have to do with the proper appreciation of music – but if by a word or two the link could be made more evident to the less careful reader – it would be advantageous.[22]

Novello's suggestion is understandable in light of the eight articles Hunt wrote for *MT*: 'Inexhaustibility on the Subject of Christmas', 'Twelfth Night', 'An Effusion upon Cream, and a Desideratum in English Poetry', 'On Poems of Joyous Impulse', 'Eating Songs', 'On the Combination of Grave and Gay', and 'An Organ in the House' (two essays).

Hunt's diversion from musical topics is not surprising in light of his career. Hunt was a prolific writer and his criticism and publications also included theatre reviews, occasional essays, fiction, and columns for various newspapers. It has been estimated that a complete collection of his works would demand at least forty volumes.[23] As early as 1828, his eccentric style of music criticism can be seen. Writing in *The Companion* for the 6 February issue, Hunt critiques the event rather than the music: 'The audience are all assembled, as grave as need be; the season, and the usual dull character of oratorios, helps to formalize them; there is a good deal of mourning in the house; and sacred music is to be performed, mixed with a little illegal profane. That is to say, there is nothing real in the business.'[24]

Finally, there is one other market to which *MT* did not address itself: the United States. Since December 1851, however, *MT* had been printing advertisements in its own journal indicating that Novello's had commissioned agencies in New York (W. Hall and Sons) and Boston (G. P. Reed) to distribute its editions and in the summer of 1852 a

---

[22]BL Add. MS 38111, fol. 101.
[23]E. D. Mackerness, 'Leigh Hunt's Musical Journalism', *The Monthly Musical Record* (1956), pp. 212–22.
[24]Ibid., p. 216.

permanent office at 389 Broadway was established.[25] Since the late 1840s Alfred had made various attempts to arrange a link with America and he no doubt believed his own headquarters would offer the ideal platform for expansion. Yet information, articles, and advertisements tailored to the American reader by *MT* were scarce. Acknowledgement of an American branch was usually limited to the addition of the New York address along with the London one in most publications. Rarely, *MT* printed small announcements/advertisements which may have been for the benefit of American readers; one example is found in the December 1852 issue.[26] Documentation concerning Novello's American connections does not appear to be extant. The only primary source material located to date with any information concerning the New York office is found in the Novello Commission Books. Within this record, a limited number of entries indicate the number of copies of specific editions in stock at 389 Broadway (see Appendix 5). Should additional information come to light it may be possible to analyse more closely *MT*'s relationship to the American branch, whether Alfred felt that publicity through *MT*, a largely British-focused journal, was not profitable, and how the house journal functioned in relation to its foreign office.

The Musical World

Despite Alfred Novello's general reluctance to highlight the activities of opera or instrumental music in *MT*, he occasionally allowed an appreciative notice to be published. In the 1 August 1848 issue, *MT* offered a review (although brief) of the Berlioz reception in England:

> Hector Berlioz has left England; and, in announcing his departure, we feel that a great and original mind has gone from amongst us, with but scant greeting and recognition of his genius from our countrymen. His productions have been received with but little general acclamation, albeit they have 'fit audience found, though few.' ... Let

---

[25]Hurd, *Vincent Novello*, p. 61. The 389 Broadway location appears to have been in use until about December 1857. In May 1858 the address of 6 Astor Place is used; 1 Clinton Hall, Astor Place is then found in an *MT* advertisement for August 1858 and seen in printed material until September 1863. In 1871 the address changes to 751 Broadway (there is a gap with no address recorded between 1863 and 1871); in 1873 the address is 599 Broadway under the agent J. L. Peters; after May 1875: 843 Broadway. The American music publisher Ditson and Co. acquired J. L. Peters in 1877 and, from July, Ditson is the Novello agent. For additional information see Hurd, *Vincent Novello*, p. 72.

[26]Quoted ibid., p. 61.

us therefore hope, that when M. Berlioz pays us his next visit, his admirable music may receive a truer welcome in England.[27]

Such brushes with Continental musical life may suggest a desire on Novello's part to introduce his readers to the artistic environment beyond the boundaries of the choral society and oratorio. Fortunately, we may also glimpse Alfred Novello's style as editor and proprietor of a music journal with an examination of his first periodical, *The Musical World*. In Alfred's initial endeavour as a journal publisher, we discover a cosmopolitan outlook and approach rarely encountered in *MT*. Although the first issue of *MW* does not state any specific editorial policy which can be compared with *MT*, later volumes suggest the style and method chosen. In 1837 Alfred sold the journal, yet the editorial interests set up in 1836 remained relatively intact for the next two years and examples given below therefore also include the years 1837 and 1838. An example of the early editorial policy is found in the 5 January 1838 issue with an announcement of the new 'enlarged series' for the journal to accommodate additional articles, reviews, and notices. In a summary of the journal's goals, a promise is made to continue an interest in Continental activities, which the editors regard as of equal importance to music in England:

> The earliest Musical intelligence from the capitals of France and Germany, and other continental places of note, with extracts from the criticisms of our foreign contemporaries on the standard works of their countrymen, will be regularly obtained and presented to the perusal of our readers. Nor shall we cease to include in our scheme the memoirs of eminent musicians, a miscellaneous register of musical anecdotes and transactions, with a weekly list of new publications; and the proprietors will spare neither expense nor exertion to contribute to the information and amusement of the professor and the amateur ... In conclusion we shall faithfully adhere to the rules laid down for the conduct of this work, at its original announcement.

With the advent of yet another new editorial hand in 1839, the journal was to move radically away from Alfred's style (see the discussion below).

From the outset, *MW* reported upon musical activities beyond England, as illustrated in their regular column, 'Chit Chat from the Continent'. Although *MW* has been defined as a 'prototype in all but size and shape to *The Musical Times*',[28] in fact, the more international flavour of *MW* would not be achieved by *MT* until the 1860s. As early as

---

[27] *MT* (1 August 1848), p. 34.
[28] Hurd, *Vincent Novello*, p. 128.

1837, *MW* refers to Chopin as 'the celebrated composer', – a strikingly different perspective from *MT*'s obituary twelve years later.[29] *MW*'s more cosmopolitan approach is found in both the small announcements and lead articles which comprised each issue. A general commitment to activities outside England is evident from the space devoted to two articles entitled 'Music in Paris in 1837' (1 December and 15 December 1837) and 'A Brief Sketch of the Present State of Music, particularly in Germany. By a German' (10 November and 17 November 1837). This kind of coverage was not special to *MW* but could be found in a number of journals, including those in the United States such as *Dwight's Journal of Music* (1858–78), but notably not in *MT*. Not only was *MW* apparently eager to report musical activities across the Channel, but frequent reviews appeared for contemporary opera and instrumental music performed within England. Thus, it is not surprising to find a review of a chamber concert in the 17 March 1837 issue which included a rather broad-minded critique of a late Beethoven quartet:

> The principal feature in the bill was Beethoven's much-talked-of posthumous quartett. With all its many phrases and passages of distinguished beauty, we must honestly confess, that hitherto we have not been able to perceive any distinctness or continuity of design in this singular composition. The fault probably lies with ourselves, and most willingly would we prefer it should be so, than that a great man should underwrite himself ... As a whole it is ultra-Beethoven, and assuredly we presume not to decide upon it after so slight an acquaintance.[30]

Coupled with the attention to contemporary instrumental music, *MW* also devoted a large portion of space to opera. The programmes of both the Italian Opera and Drury Lane were regularly reviewed under the column 'Theatres' with the London debuts often reported: 'Donizetti's opera of Belisario was performed here for the first time in this country on Saturday evening. From the reception it met with, however, we cannot anticipate that it will long maintain its ground.'[31] Moreover, the premiere of operas on the Continent also received equal notice:

> Paris. – I have heard by chance the general rehearsal of Onslow's opera in three acts, which is coming out on Tuesday next at the

---

[29]*MW* (21 July 1837).

[30]The Beethoven reception in England during the first half of the nineteenth century demands a study of its own. The quartet under review is most likely Op. 135. This quartet, and Op. 132, were each noted as 'oeuvre posthume' on the title page for the first edition. But Op. 135 contains features which more closely fit the description offered by the critic: the second movement Vivace has the character of a scherzo and the third movement Lento assai, cantante e tranquillo has the nature of a theme and variations.

[31]*MW* (7 April 1837), p. 62.

Opera Comique, and I am delighted with it. ... Whether it is likely to succeed, or not, I cannot say, as it is certainly superior to anything they are in the habit of producing at that theatre.[32]

As well as its European interest, *MW*, at least in one instance, focused attention on American musical life. The 2 December 1836 issue contains a three-page article entitled 'Music in America', which also emphasized, in the opening paragraph, the importance of an international perspective: 'As indistinct accounts, only, have hitherto been given of the progress of Music, among our transatlantic brethren, and as it is important to know the "march of sounds" in every quarter of the Globe, I beg to lay before the readers of the "Musical World" some particulars which a twelvemonth's residence in that portion of the world has enabled me to do.'

While it is not possible here to provide a complete profile of *MW*, these examples suggest an editorial policy, initiated by Alfred Novello and maintained by his successor, which promoted a cosmopolitan view. Yet, the goals set by Alfred may have been misconceived. When the journal came under new editorial management in 1839, Novello's faults as former proprietor were quickly singled out and listed in the lead article of their first issue of 3 January. This notice, entitled 'Address to the Public by the Editors: Relating to the Management of Their Magazine for the Year 1839', offered a critique of the old order and promises for future revision. The editorial is especially relevant for, within its criticism, it pinpoints the nature of *MW* under Alfred's influence. Of primary concern for the new editors was the earlier focus of the journal on the professional musician: 'It appears to us that a Musical Magazine, conducted within a manner *universally interesting* – not addressing itself merely to professionals and dilettanti, but to all those, informed or uninformed, who take an interest in Music, whether as a study, as a recreation, as a part of science and philosophy ... ought to command a circulation hardly inferior to that of any literary journal of the same relative ability ... On the other hand, however, it is a matter of notoriety amongst the publishers, that Musical Magazines have hitherto obtained only the most limited circulation.' The new editors attributed this limited subscription to the journal's as yet unrecognized market of the musical amateur:

---

[32]*MW* (2 June 1837), p. 183. The report may refer to Onslow's opera *Guise, ou Les états de Blois*; *The New Grove Dictionary of Music and Musicians*, 13: p. 544 dates the premiere as 8 September 1837. See also Viviane Niaux, 'George Onslow', *The New Grove Dictionary of Music and Musicians*, 2nd edn ed. Stanley Sadie and John Tyrrell (London: Macmillan, 2001), 18: pp. 413–14.

> There are two musical publics. There is the inner, or professional cir-
> cle; and there is the outer, or that which comprehends all the
> immense community of the lovers and learners of music. The very
> limited sale hitherto attained by Musical Magazines, taken in con-
> nexion with the technical and narrow-spirited views they generally
> expressed, indicates a well-founded belief that they have circulated
> almost exclusively in this *inner* or professional circle. We trust we
> shall not be deemed presumptuous in announcing a new ambition ...
> the ambition to obtain the ears of that larger audience – that *outer*
> circle of musical readers.

The editors also set out five causes for the general low level of interest in
the journal. Among these, two may have been aimed directly at Alfred:

> Firstly – They all more or less, bore a certain *professional* air, which
> disgusted the general reader ...
> Thirdly – They were always suspected, generally with sufficient rea-
> son, of *shop influences*; they forfeited their claim to confidence as
> guides and critics.

The first criticism most likely referred to the editorial penchant for
genres and composers seen as unfamiliar territory to the general music
enthusiast. This category especially included opera and instrumental
music from the Continent which was not easily performed or accepted by
amateurs. The point was also an invective against the various articles
which had been published on technical and specialized aspects of music
such as acoustics or theory. The second was a more personal attack:
Novello's house organ, by its very nature, was guilty of subjective journalism. In sum, the new editors promised an unbiased view of musical
activities both in England and on the Continent which would appeal to
amateur interests: 'We shall endeavour to adopt a middle course between
the professional language of the musician and the generalizing of the
mere man of letters, recommending our lucubrations to readers of all
classes by, at least, a hearty interest in the subject of them.' Through
these revisions *MW* found its larger readership and, by mid-century, represented one of *MT*'s strongest competitors. The three areas ignored by
MT – opera, contemporary instrumental music, and Continental activities – were regular features from the beginning of *MW*. It does not seem
possible that Alfred would have altered his personal journalistic preferences between his direction of *MW* and *MT* only seven years later.
Rather, *MT* was produced for a very specific audience. With its origins
as a newsletter for the amateur singer and choir member, *MT* had
already attracted and fostered a readership interested in the provincial
life of choral societies and concerts. The Continental repertoire and contemporary music were not part of these amateur activities and thus *MT*
could not focus on them.

The Music Supplements

We have seen how *MT* limited its perspective of musical life in comparison to other similar journals. In turn, these boundaries reflect the editorial policies of Novello's publishing programme. The demands and requirements of the amateur musician were the guiding factors for Novello's editions and, not surprisingly, were reflected in the house organ. Indeed, the relationship between editorial style and house journalism overlapped at an even closer level – in the music supplements added to the back of *MT* issues. With rare exception, these music supplements are arrangements for chorus and piano or organ accompaniment, suited either to small informal gatherings or choral society performances. An analysis of *MT*'s supplement repertoire suggests Novello's perception of demand and musical taste as particular composers and genres are consistently favoured.

Novello's catalogue of available music, dated August 1863, lists the contents of these supplements and through an analysis of this supplement repertoire, certain patterns can be identified. For example, in the first nine volumes of *MT* the composers published in the sacred music supplements are, in large part, from earlier periods, with the majority from the eighteenth-century English sacred repertoire: Boyce, Handel, and Battishill. Only a few are from the contemporary Continental list: Rossini (two compositions), Auber, Spohr, and Neukomm (one each). Predictably, Mendelssohn is the most frequently published contemporary composer. Moreover, the presence of contemporary composers (with the exception of Mendelssohn) does not begin until comparatively late, in volume 6, no. 110, with a piece by Neukomm. The secular music supplements are less conservative and begin, already in volumes 1 and 2, with Rossini, who is presented in five of the first ten *MT* volumes. This limited representation of contemporary Continental composers reflects the choice of composers also found in Novello's editions (see Chapter 1 for an overview of the Novello repertoire).

The popularity of *MT* music supplements, their convenient size and accessible arrangements, prompted Alfred to produce them as a new, independent editorial format and in the July 1846 issue the octavo edition was announced:

> The cheapest Musical Publication ever offered to the public, in respect both to quality and quantity!!! Handel's Sacred Oratorio, 'The Messiah' in Vocal Score. With a separate accompaniment for the Organ or Pianoforte. Arranged by Vincent Novello.[33]

---

[33]*The Musical Times* (July 1846): p. 14 and quoted in Hurd, *Vincent Novello*, p. 49.

The composition was offered for sale in a serialized form of twelve monthly issues with publication beginning the following month. As Hurd has noted, this edition was followed by similar publications, including Haydn's *Creation*, Handel's *Judas Maccabeus*, and other popular oratorios known to the choral society movement (see the discussion, in Chapter 3, of this popularity as registered in Novello's stockbooks). Since the beginning of *MT* the music supplements had proved a successful part of the journal and it is therefore not surprising that Alfred would now adopt this format as an independent publication. Nicholas Temperley has noted that *MT* was certainly not the first music journal to offer supplements and he cites as examples *The Quarterly Musical Magazine and Review* (with supplements commencing with volume 3), and *The Harmonicon*.[34]

The popularity of the piano-vocal score in octavo format, and its importance to Novello editions, cannot be underestimated. It is often, mistakenly, noted that Alfred Novello planned the octavo editions simply to follow the size of *MT* already in that format. Miriam Miller reminds us, however, that the Novello octavo edition has its roots in Mainzer's journals. *Mainzer's Musical Times* was in octavo and when Alfred took over the journal, he retained the size. It was hoped that the new journal would be bound and stored with Mainzer's and, thus, the earlier subscribers could be kept.[35] The *MT* music supplements, as part of the journal, were also in octavo size and the octavo format, piano-vocal edition was a logical successor.

The popularity of piano-vocal octavo editions had already been tested and confirmed by other publishers. Prior to Novello's publications, upright octavo scores, as opposed to oblong, did exist. These are found especially in Paris editions (of Auber and Halevy, for example) and came to be known as 'Parisian format'. Part of their identification is that two pages are printed from one plate, each with the plate number in the bottom gutter. In contrast, most of the Italian editions of similar music were still oblong format.[36] A separate study would be necessary to examine the vast German and Continental editions of octavo and related

[34]Nicholas Temperley, 'MT and Musical Journalism, 1884', *The Musical Times* 110 (1969), pp. 583–6. A comprehensive study of English music journals and their contents is Leanne Langley, 'A Descriptive Catalogue of English Periodicals Containing Musical Literature, 1665–1845' in 'The English Musical Journal in the Early Nineteenth Century' (Ph.D. diss., University of North Carolina at Chapel Hill, 1983).

[35]Miriam Miller, 'The Early Novello Octavo Editions', in O. Neighbour, ed., *Music and Bibliography: A Tribute to Alec Hyatt King* (New York and London: K. G. Saur and Clive Bingley, 1980), pp. 160–69.

[36]I am grateful to D. W. Krummel for the information he supplied concerning octavo editions.

formats. In addition to octavo editions, during the first half of the nineteenth century, the full 'miniature score' was developed. Pleyel published a selection of Haydn symphonies c.1803 in a size 8¼ × 5 inches.[37]

Following the arrival of the octavo editions, Novello then devised a marketing programme which linked the format with *MT* music supplements. Thus, an excerpt from an octavo edition, published in *MT*, could also be purchased in its complete version as one of the Novello publications. An example is seen in the 1 June 1849 issue of *MT*. The music supplement for that number is 'Cry Aloud and Shout', a chorus for five voices by William Croft. Beneath the last stave of the piece an announcement is added: 'This Chorus may be had in Vocal Score, with Organ Accompaniment by Vincent Novello. Folio size, price 1s.' Another example is found in the 1 March 1861 number: the four-voiced anthem, 'Enter Not into Judgment', by Thomas Attwood, includes a notice at the end of the piece, 'A Folio Edition of this Anthem is published by J. Alfred Novello, price 6d.' Under the umbrella of the *MT* music supplement, Novello's thus exercised the publisher's prerogative to 'puff' its own editions and sound 'the first flourish of the trumpets' as Macaulay predicted. Moreover, with the advent of the octavo editions and their close relationship to *MT* music supplements, Alfred Novello brought his journal closer than he might have intended to the Mainzer periodical style of self-promotion.

The House Journal and Editorial Policy

During the early years of publication, *MT* reflected the Novello house style in its almost complete devotion to the choral society market and amateur performer. The focus of both journal and editor on the English repertoire reflects the tastes and requirements of the Novello audience. In a Preface to volume 4 of *MT*, dated May 1852, a retrospective look at the success of the journal defines this market. This preface states in part:

> The conductors of a well-ordered periodical publication have naturally to exert a constant attention to secure an ever onward course for their paper; but it is especially on the completion of a volume that a sort of stock-taking of their position may be taken with advantage. The retrospect of the *Musical Times* now extends to eight years; and during that long period we are not aware of having made a single enemy, or intentionally given pain to any individual; and, on

---

[37]See Cecil Hopkinson, 'The Earliest Miniature Scores', *Music Review* 33 (1972): pp. 138–44; and Hans Lenneberg, 'Revising the History of the Miniature Score', *Notes* 45 (1988), pp. 258–61.

the contrary, we have received numerous assurances of hearty good-will.

We gather from the steady increase in our monthly sale, that we continue to give satisfaction to our enlarging circle of friends. The number sold of the last few Numbers has exceeded 7,000 copies – thus forming an unparalleled intercommunication amongst musical people. From our well-filled advertising columns, buyers see what new works are publishing; because sellers, knowing to how many eyes they address their announcements, take care there to make known their novelties: The amateur in search of a scarce book ... Cathedrals, in want of singers, find abundant response from candidates amongst our readers ...

We have steadily borne in mind the main objective of our work: viz., to provide concerted Vocal Music for large classes of singers, at a small cost. We gladly take this occasion to thank correspondents for suggesting various popular music for the *Musical Times*, thus giving us the advantage of their practical knowledge of what is adapted to the wants of large classes. Copyright has sometimes prevented the adoption of their proposal, but in all cases such communications are received by us with gratitude ...

Alfred Novello thus declares that *MT*'s editorial path was often *guided* by the suggestions of its readers. Such sensitivity and reception to the demands of the Novello reader and performer clearly explains the focus away from contemporary Continental music and towards the provincial repertoire. It is of note, however, that in other *MT* announcements, Alfred Novello also presented a rather different portrait of the journal's editorial policies. In his advertisements and editorial statements he projected an image of the untapped market 'invented' by his journal and publications. He states this clearly in his often-printed advertisement for the octavo editions, emphasizing the word 'invented', rather than 'discovered':

When the octavo editions of *The Messiah* and *Creation* were first printed in 1846, nothing of the kind had ever been attempted, and the success of the publications was thought hopeless when it appeared. It might have been so, but that an extended use for such books may be said to have been *invented* at the same time; namely, the use of such books by the *audience*, instead of being confined as previously to the performers.

Novello's octavo editions were also the first type of works which had the words (or texts) of a proportionate size to the music, so that both could be conveniently read at the same distance from the eye ...

These causes combined to give the octavo editions a success far beyond that sanguinely expected by their designer ...

Alfred's creation of the demand for technically accessible vocal scores (and a journal which promoted them) is a story which has been repeated throughout the Novello literature. In the second published history of the firm,[38] it is implied that the Novello family can be credited with the rise of the choral society movement: 'Thus the Novello's, father and son, can justly be claimed to be responsible for the existence today of so much good music amongst the churches, choral societies and schools of the country. In fact, as was said in *The Musical Times* for June, 1911: "It was the great merit of Vincent and Alfred Novello that by furnishing a large supply of good music they created a demand for it all over England ..."' This view is reiterated in the third, and most recent, published history of Novello's in which Alfred's talents as a publisher are praised: 'His genius as a publisher lay in his ability to sense a social and artistic trend in its outset, and then to back his instinct to the full. He recognized a need almost before it manifested itself, and promptly set about providing the material that would feed it.'[39] In a discussion of the origin of the octavo edition, Hurd notes that 'Having created a market for choral music of all kinds, Alfred Novello was quick to find new ways of feeding it'.[40] Yet, as continuing research explores the full range of Victorian musical life, the influence of Novello publications on taste and aesthetics must take a more confined place within a larger historical context: one publisher alone cannot account for the awakening and fulfilment of complete musical demand. In his study, Dave Russell urges us not to view Novello's editorial policies as a catalyst for musical activities at mid-century. He notes, 'both the company's official historian and some later writers have been too anxious to claim that the house of Novello almost *created* some aspects of popular musical life ... The revolution in publishing did not create a popular choral or any other musical tradition, but it certainly made it more varied.'[41] Russell's caveat can also be extended to include publishers' house journals. Like its parent press, *MT* was directed at an *existing* market which required reports and performance supplements grounded in the traditional repertoire. Novello's recognition that this market was already well established can be seen, for example, as early as 1849 in the 1 October issue. Under an article entitled, 'The Autumn Festivals of 1849', the contemporary desire for familiar music, and the repertoire of Handel in particular, is clearly noted: 'It is plain that while one class of amateurs are longing for novelty or things unheard before, an infinitely larger class are delighted with that which they know by heart, and precisely in that ratio. If this opens no very encouraging view to living composers, it assures the solid and progressive advancement to fame of the works of Handel.' *MT* was thus

---

[38]Swinyard, ed., *A Century and a Half in Soho*, p. 18.
[39]Hurd, *Vincent Novello*, pp. 41–2.
[40]Ibid., p. 55.
[41]Russell, *Popular Music in England*, p. 136.

fashioned and produced with the full knowledge and expectation that a market already existed for this familiar repertoire.

During the early years of publication, *MT* reflected the Novello house style in its almost complete devotion to the choral society market and amateur singer. In so doing, the journal neglected the musical life of the Continent as well as a large portion of the cultural environment of the opera and instrumental music of London. In comparison, other similar music journals offered a more cosmopolitan viewpoint, incorporating news and information from a larger field than *MT* would approach until the 1860s. By remaining well within the boundaries of prescribed house style, *MT* was a major contributor to the success of Novello's in both attracting and maintaining their market.

Conclusion

This study of a music publisher has been written with three goals in mind. The primary purpose was to chronicle the history of a chosen music publisher which began business and practised in nineteenth-century England. Novello's in particular offered a fascinating example in its first fifty years, from the founding in 1811 to the end of the 1860s. During this time, the Novello market was closely defined and publications were prepared to precise specifications to suit their audience. Through a study of specific issues and events (for example copyright law, editorial style, the house journal) a more accurate picture of these business practices emerges than can be gained through a chronological narrative. I therefore chose to examine Novello's by tracing the activities of music publishing: acquisition, editorial style, printing, relationships with composers, and response to the economic and cultural environment.[1] Through this analysis of a specific firm, my second goal was to explore how certain aspects of music publishing functioned during the period. During the first half of the century England experienced unprecedented demographic, economic, and industrial growth. The examination of a music publisher in this rapidly changing climate not only expands our understanding of this industry in particular but offers insights into the cultural history of the period.

My third goal was to suggest ways to interpret publishers' records and external evidence to form a publishing history. Publishers' policies frequently develop in reaction to external social and economic forces and examples of this cause and effect can be found in a number of documents including published notices, catalogues, record books, and the editions

---

[1]Studies of other Victorian music publishers have not taken a topical approach but have been chronological histories. Some examples are Carlene Mair, *The Chappell Story, 1811–1961* (London: Chappell, 1961): a simplified, in-house survey of the firm; Leon Plantinga, *Muzio Clementi: His Life and His Music* (Oxford: Oxford University Press, 1976): primarily a biography of Clementi as a composer; William Boosey, *Fifty Years of Music* (London: Ernest Benn, 1931): essentially a memoir. Additional studies of Victorian music contain general information on music publishing although not in-depth analyses of specific firms. See: Nicholas Temperley, ed., *Music in Britain: The Romantic Age, 1800–1914* (London: The Athlone Press, 1981); Dave Russell, *Popular Music in England, 1840–1914* (Manchester: Manchester University Press, 1987); Nicholas Temperley, ed., *The Lost Chord: Essays on Victorian Music* (Bloomington, Ind.: Indiana University Press, 1989); and William J. Gatens, *Victorian Cathedral Music* (Cambridge: Cambridge University Press, 1986).

themselves. An example is seen in Alfred Novello's caution of copyright infringement published in *The Musical Times*. It may seem curious that Alfred would quote portions of the copyright law, Act 5 & 6 Victoria c. 45 in his journal, until it is understood that the firm fought a number of infringement cases over the years. Copyright law at mid-century was ambiguous and forced publishers, in self-protection, to print warnings or to defend their rights at the Bar. In another example of a publication notice, in the December 1852 issue of *The Musical Times*, Alfred printed a list of the taxes, and the sums, he was fined as publisher of a journal (see Chapter 4). The notice was Alfred's public gesture of protest against the crippling 'taxes on knowledge'. Alfred was one of the key members of the association calling for tax repeal and at times used the house journal as a political platform.

Novello's internal business records also offer vital information concerning market perception. The Novello Commission Books (discussed in Chapter 3) provide a partial listing of the destinations of editions shipped from the warehouse. Some of the recipients were newspapers and journals, sent copies most likely for review or for publication announcements. The publisher's view of the new edition can be determined from the sorts of periodicals listed, whether popular or specialist.

One of the most informative documents for the historian is a publisher's printing record. Stockbooks, for example, are especially useful if they indicate print runs, depletion from the warehouse, and reprintings over a sizeable span of time. Print quantities, for example, suggest those compositions and composers most in demand, and, in a larger context, perhaps the taste of the market. The frequency and quantity of reprinting may indicate the level of demand or the publisher's anticipation of it. If various editorial formats, such as full score, piano-vocal, or parts, are indicated in the stockbook, one can also gauge the relative popularity of these and begin to determine which format was favoured by customers and why. Such conclusions can tell us something of music-making and performance practice of the period.

Through an analysis of source material such as printing and distribution records, publication notices, catalogues, and the house journal, the historical portrait of a publisher emerges. Novello's customer was particular: primarily demand was for choral works prepared in editions and formats suitable for the amateur and choral society member. Novello's market was not attracted to the solo piano works or operas arriving from the Continent and Alfred therefore largely avoided the repertoire. Yet correspondence and occasional articles in *The Musical Times* suggest his interest in contemporary music and no doubt Alfred would have included representative works in his catalogue had his audience wished.

After the 1860s the Novello audience gained a larger degree of sophistication. As their taste for Continental composers, contemporary music, and opera developed, Novello's, in turn, expanded the list accordingly. When Alfred signed his final contract with Henry Littleton, on 17 September 1866, the sense of a new era for the firm can almost be detected. Soon after the contractual date, the face of Novello's was to change rapidly. Now under the complete directorship of Henry Littleton, in 1867 the firm bought the entire stock of the publisher J. J. Ewer and Company, founded 1823, and the name was altered to Novello, Ewer and Company. Within the Ewer catalogue were copyrights for Mendelssohn's *Elijah*, the Violin Concerto, the 'Scottish' Symphony, and the *First Walpurgisnight*. Novello's continued its accumulation of Mendelssohn copyrights, in 1869, with the purchase from Mendelssohn's son Karl of an additional seventeen compositions, which included the *Songs without Words*, Book 8 and the 'Reformation' Symphony.[2]

In addition to the collection of pieces by composers already in the Novello catalogue, during the next twenty years Novello's acquired more contemporary music than before, with a good portion from new Continental composers. Two of the most well known to join the list were Gounod and Dvořák. Among a number of Gounod's works in the list were *La rédemption* (first performed at the Birmingham Festival, 1882), *de Profundis* (Psalm 130), and *Mors et vita* (Birmingham Festival, 1885). Novello obtained the British copyright for a number of Dvořák's works including *The Spectre's Bride*, Stabat Mater, Communion Service in D, and the Requiem.[3] At the time of their publication with Novello's, both Gounod and Dvořák were actively touring in England and on the Continent. Except for Mendelssohn, Novello's had never held such highly visible Continental composers.

As well as contemporary composers, the list also expanded to include genres rarely before published by the firm. While the catalogue previously was dominated by sacred music or secular songs, after the mid-1860s the firm published complete operas, especially in accessible piano-vocal editions. Earlier catalogues reveal that Novello's published only portions of operas, usually the most famous choruses. In a short catalogue, dated October 1856, a small section was dedicated to 'Books of Airs from Operas (Solos)'. This section included 'The overture and select airs from, *Il Seraglio* with flute ad. lib by Whitcombe, in four books', 'Select airs from *Così fan tutte*' and Spohr, 'Select airs from *Faust* with flute ad. lib. by Burrowes'. Seven years later, a much more extensive

---

[2]Michael Hurd, *Vincent Novello – and Company* (London: Novello, 1981), p. 72.
[3]Ibid., pp. 86–7.

catalogue, of August 1863, still contained only a section on 'Operatic Music and secular cantatas' not much longer than the 1856 entry. In the 1863 catalogue the choruses from *Der Freischütz* and *Oberon* were listed, but the complete works were not offered.

By the end of the decade, however, Novello's had published a complete piano-vocal edition of *Freischütz*. The addresses listed on the title page are 1 Berners Street and 35 Poultry; Novello's had opened an office in late 1867 at the Berners Street address to supplement the locations at Poultry and at 69 Dean Street,[4] so the edition probably dates from *c*.1867.[5] It is of note that Novello's maintained a different approach to opera than to oratorio piano-vocal editions. The Editor's Note, at the beginning of the *Freischütz* edition (by the translator, Natalia Macfarren, wife of the English composer George Alexander Macfarren), suggests the house style for piano-vocal editions of operas: 'No adequate idea can be formed of the musical power of this Opera without some insight into its ingenious and picturesque scoring. The list of instruments at the head of each piece may assist towards this, and wherever possible their distribution has been signified throughout the work.' Figure 6.1 illustrates the first page of the vocal-score and the indication of instruments and their entrances. This detail of orchestration can be compared with the opening of Haydn's *Creation*, 'The Representation of Chaos', from Novello's piano-vocal edition, published in the 1840s (Figure 6.2). Orchestration in the Haydn work is also elaborate and worthy of note. Yet, in Novello's piano-vocal oratorio editions, the instrumental colour was not highlighted; it was not considered a fundamental selling-point of the editions as was the clear and unobstructed presentation of the music for performance or study. Even for post-1870 Novello editions, this differentiation continued and, in general, instrumentation was not indicated in the sacred music publications. For the piano-vocal edition of Dvořák's Communion Service in D (copyright date 1894 on title page), only the instruction 'solo or small chorus' was presented in the score but instruments were not noted. Similarly, in the Magnificat (1897), by Parry, names of instruments were omitted. This example may serve as a miniature portrait of Novello's during the nineteenth century. In the 1840s, and to the end of the century, Novello's recognized the musical demands of their customers and the kinds of editions they required. When preference was for sacred music, presented in a simple, easily

---

[4]See ibid., p. 72, for details of the addresses used during this period.

[5]The edition was apparently co-published with the London firm of Simpkin, Marshall and Co. as their name appears under Novello's on the title page. Simpkins was a bookseller and publisher at 4 Stationers' Court *c*.1815–37 and known as Simpkin, Marshall and Co., *c*.1837–89 at the same location.

OVERTURE.

Weber's "Der Freischütz."—Novello, Ewer and Co.'s Octavo Edition.

Figure 6.1 Page 1, Novello, Ewer and Co., octavo edition, Weber, *Der Freischütz* (*c.*1867)

Figure 6.2 Page 1, Novello's piano-vocal edition, Haydn's *The Creation*, 'Representation of Chaos' (*c*.1840)

accessible style, Novello's prepared their editions accordingly. In the opera editions, however, orchestration was considered a key feature and names of instruments were included.

The above conclusion is obvious: Novello's correctly gauged demand and thrived. Yet that is the picture of a successful firm. An additional study could be conducted surveying music publishers who did not survive the competitive climate of mid-Victorian England. Carried further, the same documents, such as catalogues, publicity notices, and internal records could be examined to consider why the firms did not succeed. Moreover, it may be possible to analyse and compare a number of publishing houses, within a given geographical area or those publishing the same repertoire, to determine and define their levels of success.

The examination of a music publisher in nineteenth-century England is especially rewarding. When agrarian-based employment receded as the primary means of national income, it was replaced with manufacturing and service-based business. In turn, a number of new banking policies, credit laws, and working-hour legislation were established. Technological advancements created more specialized products and well-defined markets. The results were increased competition and the development of economic theories and business practices to control this volatile economic climate.[6] Music publishing was an especially vulnerable industry. Like any other business, it survived by producing an attractive product and selling it successfully. The growth and success of Novello's as a business was due in large part to the period's 'commodification of music', an excellent and apt term employed by Derek Scott in his examination of music and social class in nineteenth-century music.[7] In this regard music publishers, concert organizers, and those involved in the profession of music identified and targeted their markets and promoted their 'products' as carefully as those in other merchandise industries. Yet for Novello's this was also coupled with the commitment to disseminate music of educational and artistic value. By observing Novello's development and survival and the balance struck between these two poles, we may begin to place music publishing within the larger context of Victorian history.

---

[6]See S. G. Checkland, *The Rise of Industrial Society in England, 1815–1885* (Harlow: Longman, 1971), pp. 189ff.

[7]Derek B. Scott, 'Music and Social Class', in Jim Samson, ed., *The Cambridge History of Nineteenth-Century Music* (Cambridge: Cambridge University Press, 2002), pp. 544–67.

Contract between J. Alfred Novello and Henry Littleton, 28 October 1861*

Articles of Partnership made this twenty eighth day of October One thousand eight hundred and sixty one between Joseph Alfred Novello of 69 Dean Street Soho in the County of Middlesex of the one part and Henry Littleton of 10 College Place Camden Town in the said County of the other part. Whereas the said Joseph Alfred Novello has for some years past carried on the business of a Music publisher and Typographical Music and General printer at Dean Street aforesaid and at Dean's Yard Soho and at No. 35 Poultry in the City of London. And Whereas the said Joseph Alfred Novello in consideration of his confidence in and good opinion of the said Henry Littleton has agreed to enter into a partnership with him for the time and upon the terms hereinafter contained.

Now these present witness that in pursuance of the said Agreement and in consideration of the premises each of the said parties hereto for himself his executors, administrators and assigns doth promise and agree with the other of them his executors, administrators and assigns as follows: that is to say

1.   The said parties shall be partners under the style or firm of "J. A. Novello and Co." or under such other style or firm as shall be from time to time agreed upon between them in the said business of a Music publisher and Typographical Music and General Printer for twenty half-years from the first day of November One thousand eight hundred and sixty one subject to the provisions hereinafter contained.

2.   The property of the partnership shall consist of the Copyright plates and Stock in Trade on the premises at Dean Street and in the Poultry. And also the Types and Plant at the premises in Dean's Yard and also the fixtures at each of the said three places and also the respective Leases of the premises at Dean Street and in the Poultry and also all Book Debts unpaid on the said first day of November One thousand eight hundred and sixty one and also the Bills receivable unmatured and unpaid at

---

Source: The Cowden Clarke Collection, Brotherton Library, Leeds University.

that date and also the sum of Five hundred pounds in Cash on the current Account at the Bank of London Western Branch and also the general goodwill of the said Businesses all now belonging to the said Joseph Alfred Novello. And Also of the Copyright and plates of the Irish Melodies now belonging to the said Henry Littleton.

3.   The said Joseph Alfred Novello shall not be requested to devote to the said businesses any portion of his personal time and attention but the said businesses shall be carried on essentially in the same manner in which they have been carried on since the said Joseph Alfred Novello went abroad in the year One thousand eight hundred and fifty six with the intention of extending the production of new publications. And the said Henry Littleton shall devote to the [condition?] and management of the said business the whole of his business time and attention and shall have the entire control and management of the said business except that the present Book Keeper Mr. William Humphrys shall not be dismissed without the consent in writing of the said Joseph Alfred Novello who shall also have the sole right to nominate the Book Keeper of the said partnership for the time being provided that the said Henry Littleton shall be at liberty to continue the separate business of a Music printer from engraved metal plates heretofore carried on by him at 24 Cornwall Road, Lambeth.

4.   At the termination of each of the said twenty half years the said Joseph Alfred Novello shall have the right to draw out in Cash from the said partnership the sum of Two thousand five hundred pounds and the said Henry Littleton shall have the right to draw out in Cash from the said partnership the sum of Two hundred pounds.

5.   In the case at the end of any half year after such sums as aforesaid have been drawn out by the said partners there shall be a surplus beyond the sum of Five hundred pounds standing to the credit of the partnership Banking Account the said Henry Littleton shall be at liberty to pay such sum as he shall think proper out of such surplus to the said Joseph Alfred Novello on account of the next one or more of such half yearly payments of Two thousand five hundred pounds so as aforesaid to become due to the said Joseph Alfred Novello. And the said Henry Littleton shall thereupon be entitled to take credit with the said Joseph Alfred Novello on account of such future payment or payments for the sums so paid together with interest thereon at the rate of Five per cent per annum from the day of such payment to the day upon which the said Joseph Alfred Novello would otherwise under these Articles have been entitled to draw the sum on account of which such payment shall be made.

6.   In case at the end of two successive half years the balance of the partnership Banking Account beyond the sum of Five hundred pounds shall not be sufficient to allow the partners to draw the respective sums of Two thousand five hundred pounds and Two hundred pounds as aforesaid then the said Joseph Alfred Novello is to be at liberty to terminate the partnership by a written notice under his hand delivered to or left at the Counting House of the said business for the said Henry Littleton.

7.   In case of the termination of the said partnership in pursuance of the last Article or otherwise or in Case the said Henry Littleton shall die before the termination of the said partnership the entire property belonging to the said partnership shall be sold within the subsequent six months and the proceeds shall be divided into Twenty equal parts of which the said Henry Littleton or in case of his death his executors or administrators shall be entitled to have a number equal to the number of half years that shall have been completed at the time of such dissolution or death respectively and the said Joseph Alfred Novello shall be entitled to a number equal to the number of half years of the said intended partnership that shall then remain uncompleted. And for the purpose of making such division no half year shall be considered a completed half year in which the balance of the partnership Banking Account shall both have enabled the said partners to draw out the respective sums of Two thousand five hundred pounds and Two hundred pounds.

8.   In case of the death of the said Joseph Alfred Novello before the termination of the said partnership the said Henry Littleton shall continue to conduct the said business as near as circumstances will permit under the terms hereof as if the said Joseph Alfred Novello were still living the said Joseph Alfred Novello being thereupon represented by his executors or administrators who shall enjoy all the rights, privileges and advantages hereby secured to the said Joseph Alfred Novello.

9.   In case the result of any half year of the said partnership shall be an absolute loss the amount of every such loss shall be borne by the partners in the proportion of Two thousand five hundred pounds as the share of the said Joseph Alfred Novello to Two hundred pounds as the share of the said Henry Littleton.

10.   All premiums and fees taken with Apprentices or the like shall be taken as the partnership profits.

11.   All the pecuniary and other transactions of the said partnership shall be duly entered and recorded in proper Books in accordance with the practice which has been hitherto observed in the said business and all such Books together with all securities and Vouchers shall be open to the inspection of each partner.

12.   The Banking Account of the said partnership shall continue to be kept at the Western Branch of the Bank of London and shall not be removed without the consent of both partners.

13.   Neither of the said partners shall engage or pledge the partnership name on any negotiable or other security or make himself or the said partnership liable as Bail or Security for any person or any accommodation, Bill or Note [or?] Policy of Insurance or enter into any Wageing Contract or assign his share and interest in the partnership or withdraw any money from the partnership except as aforesaid or expose the partnership effects to the danger of being taken in execution.

14.   After the termination of the said partnership and after the whole of the payments herein provided shall have been made to the said Joseph Alfred Novello the whole of the partnership property shall belong exclusively to the said Henry Littleton who after advertizing the termination of the said partnership in the London Gazette shall be entitled to continue to carry on the said business under the said Firm of Novello and Co. or under the Firm of Novello and Littleton but shall not be entitled in any other way to use the name of the said Joseph Alfred Novello.

15.   If any difference or dispute shall at any time or times arise between the said partners or their legal representatives respecting anything contained in these presents or otherwise concerning the said partnership the same shall upon the request of either of the parties be reduced into writing and referred to the Arbitration of three indifferent persons one to be chosen by each of the parties in dispute within seven days from such request and the third to be chosen within the next seven days by the two persons so first chosen before entering upon such reference and the award of such three persons or of the majority of them shall be final and conclusive upon the said parties in difference and their respective heirs, executors and administrators so as such award to be made in writing under the hands and seals of such three persons ready to be delivered to the party requiring it within fourteen days after the appointment of the third of such three persons or within such further time as the said three persons or the majority of them shall by any writing determine and appoint Provided that if either of the said parties in difference shall

refuse or omit to appoint such referees as aforesaid within the time herein limited for such appointment then the Referee appointed by the other party in difference shall and may appoint a second Referee to act with him in the choice of the third Referee and in the Arbitration herein provided for. Provided Also that in case such three Referees or the majority of them shall not make their Award within the time herein limited for that purpose the matter in difference shall be referred upon the written request of either of the said parties in difference to the decision of a Solicitor to be nominated by the Secretary for the time being of the Incorporated Law Society and the Award to be made by such Solicitor within such time as he shall on hearing of the parties appointed shall be binding and conclusive. And every such Award shall from time to time be made a Rule of Her Majesty's Court of Queen's Bench according to the provisions of the Statute in that case made and provided. And the said Referees shall have power to examine the said parties on oath and to call for a discovery of all documents and matters relating to the matters referred and no Action or Suit shall be brought against either party in respect of any matter in difference until the time for making such award shall have expired. As Witness our hands the day and year first above written.

Contract between J. Alfred Novello and Henry Littleton, 17 September 1866*

This Indenture made the seventeenth day of September One thousand eight hundred and sixty six Between Joseph Alfred Novello, of the Villa Novello, Genoa, in the Kingdom of Italy, of the one part and Henry Littleton, of Number 69 Dean Street Soho in the County of Middlesex, of the other part, Whereas the said Joseph Alfred Novello and Henry Littleton have for some years past carried on business in copartnership under the style or firm of "J. A. Novello and Co." under the provisions of certain Articles dated on or about the twenty eighth day of October One thousand eight hundred and sixty one and by the same Articles it is provided that the property of the Partnership shall consist of the Copyrights, Plates and Stock in trade on the premises in Dean Street and in the Poultry. And also the types and plan at the premises in Dean's Yard. And also the fixtures at each of the said three places. And also the respective Leases of the premises at Dean Street and in the Poultry. And also all book debts unpaid on the first day of November One thousand eight hundred and sixty one. And also the Bills receivable unmatured and unpaid. And also the sum of Five hundred pounds in Cash on the current account at the Bank of London Western branch. And also the general goodwill of the several businesses therein mentioned. All then belonging to the said Joseph Alfred Novello. And also of the Copyright and Plates of the Irish Melodies then belonging to the said Henry Littleton. And by the same Articles it is further provided that at the termination of each half year of the said Partnership (which was calculated to endure for twenty of such half years) the said Joseph Alfred Novello should be at liberty to draw out in cash from the said Partnership the sum of Two thousand five hundred pounds and the said Henry Littleton the sum of Two hundred pounds and that if after payment of such sums at the end of any half year there should be a surplus beyond the sum of Five hundred pounds to the credit of the Partnership Banking Account the said Henry Littleton should be at liberty to pay such sum as he should think proper out of such surplus to the said Joseph Alfred Novello on account of the next one

---

*Source: The Cowden Clarke Collection, Brotherton Library, Leeds University.

or more of such half yearly payments of Two thousand five hundred pounds so as aforesaid to become due to the said Joseph Alfred Novello.

And that the said Henry Littleton should therefrom be entitled to take credit with the said Joseph Alfred Novello on account of such future payment or payments for the sum so paid with interest thereon at the rate of Five per cent per annum from the day of such payment to the day upon which the said Joseph Alfred Novello would otherwise under the Articles have been entitled to draw the sum on account of which such payments should be made. And by the same Articles it is further provided that after the termination of the said Partnership and after the whole of the payments therein provided should have been made to the said Joseph Alfred Novello the whole of the Partnership property should exclusively belong to the said Henry Littleton who after advertising the termination of the said Partnership in the London Gazette should be entitled to continue to carry on the said business under the said firm of "J. A. Novello and Co." or under the firm of "Novello and Littleton" but should not be entitled in any other way to use the name of the said Joseph Alfred Novello. And Whereas the said Henry Littleton has from time to time made various payments to the said Joseph Alfred Novello in addition to the several half yearly payments mentioned in the said Articles which have fallen due and such payments with the interest thereon allowed as provided for by the said Articles amount to the sum of Fifty thousand pounds being the full amount of the twenty half yearly payments of Two thousand five hundred pounds each by the said Articles agreed to be paid by the said Henry Littleton to the said Joseph Alfred Novello as the said Joseph Alfred Novello doth hereby acknowledge. And whereas the said Henry Littleton has called on the said Joseph Alfred Novello to terminate the said Partnership and to transfer to him All the part and share of him the said Joseph Alfred Novello of and in the partnership properly and to invest him the said Henry Littleton his executors and administrators with the several powers and to enter into the several covenants on his part hereinafter contained which the said Joseph Alfred Novello has agreed to do on the said Henry Littleton agreeing to pay the several debts owing from or by the said parties in respect of the said Partnership and to indemnify the said Joseph Alfred Novello his heirs, executors and administrators from and against the same and from and against all costs and expenses relating thereto and to enter unto the several covenants on the part of the said Henry Littleton his executors, administrators and assigns to be performed hereinafter obtained. Now This Indenture Witnesseth that in pursuance of the said Agreement They the said Joseph Alfred Novello and Henry Littleton have mutually determined and dissolved And by these presents Do mutually determine and dissolve the said Partnership and joint trade and do hereby declare that the same and the said

Articles of Partnership and every Clause Article Matter and thing therein contained shall (except as appears by these presents henceforth absolutely cease and be void). And It Is hereby agreed and declared between and by the said Joseph Alfred Novello and Henry Littleton that a proper notice or advertisement of the dissolution of the Partnership shall forthwith be inserted and published in the London Gazette. And this Indenture further witnesseth that in further pursuance of the said Agreement and in consideration of the premises He the said Joseph Alfred Novello Doth grant, bargain, sell, assign and transfer unto the said Henry Littleton his executors, administrators and assigns All the share and interest of him the said Joseph Alfred Novello of and in All and Singular the goods, wares and merchandize stock in trade, credits, effects, matter and things belonging and owing to them the said Joseph Alfred Novello and Henry Littleton as Partners and Joint Traders as aforesaid. And all the estate, right, title, interest, property, claim and demand whatsoever both by law and in equity of him the said Joseph Alfred Novello of and in the same premises To Have, receive, take and enjoy the same premises unto the said Henry Littleton, his executors, administrators and assigns of this and their proper use and benefit and for more effectually enabling the said Henry Littleton his executors or administrators to receive and recover the said several credits and effects of the said Partnership. He the said Joseph Alfred Novello Doth by these presents absolutely and irrevocably constitute and appoint the said Henry Littleton his executors or administrators his true and lawful attorney and attornies in the joint names of the said Joseph Alfred Novello and Henry Littleton or in the name or names of the said Joseph Alfred Novello his executors or administrators but for the exclusive benefit and at the sole costs and risk of the said Henry Littleton his executors or administrators to demand and call in and receive from all persons whom it may concern All and singular the credit sums of money and effects of the said Partnership and to give receipts and other sufficient discharges for the same respectively and to use or adopt all such legal or equitable remedies or proceedings for recovering and getting in the said credits and effects as may be deemed expedient. And for all or any of the purposes aforesaid from time to time to appoint a substitute or substitutes and such substitution to revoke and generally to do or cause to be done whatsoever shall be requisite for giving to the said Henry Littleton his executors or administrators the full benefit of the assignment hereby made. And the said Joseph Alfred Novello for himself, his heirs, executors and administrators doth hereby covenant with the said Henry Littleton, his executors and administrators and any other partners whom he or they shall take into the said Partnership business shall be at liberty to carry on the said business under the said style or firm of "J. A. Novello and Co." or under the style or firm of "Novello and Littleton" as long as he or they shall think expedient. And the said Joseph Alfred Novello for himself, his heirs, executors and administrators doth hereby covenant with the said Henry Littleton his executors, administrators and assigns That he the said Joseph Alfred Novello hath not at any time heretofore contracted any debt or debts or become bound or engaged to pay any sum or sums of money which can or may be charged or affect the stock in trade, goods, credits or effects of the said Partnership or any part or parts thereof respectively or for the recovery whereof he the said Henry Littleton his executors or administrators shall or may be liable to be sued in any Court of Law or Equity whatsoever other than such debts or sums of money as are duly entered in books kept by the said Henry Littleton and Joseph Alfred Novello for that purpose. And that he the said Joseph Alfred Novello hath not at any time heretofore assigned, released, discharged or received any of the credits of the said Partnership other than and except such as are entered as received in the books of the said Partnership or done any other act whereby the credits and effects hereby assigned or intended so to be or any part thereof have or has been or can or may be charged or incumbered in any manner howsoever. And that he the said Joseph Alfred Novello his executors or administrators will allow, ratify and confirm whatsoever the said Henry Littleton his executors, administrators or assigns shall lawfully do by virtue of the power hereinbefore contained and will from time to time and at all times hereafter at the request and costs of the said Henry Littleton his executors, administrators and assigns made do and execute all such further and other assignments, assurances, powers and things for the more effectually assigning to and empowering the said Henry Littleton his executors, administrators and assigns to recover and receive all or any of the said Partnership property for his and their own proper use and benefit as by the said Henry Littleton his executors, administrators or assigns or his or their Counsel in the law shall be reasonably advised, devised and required. And further that he the said Joseph Alfred Novello his executors or administrators will not at any time hereafter revoke or make void the power of attorney hereinbeforegiven to the said Henry Littleton his executors and administrators nor compound or release any action or suit commenced or instituted by him or them by virtue thereof nor do any other act or thing whereby the recovery of the credits and effects hereby assigned or intended so to be or by part thereof may be impeded or delayed. And for the consideration aforesaid the said Henry Littleton for himself, his heirs, executors and administrators doth hereby covenant and agree with the said Joseph Alfred Novello his executors and administrators that he the said Henry Littleton will pay or cause to be paid All and singular the debt and debts owing from or by the said Henry

Littleton and Joseph Alfred Novello in respect of their said late Partnership and which have been duly entered in the partnership Books or are otherwise known to the said Henry Littleton and shall and will save and keep harmless and indemnified the said Joseph Alfred Novello his heirs and executors and administrators and his and their lands and tenements, goods and chattels of, from and against all costs, charges, damages and expenses by reason or in respect of any action or suit which shall or may be brought or prosecuted by the said Henry Littleton his executors or administrators herein the name of the said Joseph Alfred Novello his executors or administrators shall be used in pursuance of any power given to the said Henry Littleton his executors, administrators or assigns by virtue of these presents. And This Indenture Lastly Witnesseth that in consideration of the premises each of them the said Joseph Alfred Novello and Henry Littleton for himself, his heirs, executors and administrators doth hereby remise and release and forever quit claim unto the other of them his heirs, executors, administrators and assigns all actions, suits, accounts, claims and demands whatsoever at law or in equity which either of them the said parties his heirs, executors or administrators now hath or hereafter may have against the other of them his heirs, executors, administrators or assigns for or by reason of the hereinafter mentioned Articles of Partnership or any clause covenant, agreement, matter or thing therein contained or any other matter or thing whatsoever relating to the said Partnership Subject and without prejudice to the covenants and clauses herein contained. In witness whereof the said parties to these presents have hereunto set their hands and seals the day and year first above written.

Signed, sealed and delivered by the above named Joseph Alfred Novello and Henry Littleton in the presence of Joseph Barnby. The Cloisters, Westminster Abbey, London S.W.

Preliminary Remarks in Novello's Edition, *The Collected Masses of Joseph Haydn* (Orchestral Accompaniment Edition, 1828)

Preliminary Remarks

The following are the objects which the Editor has proposed to attain by the publication of the present Edition.

First   To afford an opportunity of having these Masterly Compositions performed by a *complete Orchestra*, by giving the *whole* of the Accompaniments exactly as they were originally written and intended to be performed by the Composer.

Second   To enable a *small* Band to execute them in Amateur Societies, or domestic private Parties, when a *full* Orchestra cannot be obtained – For this purpose, instead of having the *stringed* Instruments engraved with *rests* upon the old plan – the prominent passages of the *Wind Instruments* and *Voices* are inserted in a smaller character, wherever the rests formerly occurred – so that the Leader may not only *see* what is going forward in the other parts, but will also be able to supply the place of the Flute, Oboe, Clarinett &c. – in case those Instruments should be deficient: – in the same manner, the Second Violin will be enabled to supply the obligato parts of the Second Flute &c. when necessary – The Viola of the Horns &c. – and the Violoncello, of the Bassoon, when requisite. –

Third   To accord an opportunity for their performance by the *Voices* and *Piano Forte* alone – for which purpose the whole of the Accompaniment for the latter Instrument has been re-written and arranged so as to introduce several more of the features of the Score (especially of the *Violin* passages) than could have been included with propriety in the *Organ* Accompaniment of the former Edition, from which the present Work is quite distinct.

Fourth   To enable the Leader to know exactly what Instruments are requisite for the different Accompaniment of the various Masses – so that he may be aware of what performers are wanted, and whether they are ready at their desks. With this view, in the Book for the First Violin, at the commencement of every Mass, is given a complete List of all the Instruments required for its Accompaniment according to the original Score.

Fifth   To empower the Copyist to check and correct the parts he may have to write out for a numerous Orchestra – for which end, there will be found affixed to the termination of every Movement, *the exact number of Bars* contained in it.

Sixth   In laying out the Work for the Engraver, the greatest care has been taken to contrive convenient *turnings*; so that in no case will the Performers have to turn over, except at the occurrence of a Pause, or when there are several Bars rest (for their own Instrument) or at the conclusion of a Movement.

It is hoped that the above deviations from the usual plan of engraving separate Accompaniments, will be considered as improvements – and if they should be found conductive to the clearer understanding the intentions of the Composer, or facilitate the performance of them with greater precision and effect, the object and wishes of the Editor will be fully accomplished; and he will feel encouraged to proceed in the publication of the whole "MOZART'S MASSES", arranged upon a similar plan.

V. Novello, No. 66, Great Queen Street, Lincoln's Inn, Octr. 1828.

The Editor has also the pleasure of announcing, that, from a Letter which he has received from His Serene Highness The Prince Esterhazy, he anticipates the gratification of being able to add to this Edition several other M.S. Masses written by HAYDN while Maestro di Capella to the ESTERHAZY Family – and which have never before been published.

Partial Transcription of the Novello Stockbook, November 1858–May 1869

Note: Assumes octavo format unless otherwise stated. Parentheses indicate mathematical and dating corrections.

Novello Stockbook now part of the British Library, Novello Business Archive, Deposit 1996/09 Part E

Noted in stockbook at points as cl = cloth and pa = paper (cl = hardcover binding and pa = paperback binding)

No. printed	When printed	No. sent away	When sent	Left in stock	Remarks
Messiah:				(1000)	
5,000	12/58	1,000	12/1/58		750pa;250cl
		1,000	12/28/58	4,000	
		500	1/12/59	3,500	200pa;300cl
		1,000	2/18/59	2,500	All paper
		1,250	3/10/59	1,250*	1,000pa; 250cl
6,000	5/59 by Saville	5,000	5/59	1,000	Paper
		750	11/16/59	250	Paper
6,000	11/59	3,000	12/7/59	3,000 (3,250)	Paper
		250	12/29/59	3,000	Cloth
		300	2/2/60	2,700	Cloth
		300	4/13/60	2,400	Cloth
		1,500	8/4/60	900	Paper
		300	8/6/60	600	Cloth
		500	9/22/60	100	Paper
		175	11/6/60	0	Cloth

No. printed	When printed	No. sent away	When sent	Left in stock	Remarks
6,000	12/60 by Saville	3,500	1/61	2,500	Paper 3,100 cl;400pa
		300	3/26/61	2,200	Cloth
		400	7/20/61	1,800	Cloth
		1,000	8/9/61	800	Paper
		500	11/4/61	300	Paper
		250	12/7/61	50	Paper
		141	12/11/61	0	Cloth
6,000	12/61	2,000	3/62		
		500	3/24/62	3,500	Paper
		2,000	4/9/62	1,500	Paper
		1,000	5/62		Paper
5,000	5/62	3,000	5/7/62		
		300	12/24/62		
		250	4/8/63		Cloth
		250	8/27/63	1,200	Cloth
		500	10/28/63		Paper
		250	11/30/63	450	Paper
		250	11/20/63	200	Cloth
		370	1/13/64		Paper
5,000 (6,000)	1/22 by Kenny	1,000	2/24/64		
		1,000 from Kenny	7/10/64	4,000	750pa;250cl
		500	9/12/64		Paper
		100	11/30/64	3,400	Cloth
		1,000	12/23/64		750pa;250cl

[Record continues through 1868]
*1,250 removed before 5/59 printing.

No. printed	When printed	No. sent away	When sent	Left in stock	Remarks
Messiah (folio edition):				704? (110)	
500	11/59	100	12/17/58		50cl;50pa
		77	12/3/59	433	48cl;29pa
		50	8/6/60	383	Cloth
		100	2/10/(61)?	(283)	Paper
		50	1/17/62	(233)	Cloth
		50	8/6/62	(183)	Paper
		50	11/22/62	(133)	Cloth
		50	6/2/63	(83)	Cloth
		60	2/2/64	(23)	20pa;20cl
Messiah (parts):					
500	?	250-soprano & tenor	4/13/63	250	S&t: soprano & tenor
		200-(s&t?)	12/18/63	50	(S&t?)
500-alto & bass	?	200-a&b	12/18/63	300	A&b
		58-soprano	3/14/65	0	S
500-soprano	9/65	250-soprano	10/2/65	250	S
		55-A&B	10/4/65	245	A&b
		150-soprano	12/18/65	100	S
		56-tenor	12/18/65	(0)	T
		150-bass	12/22/65	95	B
		150-alto	1/20/66	95	A
500-tenor	8/66	104-soprano	11/2/66	0	S
		98-alto	11/2/66	0	A
		250-tenor	11/2/66	250	T
		104-bass	11/2/66	0	B
500-alto	12/66	—	—	500	A
500-bass	12/66	—	—	500	B
500-soprano	2/67	—	—	500	S

No. printed	When printed	No. sent away	When sent	Left in stock	Remarks
Messiah (pocket edition):					
7,500	5/59	5,000	5/59	2,500	
		1,000	8/3/60	1,500	
		250	10/29/60	1,250	Cloth
		750	12/21/60	500	Paper
		400	3/25/61	100	Paper
		190	4/4/61	0	Cloth
5,000	10/61	1,000	10/61	4,000	
		1,000	1/15/62	3,000	Paper
		250	3/24/62	2,750	Cloth
		750	5/6/62	2,000	Paper
		500	5/8/62	1,500	Cloth
		1,554	5/29/62	0	Paper
Mendelssohn, *St Paul*:				1,500	
		500	11/19/58	1,000	
		500	12/22/58	500	400pa;100cl
		220	1/17/59	280	Paper
		288	3/59	0	
1,500	4/59	500	4/15/59	1,000	
		200	4/18/59	800	Cloth
		500	8/8/59	300	Paper
1,500	10/59	500	11/12/59	1,300	Paper
				1,000	
		300	12/9/59	1,000	Cloth
		774	2/14/60	226	Paper
3,000	11/60 by Saville	500	11/23/60	2,500	Paper
		1,250	5/22/61	1,250	1,000pa; 250cl
Mendelssohn, *St Paul* (vocal parts):					
500 (treble parts)	11/8/67	250	11/8/67	250	Treble
500 (bass)	11/8/67	250	11/8/67	250	Bass
		84	5/11/69	166	Treble

No. printed	When printed	No. sent away	When sent	Left in stock	Remarks
		40	5/11/69	400	Alto
				210	
		60	5/11/69	190	Tenor
		74	5/11/69	176	Bass

Mendelssohn,
Elijah
'Ewer's'
(Acquired by Novello's with purchase of Ewer's)

No. printed	When printed	No. sent away	When sent	Left in stock	Remarks
2,000	1/60	500	1/6/60	1,500	
		1,500	4/28/60	0	
2,000	8/60	2,000	8/60	0	
2,000	12/61	250	12/61	1,750	
		1,000	4/21/62	750	
		750	10/27/62	0	
2,000	3/63	'all sent away'			
2,000 by Saville	7/63	500	8/1/63	1,500 + 500?	

Mendelssohn,
'*Come let us Sing*'
Psalm 95:

No. printed	When printed	No. sent away	When sent	Left in stock	Remarks
1,000	11/58	160	11/19/58	840	
		300	2/11/59	540	
		300	5/3/59	240	'for paper'
		150	4/25/60	90	Paper
1,000	12/60	590	12/14/60	500	Paper

Mendelssohn,
Lobgesang

No. printed	When printed	No. sent away	When sent	Left in stock	Remarks
		100	10/27/58	550	'for cloth'
		460	11/5/58	90	'paper covers'
		90	3/18/59	0	
3,000	4/59 by Saville & Co.	500	4/21/59	2,500	Paper
		618	11/2/59	1,882	200cl;418pa
		500	2/2/60	1,382	Paper
		500	8/13/60	882	Paper

No. printed	When printed	No. sent away	When sent	Left in stock	Remarks
Rossini, Stabat Mater:				400	
		300	2/25/59	100	
		100	4/19/59	0	
2,000	4/59	500	4/21/59	1,500	Paper
		300	9/12/59	1,200	Paper
		100	10/10/59	1,100	Cloth
		330	11/2/59	770	Paper
		500	2/17/60	270	Paper
		150	8/6/60	120	Cloth
		120	8/13/60	0	Paper
1,500	9/60	389	9/22/60	1,200 (1,111+89)	Paper
		500	3/12/61	700 (611+89)	
		250	6/12/61	361 (450−89)	150pa;100cl
		250	7/27/61	111 (200−89)	Paper
		124	12/12/61	0	Paper
2,500	2/62 by Saville	700	2/1/62	1,800	500pa;200cl
		528	3/7/62	1,300 (1,272?)	Paper
		500	8/19/62	800 (772?)	paper
		500	1/19/(63)?	300 (272?)	Paper
		332	5/26/(63)?	0	232pa;100cl
3,000	7/63 by Saville				
Mozart, '12th Mass'					
		500	2/25/63	350	Paper
		200	4/24/63	150	Paper
		211	5/14/63	0	Paper
4,000	6/63 by Saville	750	6/3/63	3,250	
		500	9/22/63	2,750	250pa;250cl

No. printed	When printed	No. sent away	When sent	Left in stock	Remarks
		500	10/16/63	2,250	Paper
		500	11/20/63	1,750	Paper
Haydn, *Seasons* (complete edition):				0	
1,000	12/58	400	1/22/59	600	
		230	3/25/59	370	
		250	6/6/59	120	Paper
		120	11/28/59	120	Paper
2,000	12/59	238	12/27/60	1,762	138pa;100cl
		500	3/9/60	1,264* (1,262?)	Paper
		720	8/6/60	544	520pa;200cl
		250	8/23/62	294	Paper
		200	5/14/63	94	Paper
		62	11/23/63	32	Paper

*following assumes '1,264' as correct.

No. printed	When printed	No. sent away	When sent	Left in stock	Remarks
Haydn, *Seasons* (Spring):				0	
1,000	11/59	250	11/25/(59)?	750	
		250	4/12/61	500	
		250	3/17/62	500 (250)	
		250	2/13/63	250 (0)	
		60	10/3/63	0	
1,000	10/63	250	10/9/63	750	Paper
Alexander's Feast:				700	
		200	2/8/59	500	Paper
		100	3/3/59	400	Cloth
		300	6/6/59	100	Paper
		100	11/4/59	0	Cloth
1,500	11/59	500	11/24/59	1,000	Paper
		100	7/6/60	900	'w/ *Acis & Galatea*, etc.'
		400	12/9/61	500	Paper

No. printed	When printed	No. sent away	When sent	Left in stock	Remarks
		200	10/30/(62)	300	Paper
2,000	5/63 by Saville	200	4/24/63	2,100	Paper
Last Judgement: 'First published in octavo form, December, 1854'				1,000	
		500	11/22/58	500	Paper covers
		200	4/29/59	300	Cloth
		315	8/9/59	0	Paper
1,000	10/59	400	11/18/59	600	Paper
		500	7/20/61	100	Paper
		115	8/16/62	0	Paper
Mendelssohn, 'As the Hart Pants' Psalm 42:				350	
		350	3/1/59	0	Paper
1,000	7/59	150	7/29/59	850	Paper
		500	11/3/59	350	Paper
		250	8/13/(60)?	100	Paper
		118	12/24/60	0	Paper
1,000	1/61	180	1/23/61	820	Paper
		100	4/9/61	720	Paper
		500	4/19/61	220	Paper
		100	7/27/61	120	Cloth
		140	11/29/61	0	Paper
1,000	3/62	300	3/8/62	700	Paper
Samson:				100	75pa;25cl
		100	1/6/59	0	
1,500	2/59	400	2/25/59	1,100	Paper
		150	3/14/59	950	Cloth
		450		500	
		316	7/23/59	184	Paper
		44	10/10/59	140	Cloth

No. printed	When printed	No. sent away	When sent	Left in stock	Remarks
		146	10/18/59	0	Paper
1,500	11/59	250	11/5/59	1,250	Cloth
		250	11/8/59	1,000	Paper
		615	12/30/59	(385)	
		250	2/14/60	(135)	Cloth
		150	4/3/60	0	Paper
750	4/60	500	4/18/50	250	Paper
		200	12/6/60	50	Paper
		113	2/6/61?	0	
2,000	2/61 by Saville	500		1,500	
Acis and Galatea:				864	
		156	12/4/58	708	Paper
		500	2/3/59	208	Paper
		208	4/4/59	0	
1,500	5/59	500	5/10/59	1,000	Paper
		200	2/14/60	800	Cloth
		318	4/3/60	482	Paper
		400	7/4/60	100 (82)	Paper
		100	7/6/60		'w/ *Alexander's Feast*, etc.'
1,500	11/60	620	2/22/61	880	Paper
		500	12/6/61	380	Paper
		150	5/14/62	230	Cloth
		150	7/20/62	80	Paper
		100	9/22/62	0	Paper
1,000	10/62				
Solomon:				498	
		350	12/22/58	148	
		86	3/1/59	62	Paper
		57	3/14/59	(5)	Cloth
1,000	3/59	500	4/14/59	500	Paper
		250	11/12/59	250	Cloth
		200	8/13/60	50	Paper
		54	11/28/60	0	
1,000	5/61	276	5/8/61	724	Paper

No. printed	When printed	No. sent away	When sent	Left in stock	Remarks
		500	3/19/62	224	400pa;100cl
		150	10/3/63	74	Paper
		73	8/8/64	(1)	Paper
Judas Maccabeus:			1/25/59	100	
3,000	3/59 by Saville	500	3/4/59		
		200	3/16/59		
		1,000	3/25/59	1,400	
		200	5/27/59	1,200	
		500	8/8/59	(700)	
		500	10/18/59	200	
		205	11/2/59	0	
3,500	11/59 'all but 1 by Saville'	1,000	11/17/59	2,500	Paper
		250	2/9/60	2,250	Cloth
		750	2/14/60	1,500	Paper
		796	4/25/60	704	Paper
		200	8/6/60	504	Cloth
		543	10/30/60	0	Paper
'Parts of Judas Maccabeus':					
500-s,a,t,b	?	300-satb	6/8/63	200	satb
		150-satb	11/16/64	50	satb
		50-s	11/2/66	0	S
500-s	12/66	250-s	4/8/67	250	S
		60-t	4/8/67	0	T
		60-b	4/8/67	0	B
		150-s	10/4/67	100	S
		54-a	10/4/67	0	A
500-t	11/14/67	250-t	11/14/67	250	T
Israel in Egypt:					
3,000	4/59 by Saville	3,047	5/12/59	0	

No. printed	When printed	No. sent away	When sent	Left in stock	Remarks
4,000	5/59 by Saville	3,300	6/59	700	
		500	12/31/59	200	Cloth
		233	2/2/60	0	Paper
1,000	3/60	500	4/12/60	500	Paper
		428	4/9/61	72	Paper

The Creation:

2,500	11/58	300	11/22/58	2,200	For cloth
		1,000	11/25/58	1,200	For paper
		500	2/4/59	700	200pa;300cl
		500	3/1/59	200	Paper
		200	4/18/59	0	Paper
5,000	4/59 by Saville	1,000	5/16/59	4,000	Paper
		300	5/27/59	3,700	Cloth
		1,012	9/6/59	2,688	Paper
		300	10/25/59	2,388	Cloth
		400	12/9/59	1,988	Cloth
		1,533	12/31/59	435 (455)	Paper
		250	4/26/60	185*	Cloth
		266	8/6/60	0	Paper
4,000	8/60 by Saville	1,500	9/14/60	2,500	1300pa;200cl
		500	9/22/60	2,000	Paper
		300	11/6/60	1,700	Cloth
		1,500	1/14/61	200	Paper
		244	2/26/61	0	Cloth

*185 correct for '435' in stock.

Boyce/
Arnold,
*Cathedral
Music*:

1,500	11/59	1,000	11/4/59	500	
		500	7/27/61	0	
1,500	2/62	500	2/62	1,000	
		500	9/5/62	500	
		400	5/14/63	100	

No. printed	When printed	No. sent away	When sent	Left in stock	Remarks
		118	10/29/63	0	
2,500 by Saville	11/63	500	11/27/63	2,000	
Dr Monk's Anglican Chants:					
1,000	10/60	500	10/2/60	500	
	8/61	250	8/21/61	250	
		275	3/22/61	0	
1,000	8/62	135	8/15/62	865	
		300	11/5/62	565	
		210	4/29/63	355	
		200	9/17/63	155	
		100	9/22/63	55	
		60	11/3/63	0	
1,000	11/63	300	11/27/63	700	
Kent's Anthems No. 1:				300	
			9/12/59	100	
500	(between 9/59– 2/60)	(200)	2/2/60	300	
		100	12/9/61	200	
		100	8/18/62	100	
		100	5/19/63	0	
1,000	8/63	150	8/6/63	850	
		100	10/20/63	750	
Kent's Anthems No. 10:				550	
		200	12/28/58	350	
		200	7/7/59	150	
		150	9/24/59	0	

No. printed	When printed	No. sent away	When sent	Left in stock	Remarks
1,000	11/59	200	11/30/59	800	
		100	2/2/60	700	
		200	3/13/60	500	'to
		200	5/29/60	300	Dean
		100	8/29/60	200	Street'
		100	11/20/60	100	
		100	2/13/61	0	
1,500	2/26/61	226	2/27/61	1,274	
Westminster Chants:					
1,000	8/60	250	8/28/60	750	
		250	6/14/61	500	
		300	11/6/61	200	
1,000	12/61	250	1/20/62	950	
		214	4/4/62	736	
		500	4/30/62	236	
		150	9/5/62	86	
		100	11/16/63	0	
1,000	4/63	250	4/8/63	750	
		400	6/2/63	350	
		150	9/5/63	200	
		125	10/31/63	75	
		25	10/31/63	50	
1,500	11/63	350	11/3/63	1,200	
		374	12/28/63	826	
		40	1/6/64	786	
		17	2/10/64	769	'sent in sheets'
		500	2/26/64	269	'sent in sheets'

Partial Transcription of the Novello Commission Book

Reeves. On the Science of Music   J. Stephen
10/6 trade   7/10 with 15 per cent to us

1853

July	13	1 to M. Stephen
Aug.	9	12 Do [ditto]
Oct.	20	1 Do
Nov.	3	3 Do
	15	4 Do
	21	14 Do & Res [?]
Dec.	6	4 Do & self
	31	60 on hand
	14	sold

113

1854

April	4	5 Stationers' Hall & British Museum
	10	1 Miss Stephen
		1 Miss Garratt
	19	2 to a Lady
	21	1 Library Bristol
June	5	1 self
	Do	1 Cip[riani]. Potter
July	11·	1 Sir H[enry] Bishop
	Do	1 T. A. Walmisley

Millennial Cantata   William Johns
3/-   2/3   less 15 per cent

1852

Dec.	17	100 self
	23	300 self

Source: British Library, The Novello Business Archive, Add. MS 69516, vol. 1

1853
June   4   1000 printed
1854
April   5   451 self
July   1   British Museum
1855
Sept.   12   141 on hand
                7 sold *5/7 1/2* less 15%
                _____

                1000

[pencilled note across bottom of page:]
"Author has sold *all* copies, and the Cantata will not be reprinted."

[Letter stuck in book from William Johns, dated 24 January 1859:]

"Dear Sir: With respect to the price of the "Cantata" – I will leave to your judgement hoping a good sale – I counted the Books over finding all is right, much obliged for the Post office Order. I remain dear sir, your obliged William Johns."

Evening Service   J. Wells 4/6
1852   Aug. 28 250 copies printed
Aug.   31   200 self
                1 Musical World
                1 Illustrated News
                1 Athenaeum
                1 Atlas
                1 Advertiser
                1 Spectator
                1 Examiner
                1 Daily News
                18 self
Dec.   31   23 on hand

1853   Jan. 1   23 on sale
Mar.   30   19 self
[end of entry]

Sacred Music for Schools   J. Tilleack at 1/- net

1852
Feb.   17   349 on sale 211 sewed

Mar.   5   1 Paper for Schoolmasters
                1 Educator
                1 Educational Record
Apr.   15   12 Wm Cope
May   6   [?]
Oct.   15   24 Wm Liddle
                1 Scot. Educ. Journal
Nov.   11   13 Wm Cope

1853
Jan.   1   222 on hand
                273 sold
Jan.   19   1 Adamson
Mar.   4   1 Longmans
         30   100 Longmans
July   30   31 Insp. Schools
                1 I [?] Goddall Esq

Lord Who Shall   Mrs May
1854
Feb.   18   1 Prince Albert

Hymn of Praise   T. L. Fowle   7/6   3/9   3/6   1/2 net

1851
May   15   20 self
         16   5 Miss Fo [?]
         22   1 Mr Brabant
         30   Rev. Hessey
[...]
Nov.   4   1 Musical World
         6   1 British Museum
                4 Stationers' Hall

1852
Oct.   29   3 on sale to 389 Broadway
Dec.   31   7 on hand and 3 at Broadway

Transcription of Deposition in Court Case Taylor vs. Novello*

Mr. Henry Gauntlett organist of Christ Church has heard Mr. Hobbs say, when enquiring of him, as secretary and general manager of the Purcell dinner, given at the Westminster Hotel in Autumn 1836, why Mr. A. Novello did not succeed in getting a ticket, that, *"Taylor says Alfred Novello is a Thief."* That he (Mr. Gauntlett) is quite sure that those were the words, having often heard Mr. Hobbs repeat them since. *Mr. Edward Gauntlett*, brother to the above, heard Mr. Hobbs use the same words on that occasion and since. [amended note: This will not do – there must be proof ...? Who heard Taylor say it?]

Mr. Enoch Hawkins has often heard Mr. Taylor state at the Concentorie Society and other public places that he (Mr. Taylor) was confident many more copies of the *Last Judgt.* had been printed than he (Mr. Taylor) had any knowledge of. That he (Mr. Taylor) was the more convinced of this from having met with copies in the country not containing the letter press. That Mr. Taylor did not wish to obtrude his opinion but that whenever it was asked he should say the same thing. Mr. Hawkins had no doubt that Mr. Taylor would tell Mr. A. Novello the same thing if he was asked or wrote to him as he (Mr. Taylor) seemed to have no doubt as to the truth of his allegations. Mr. Hawkins also informed Mr. Novello, that his supposed conduct to Mr. Taylor was the real reason why he did not succeed in getting a ticket for the Purcell dinner. Mr. Hawkin's brother is connected with the Psalmist, a work published for the proprietors by Mr. A. Novello, and now in course of Publication.

Mr. Emanuel Walton Professor of Music, Leeds, was told by Mr. Taylor in a large company at the Literary Institution, Leeds, that he (Mr. Taylor) now had the Plates of his works in his own Possession and could now tell how many copies were sold, that for a work that was so well known as the *Last Judgment* and done at all the Festivals, *many more copies must have been sold than he had any account of, and notwithstanding* Mr. Walton said he had long known Mr. Novello and had great confidence in him, Mr. Taylor still *represented Mr. A. Novello as a person wholly unfit to be trusted.* Mr. Walton also *understood*

Source: The Cowden Clarke Collection, Brotherton Library, Leeds University.

Mr. Taylor to say that *Mr. A. Novello had defrauded him with respect to some parts to Madrigals published for the Vocal Society. NB* The Plates of these Madrigals were never in the possession of Mr. Novello nor was he further concerned in the Madrigals than by selling a certain number of copies sent from Mr. Taylor, and of which Mr. Taylor in the capacity of the Secretary of the Vocal Society always received a regular account. Mr. *Walton* requested his name should not *be used as Mr. Taylor "seemed a dangerous Man and spared no pains to sow his seed deep against those with whom he was at variances."* Mr. Walton has published extensively with Mr. A. Novello and has now many works in his hands.

Charles Cowden Clarke [Alfred Novello's brother-in-law, married to his sister Mary Victoria], resides with Mr. Novello and has kept his Ledgers since 1831 and can speak to the general accuracy of the accounts, he has carefully extracted from Mr. Pearman's accounts for music Printing, every time that each work of Mr. Taylor's has been printed, and finds that not only the number exactly corresponds with the accounts delivered to Mr. Taylor but also that the printing of the same has always been charged to Mr. Taylor *at the time*, as is proved by the subjoined list of dates.

Mr. Pearman The music printer will speak to the number and dates upon which copies of the various works have been printed and also to his being the only Music Printer employed by Mr. Novello since the publication of the *Last Judgment* in April/31, he having the care of the plates in Dean Street.

Mr. Frederick Hehl Mr. Novello's foreman will speak to his (Mr. Hehl's) having charged Mr. Taylor's account with the printing of his works, every time they have been printed, and also to the fact of Mr. Novello's employing no other music printer than Mr. Pearman.

Mr Edward Taylor from his travelling about the country to give Lectures has great opportunities of spreading his calumnies and from his connection with Festivals and choral Societies, the false reports circulated by him are additionally pernicious, those channels being precisely where most of Mr. A. Novello's business lies.

The Last Judgment was always sent to Mr. Richard Taylor, in Fleet Street (brother of Edward Taylor) in order that he should add the letter press and Board the work. Mr. Edward Taylor always kept the Engraved Title of *The Christian's Prayer* which was engraved by his own Engraver and printed by his own printer and was added to the work, when sent to Fleet Street, with the letter press and sewed by his brother Richard. These precautions, altho' they ought [to] have satisfied Mr. Edward Taylor, gave Mr. A. Novello no cause to suppose his integrity doubted, as the reason given was that Mr. Edward Taylor's brother would do that part of the work very cheaply being a printer.

Mr. Taylor did not even give Mr. A. Novello a hint of his present extraordinary charges, when he (Mr. Taylor) removed his plates from Dean Street in the Spring of 1836 but said only that he had a room fitted up in Regent Square and was having his plates from all his publishers in order to keep them together. Such is his apparent courtesy that he addressed a letter on business to Mr. A. Novello so lately as the 27th Jany. 1837 beginning *Dear Sir* and concluding *Yours truly*!!! To a man he was so traducing!

Mr. Novello expected he should still have the plates sent to him when more copies were wanted, as Mr. Edward Taylor derived great benefit for his works, by their being revised and rearranged by Mr. Vincent Novello, that name being of itself a passport for the adaptations of the then unknown Mr. Taylor and Mr. A. Novello expects for some compensation for their being removed.

Mr. A. Novello has the right of printing the Overtures to the 1st and 2nd Parts of the *Last Judgment* from Mr. Taylor's plates, and he wishes to have this secured to him or a compensation made in case Mr. Taylor wishes to withdraw that right. Mr. A. Novello has taken the greatest pains to forward the sale of the works in general and obtained the publication of the orc. Parts of the *Last Judgment* which Mr. Taylor could not do for himself in consequence of his connection with the Norwich festival, and by these means Mr. A. N. [Alfred Novello] introduced the work extensively as also by Mr. A. Novello's great influence and connection with choral societies and he now thinks himself entitled to some compensation for their removal particularly coupled with the reports against his character.

The copies of the *Christian's Prayer* which were sent to Mr. Taylor first in February and March 1832 had the words torn out, for the purpose of printing them in a 12mo entitled "Novello's Words of Classical Sacred Music" and a copy of the *Last Judgment* was served in the same way for the same purpose, this Book is well known to Mr. Taylor and Mr. Novello had his thanks at the time for the constant advertisement thus afforded to his work.

Bibliography

Primary Sources

Leeds. The Cowden Clarke Collection, The Brotherton Library, Leeds University:
  primarily family papers. Business documents include contracts between Alfred Novello and Henry Littleton (28 October 1861 & 17 September 1866); transcription of court case Taylor vs. Novello.
London. British Library: Vincent Novello's 'Workbooks': Add. MS 9071–4; 9076, 9077; 17856; 17857; 17858; 31120; 33239.
London. British Library. Add. MS 65433, vol. 52: Collections of music from Vincent Novello's private library.
London. British Library. Novello Collection Add. MS 65462, vol. 81: Vincent Novello's correspondence, including letter to Alfred Novello, 23 June 1849.
London. British Library. Add. MS 11730; Add. MS 14396: Correspondence to Vincent Novello and Mendelssohn Organ Fugue, fols 33–4.
London. British Library. The Novello Business Archive, Add. MS 69516–69792 (c.1840–c.1974, primarily post-1870s); Stockbook: Deposit 1996/09 Part E.
London. The Royal College of Music: Vincent Novello's 'Workbooks', uncatalogued.
London. St Bride's Printing Library: Collection of primary and secondary sources: printing history and typography.
London. Stationers' Hall. Copyright registration books, 1830–42.
London, Kew. Public Record Office. Stationers' Hall copyright registration books, 1843–69.
New York. The Pierpont Morgan Library. The Mary Flagler Cary Music Collection, series 2: Letter: Vincent Novello to George Swilt, 22 November 1828.
Oxford. The Bodleian Library. The Deneke Collection: Correspondence between Mendelssohn and Vincent Novello/Alfred Novello:
JAN = J. Alfred Novello VN = Vincent Novello
MS M.D.M.d. 32,155: JAN to Mendelssohn: 12 Dec. 1837
33,31: JAN to Mendelssohn: 30 Jan. 1838
34,3: JAN to Mendelssohn: 2 July 1838
34,104: JAN to Mendelssohn: 6 March 1838
34,119: JAN to Mendelssohn: 15 May 1848

36,105: JAN to Mendelssohn: 28 Oct. 1839
37,63: JAN to Mendelssohn: 18 Feb. 1840
37,164: JAN to Mendelssohn: 29 May 1840
37,215 JAN to Mendelssohn: 26 June 1840
38,147: JAN to Mendelssohn: 27 Nov. 1840
39,199: JAN to Mendelssohn: 23 April 1841
39,211: JAN to Mendelssohn: 30 April 1841
40,35: JAN to Mendelssohn: 14 Aug. 1841
40,152: JAN to Mendelssohn: 5 Nov. 1841.

Secondary Sources

Altmann, W., ed. *Richard Wagners Briefwechsel mit seinen Verlegern: Briefwechsel mit Breitkopf und Härtel*. Berlin: Breitkopf and Härtel, 1911.
—— ed. *Richard Wagners Briefwechsel mit seinen Verlegern: Briefwechsel mit B. Schotts Söhne*. Mainz: B. Schott's Söhne, 1911.
Bailey, Peter. *Leisure and Class in Victorian England: Rational Recreation and the Contest for Control, 1830–1885*. London, New York: Methuen, 1987.
Bank, Chris. 'From Purcell to Wardour Street: A Brief Account of Music Manuscripts from the Library of Vincent Novello now in the British Library'. *The British Library Journal* 21 (1995): 239–58.
Beedell, A. V. *The Decline of the English Musician, 1788–1888: A Family of English Musicians in Ireland, England, Mauritius, and Australia*. Oxford: Clarendon Press, 1992.
Bennett, Joseph. 'A History of *The Musical Times*'. *The Musical Times* 35 (1894): 9–11.
[—— ed.] *A Short History of Cheap Music, as Exemplified in the Records of the House of Novello, Ewer & Co.* London and New York: Novello, Ewer and Co., 1887.
Best, Geoffrey. *Mid-Victorian Britain, 1851–1875*. London: Fontana Press, 1971.
Bledsoe, Robert Terrell. *Henry Fothergill Chorley: Victorian Journalist*. Aldershot: Ashgate, 1998.
Boorman, Stanley, Selfridge-Field, Eleanor, and Krummel, Donald W. 'Printing and Publishing of Music'. *The New Grove Dictionary of Music and Musicians*. 2nd edn ed. Stanley Sadie and John Tyrrell. London: Macmillan, 2001. 20: 326.
Boosey, William. *Fifty Years of Music*. London: Ernest Benn, 1931.

Branscombe, Peter. 'Ignaz (Xaver) Ritter von Seyfried'. *The New Grove Dictionary of Music and Musicians*, 2nd edn ed. Stanley Sadie and John Tyrrell. London: Macmillan, 2001. 18: 184.

Breitkopf and Härtel. *Pasticcio auf das 250jährige Bestehen des Verlages Breitkopf und Härtel: Beitrage zur Geschichte des Hauses.* Leipzig: Breitkopf and Härtel, 1968.

Brett, Philip. 'Text, Context, and the Early Music Editor'. In Nicholas Kenyon, ed. *Authenticity and Early Music: A Symposium.* Oxford: Oxford University Press, 1988.

Brown, Clive. *Louis Spohr: A Critical Biography.* Cambridge: Cambridge University Press, 1984.

Brown, Philip A. H. *London Publishers and Printers c.1800–1870.* London: The British Library, 1982.

Chalklin, Christopher. *The Rise of the English Town, 1650–1850.* Cambridge: Cambridge University Press, 2001.

Checkland, S. G. *The Rise of Industrial Society in England, 1815–1885.* Harlow: Longman, 1971.

Chorley, Henry Fothergill. *Modern German Music.* New Introduction and Index by Hans Lenneberg, 2 vols. New York: Da Capo, 1973.

Clark, Peter. *The Cambridge Urban History of Britain*, vol. 2: *1540–1840.* Cambridge: Cambridge University Press, 2000.

Coleman, D. C., and Mathias, Peter. *Enterprise and History: Essays in Honour of Charles Wilson.* Cambridge: Cambridge University Press, 1984.

Cooper, Victoria L. 'The Novello Stockbook, 1858–1869: A Chronology of Publishing Activity'. *Notes: The Quarterly Journal of the Music Library Association* 44 (1987): 240–51.

Coral, Lenore. 'Music Dealers and Antiquarians'. *The New Grove Dictionary of Music and Musicians*, 2nd edn ed. Stanley Sadie and John Tyrrell. London: Macmillan, 2001. 17: 477–80.

Cox, Jeffrey N. *Poetry and Politics in the Cockney School: Keats, Shelley, Hunt and their Circle.* Cambridge: Cambridge University Press, 1998.

Crum, Margaret. *Catalogue of the Mendelssohn Papers in the Bodleian Library, Oxford.* Oxford: Oxford University Press, 1980.

Cunningham, H. *Leisure in the Industrial Revolution, c.1780–c.1880.* London: Croom Helm, 1980.

Dahlhaus, Carl, ed. *Das Problem Mendelssohn.* Regensburg: Bosse Verlag, 1974.

Davis, Tracy C. *The Economics of the British Stage, 1800–1914.* Cambridge: Cambridge University Press, 2000.

Deathridge, John, Geck, Martin, and Voss, Egon, eds. *Verzeichnis der musikalischen Werke Richard Wagners und ihrer Quellen*. Mainz: B. Schotts Söhne, 1986.

Dibble, Jeremy. 'The RCM Novello Library'. *The Musical Times* 124 (1983): 99–101.

Dougherty, Charles T., and Welsh, Homer C. 'Wiseman on the Oxford Movement: An Early Report to the Vatican'. *Victorian Studies* (1958): 149–54.

Ehrlich, Cyril. *The Music Profession in Britain Since the Eighteenth Century*. Oxford: Clarendon Press, 1985.

—— *The Piano: A History*. rev. edn. Oxford: Clarendon Press, 1990.

Elvers, Rudolf. *Breitkopf und Härtel, 1719–1916: Ein historischer Überblick zum Jubilaeum*. Wiesbaden: Breitkopf and Härtel, 1969.

—— ed. *Felix Mendelssohn Bartholdy: Briefe an deutsche Verleger*. Wiesbaden: Breitkopf and Härtel, 1968.

—— *Pasticcio auf das 250jährige Bestehen des Verlages Breitkopf und Härtel: Beiträge zur Geschichte des Hauses*. Leipzig: Breitkopf and Härtel, 1968.

Fellinger, Imogen. *Verzeichnis der Musikzeitschriften des 19. Jahrhunderts*. Regensburg: Bosse Verlag, 1968.

Flood, Roderick, and McCloskey, Deirdre. *The Economic History of Britain Since 1700*, vol. 1: *1700–1860*, 2nd edn. Cambridge: Cambridge University Press, 1994.

Foster, John. *Class Struggle and the Industrial Revolution: Early Industrial Capitalism in three English Towns*. London, New York: Methuen, 1974.

Fuld, James. 'The Ricordi "Libroni"'. In Rudolf Elvers, ed. *Festschrift Albi Rosenthal*. Tutzing: Hans Schneider, 1984.

Gatens, William J. *Victorian Cathedral Music in Theory and Practice*. Cambridge: Cambridge University Press, 1986.

Grace, Harvey, and Jones, Peter Ward. 'Novello and Co.'. *The New Grove Dictionary of Music and Musicians*, 2nd edn ed. Stanley Sadie and John Tyrrell. London: Macmillan, 2001. 18: 218–19.

Gregg, Pauline. *A Social and Economic History of Britain 1760–1965*, 5th edn rev. London: G. Harrap, 1965.

Harris, Michael, and Lee, Alan, eds. *The Press in English Society from the Seventeenth to the Nineteenth Centuries*. London: Associated University Presses, 1987.

Himmelfarb, Gertrude. *The Idea of Poverty: England in the Early Industrial Age*. New York: Vintage Books, 1985.

Hoboken, Anthony van. *Joseph Haydn: thematisch-bibliographisches Werkverzeichnis*. Vol. 3. Mainz: B. Schotts Söhne, 1978.

Hobsbawm, E. J. 'The Standard of Living during the Industrial Revolution: A Discussion'. *The Economic History Review* 15 (1963): 119–34.

Holmes, Edward. 'Critical Notice'. *Mozart's Twelfth Mass*. London: Novello, [1850].

Holoman, D. Kern. *Catalogue of the works of Hector Berlioz*. Kassel, Basel, London, New York: Bärenreiter, 1987.

Hopkinson, Cecil. 'The Earliest Miniature Scores'. *Music Review* 33 (1972): 138–44.

Hughes, Rosemary, ed. *A Mozart Pilgrimage: Being the Travel Diaries of Vincent and Mary Novello in the Year 1829*. Compiled and transcribed by Nerina Medici. London: Ernst Eulenberg, 1975.

—— 'The Novello Family'. *The New Grove Dictionary of Music and Musicians*, 2nd edn ed. Stanley Sadie and John Tyrrell. London: Macmillan, 2001. 18: 214–17.

Humphries, Charles, and Smith, William C. *Music Publishing in the British Isles: from the Beginning until the Middle of the Nineteenth Century*, 2nd edn. Oxford: Basil Blackwell, 1970.

Hurd, Michael. 'The Novello Archives'. *The Musical Times* 126 (1986): 687–8.

—— *Vincent Novello – and Company*. London: Novello, 1981.

Jensen, Luke. *Giuseppe Verdi and Giovanni Ricordi, with notes on Francesco Lucca: From 'Oberto' to 'La Traviata'*. New York: Garland, 1989.

Jones, Peter Ward. 'Mendelssohn and his English Publishers'. In R. Larry Todd, ed. *Mendelssohn Studies*. Cambridge: Cambridge University Press, 1992: 240–55.

Jost, Christa. *Mendelssohns 'Lieder Ohne Wörte'*. Frankfurter Beiträge zur Musikwissenschaft, vol. 14. Tutzing: Hans Schneider Verlag, 1988.

Kainen, Jacob. *George Clymer and the Columbian Press*. New York: The Typophiles, 1950.

Kallberg, Jeffrey. 'Chopin in the Marketplace: Aspects of the International Music Publishing Industry in the First Half of the Nineteenth Century'. *Notes: The Quarterly Journal of the Music Library Association* 39 (1982–3): 535–69; 795–824.

Kidson, Frank. *British Music Publishers, Printers and Engravers: London, Provincial, Scottish, and Irish, from Queen Elizabeth's Reign to George the Fourth's*. London: 1900; New York: Benjamin Blom, 1967.

King, Alec Hyatt. *A Mozart Legacy: Aspects of the British Library Collections*. London: The British Library, 1984.

—— *Some British Collectors of Music, c.1600–1960*. Cambridge: Cambridge University Press, 1963.

Kinsky, Georg, and Halm, Hans, eds. *Das Werk Beethoven: thematisch-bibliographisches Verzeichnis seiner sämtlichen vollendeten Kompositionen*. Munich and Duisberg: G. Henle Verlag, 1955.

Kitson, Richard. 'James William Davison, Critic, Crank and Chronicler: A Re-evaluation'. *Nineteenth-Century British Music Studies* 1 (Aldershot: Ashgate, 1999): 303–10.

Kobylanska, Krystyna. *Frederic Chopin: thematisch-bibliographisches Werkverzeichnis*. Munich: Henle Verlag, 1979.

Köchel, Ludwig, ed. *Chronologisch-thematisches Verzeichnis sämtlicher Tonwerke Wolfgang Amade Mozart*, 6th edn. Wiesbaden: Breitkopf and Härtel, 1964.

Koehler, Karl-Heinz, and Bartlitz, Eveline. 'Mendelssohn'. In Stanley Sadie, ed. *The New Grove Dictionary of Music and Musicians*. London: Macmillan, 1980. 12: 134–59.

Krummel, D. W. 'Searching and Sorting on the Slippery Slope: Periodical Publication of Victorian Music'. *Notes: The Quarterly Journal of the Music Library Association* 46 (1990): 593–608.

—— ed. *Guide for Dating Early Published Music: A Manual of Bibliographical Practices*. Hackensack, NJ: Joseph Boonin Inc., 1974.

—— and Sadie, Stanley, eds. *Music Printing and Publishing*. The New Grove Handbooks in Music. London: Macmillan, 1990.

Kubler, George A. *A New History of Stereotyping*. New York: George A. Kubler, 1941.

Landon, H. C. Robbins. 'Mozart fälschlich zugeschriebene Messen'. *Mozart Jahrbuch* (1957): 85–95.

Lang, Paul Henry. *George Friedrich Handel* (New York: Norton, 1977).

Langley, Leanne. 'The English Musical Journal in the Early Nineteenth Century'. Ph.D. dissertation, University of North Carolina at Chapel Hill, 1983.

—— 'The Musical Press in Nineteenth-Century England'. *Notes: The Quarterly Journal of the Music Library Association* 46 (1990): 583–92.

—— 'Edward Holmes'. In *The New Grove Dictionary of Music and Musicians*, 2nd edn ed. Stanley Sadie and John Tyrrell. London: Macmillan, 2001. 11: 642–3.

Lawson, Colin, and Stowell, Robin. *The Historical Performance of Music: An Introduction*. Cambridge: Cambridge University Press, 1999.

Lenneberg, Hans. 'Early Circulating Libraries and the Dissemination of Music'. *Library Quarterly* 52 (1982): 122–30.

—— 'The Haunted Bibliographer'. *Notes: The Quarterly Journal of the Music Library Association* 40 (1984): 239–48.

—— 'Music Publishing and Dissemination in the Early 19th Century: Some Vignettes'. *The Journal of Musicology* 2 (1983): 174–83.

—— 'Revising the History of the Miniature Score'. *Notes: The Quarterly Journal of the Music Library Association* 45 (1988): 258–61.

Levy, David B. 'Thomas Massa Alsager, Esq.: A Beethoven Advocate in London'. *19th-Century Music* 9 (1985): 119–27.

Lindert, Peter H. 'Unequal Living Standards'. In Roderick Flood and Deirdre McCloskey, eds. *The Economic History of Britain Since 1700*, vol. 1: *1700–1860*, 2nd edn. Cambridge: Cambridge University Press, 1994: 357–86.

Lindert, Peter H., and Williamson, Jeffrey G. 'English Workers' Living Standards during the Industrial Revolution: A New Look'. *The Economic History Review 1* 36 (1983): 1–25.

—— 'Revising England's Social Table, 1688–1812'. *Explorations in Economic History*, 19 (1982): 385–408.

Loesser, Arthur. *Men, Women and Pianos: A Social History*. London: Gollancz, 1955.

Logan, Thad. *The Victorian Parlour: A Cultural Study*. Cambridge: Cambridge University Press, 2001.

Long, Kenneth R. *Music of the English Church*. London: Hodder and Stoughton, 1971.

McCalman, Iain, ed. *An Oxford Companion to the Romantic Age: The British Culture, 1776–1832*. Oxford: Oxford University Press, 1999.

MacIntyre, Bruce G. 'Haydn's Doubtful and Spurious Masses: An Attribution'. *Haydn-Studien* 5 (1982): 42–54.

Mackenzie-Grieve, Averil. *Clara Novello, 1818–1908*. London: Geoffrey Bles, 1955.

Mackerness, E. D. 'Leigh Hunt's Musical Journalism'. *The Monthly Musical Record* (1956): 212–22.

Mactaggart, Peter, and Mactaggart, Ann, eds. *Musical Instruments in the 1851 Exhibition: A Transcription of the Entries of Musical Interest from the Official Illustrated Catalogue of the Great Exhibition of the Art and Industry of All Nations, with additional Material from Contemporary Sources* (Welwyn, Herts: Mac and Me Ltd, 1986).

McVeigh, Simon. *Concert Life in London from Mozart to Haydn*. Cambridge: Cambridge University Press, 1993.

Mainzer, Joseph. *Singing for the Million: A Practical Course of Musical Instruction*. London, 1841.

Mair, Carlene. *The Chappell Story, 1811–1961*. London: Chappell, 1961.

Miller, Miriam. 'The Early Novello Octavo Editions'. In O. Neighbour, ed. *Music and Bibliography: A Tribute to Alec Hyatt King*. New York and London: K. G. Saur and Clive Bingley, 1980.

Moran, James. *Printing Presses: History and Development from the 15th Century to Modern Times*. London: Faber and Faber, 1973.

Moscheles, Felix, ed. and trans. *The Letters of Felix Mendelssohn to Ignaz and Charlotte Moscheles*. London, 1888.

Music, Musicians, Publishing: 175 Years of Casa Ricordi, 1808–1983. Milan: Ricordi, 1983.

Neale, R. S. 'Class and Class-consciousness in early Nineteenth-Century England: Three Classes or Five?' *Victorian Studies* (1968): 5–32.

Niaux, Viviane. 'George Onslow'. In *The New Grove Dictionary of Music and Musicians*, 2nd edn ed. Stanley Sadie and John Tyrrell. London: Macmillan, 2001. 18: 413–14.

Novello, Alfred. *Some Accounts of the Methods of Musick Printing, with Specimens of the Various Sizes of Moveable Types; and of Other Matters*. London: Novello, 1847.

Nowell-Smith, Simon. *International Copyright Law and the Publisher in the Reign of Queen Victoria*. Oxford: Clarendon Press, 1968.

Palmer, Fiona M. *Dragonetti in England (1794–1846): The Career of a Double Bass Virtuoso*. Oxford: Clarendon Press, 1997.

—— 'Vincent Novello and the Philharmonic Society of London'. In Bennett Zon and Peter Horton, eds. *Nineteenth-Century British Music Studies* 3. Aldershot: Ashgate, 2003: 207–23.

—— 'Vincent Novello in 1811: Entrepreneur or Antiquarian?', paper given at the Music in Britain Social History Seminar, February 2002.

Patten, Robert L. *Charles Dickens and his Publishers*. Oxford: Clarendon Press, 1978.

Plantinga, Leon. *Muzio Clementi: His Life and His Music*. Oxford: Oxford University Press, 1976.

Poole, Edmund H., and Krummel, D. W. 'Printing and Publishing of Music'. In Stanley Sadie, ed. *The New Grove Dictionary of Music and Musicians*. London: Macmillan, 1980.

Pritchard, Brian. 'The Musical Festival and the Choral Society in England in the 18th and 19th Centuries: A Social History'. Ph.D. dissertation, University of Birmingham, 1968.

Rainbow, Bernarr. *The Choral Revival in the Anglican Church (1830–1872)*. London: Barrie and Jenkins, 1970.

—— 'Joseph Mainzer'. In Stanley Sadie, ed. *The New Grove Dictionary of Music and Musicians*. London: Macmillan, 1980. 11: 539–40; also 2nd edn ed. Stanley Sadie and John Tyrrell. London: Macmillan, 2001. 15: 642.

—— 'The Rise of Popular Music Education in Nineteenth-Century England'. *Victorian Studies* (Autumn 1986): 25–49.

[Ricordi]. *Music, Musicians, Publishing: 175 Years of Casa Ricordi, 1808–1983*. Milan: Ricordi, 1983.

Riemann, Hugo. *Musik Lexikon*. 10th edn, ed. Alfred Einstein. Berlin: Max Hesses Verlag, 1922.

Russell, Dave. *Popular Music in England, 1840–1914: A Social History*. Manchester: Manchester University Press, 1987.

Sadie, Stanley, ed. *The New Grove Dictionary of Music and Musicians*. London: Macmillan, 1980.

—— and Tyrrell, John, eds. *The New Grove Dictionary of Music and Musicians*. 2nd edn. London: Macmillan, 2001.

Sartori, Claudio. *Casa Ricordi*. Milan: Ricordi, 1958.

Scholes, Percy. *The Mirror of Music, 1844–1944: A Century of Musical Life in Britain as Reflected in the Pages of The Musical Times*, 2 vols. Oxford: Oxford University Press, 1947; repr. Freeport, New York: Books for Libraries Press, 1970.

Scott, Derek B. 'Music and Social Class'. In Jim Samson, ed. *The Cambridge History of Nineteenth-Century Music*. Cambridge: Cambridge University Press, 2002: 544–67.

Seville, Catherine. *Literary Copyright Reform in Early Victorian England: The Framing of the 1842 Copyright Act*. Cambridge: Cambridge University Press, 1999.

Sutherland, J. A. *Victorian Novelists and Publishers*. Chicago: University of Chicago Press, 1976.

[Swinyard, Laurence, ed.] *A Century and a Half in Soho: A Short History of the Firm of Novello, Publishers and Printers of Music, 1811–1961*. London: Novello, 1961.

Temperley, Nicholas. 'Beethoven in London Concert Life, 1800–1850'. *Music Review* 21 (1960): 207–14.

—— 'Domestic Music in England: 1800–1860'. *Proceedings of the Royal Musical Association* 85 (1958/9): 31ff.

—— 'The English Romantic Opera'. *Victorian Studies* (1966): 293–301.

—— 'The Lost Chord'. *Victorian Studies* (1986): 7–23.

—— ed. *The Lost Chord: Essays on Victorian Music*. Bloomington, Ind.: Indiana University Press, 1989.

—— 'MT and Musical Journalism, 1844'. *The Musical Times* 110 (1969): 583–6.

—— ed. *Music in Britain: The Romantic Age, 1800–1914*. The Athlone History of Music in Britain, vol. 5. ed. Ian Spink. London: The Athlone Press, 1981.

—— *The Music of the English Parish Church*, 2 vols. Cambridge: Cambridge University Press, 1979.

Thistlethwaite, Nicholas. *The Making of the Victorian Organ*. Cambridge: Cambridge University Press, 1990.

—— and Webber, Geoffrey, eds. *The Cambridge Companion to the Organ*. Cambridge: Cambridge University Press, 1998.

Todd, William B. *A Directory of Printers and Others in Allied Trades: London and Vicinity, 1800–1840*. London: Printing Historical Society, 1972.

Tyson, Alan. *The Authentic English Editions of Beethoven*. London: Faber and Faber, 1963.

von Hase, Otto. *Der Bär: Jahrbuch von Breitkopf und Härtel*. Leipzig: Breitkopf and Härtel, 1930.

—— *Breitkopf und Härtel: Gedenkschrift und Arbeitsbericht*, 3 vols. Leipzig: Breitkopf and Härtel, 1917–19.

Warrack, John. 'Edward Holmes'. In Stanley Sadie, ed. *The New Grove Dictionary of Music and Musicians*. London: Macmillan, 1980.

Weber, William. 'The Muddle of the Middle Classes'. *19th-Century Music* 3 (1979): 175–85.

—— *Music and the Middle Class: The Social Structure of Concert Life in London, Paris and Vienna*. London: Croom Helm, 1975. Reissued Aldershot: Ashgate, 2003.

Weedon, Alexis. *Victorian Publishing: The Economics of Book Production for a Mass Market, 1830–1916* (forthcoming).

Weliver, Phyllis. *Women Musicians in Victorian Fiction, 1860–1900: Representations of Music, Science and Gender in the Leisured Home*. Aldershot: Ashgate, 2000.

Wood, Caroline. 'Music-Making in a Yorkshire Country House'. *Nineteenth-Century British Music Studies* 1 (1999): 209–24.

Zon, Bennett. *The English Plainchant Revival*. Oxford: Oxford University Press, 1999.

—— *Music and Metaphor in Nineteenth-Century British Musicology*. Aldershot: Ashgate, 2000.

Index